jBPM6 Developer Guide

Learn about the components, tooling, and integration points that are part of the JBoss Business Process Management (BPM) framework

Mariano Nicolas De Maio

Mauricio Salatino

Esteban Aliverti

[PACKT] open source✻

community experience distilled

PUBLISHING

BIRMINGHAM - MUMBAI

jBPM6 Developer Guide

First published: December 2009

Third edition: August 2014

Production reference: 1120814

Published by Packt Publishing Ltd.
Livery Place
35 Livery Street
Birmingham B3 2PB, UK.

ISBN 978-1-78328-661-4

www.packtpub.com

Cover image by Eugenio Dal Monte (e_dm@fastwebnet.it)

Credits

About the Author

Mariano Nicolas De Maio is a software engineer who graduated from the Argentinian Enterprise University (UADE). He has been working on Java-based projects and open source frameworks for over a decade. He became involved in the jBPM and Drools projects as a community contributor 4 years ago—first as a project architect for a company investigating the feasibility of a few rules and processes, and eventually as a community contributor on several components that are now part of the open source release components of jBPM, such as the jBPM5 JMS connectors for Human task services, the Infinispan implementations of Drools and the jBPM6 persistence scheme, the Form Builder project and its initial migration to UberFire, the jBPM rollback API, and a number of bug fixes for the core components of several other projects.

For the last 3 years, he has been teaching and consulting for jBPM and Drools. Currently, he is the CTO at Plugtree (`http://www.plugtree.com`), a company that provides consultancy and training around the world on Drools, jBPM, and any artificial intelligence concept where they can lend a hand to different companies. Since then, he has provided both private and public training on both Drools and jBPM to a large number of companies all over the world.

He lives in Buenos Aires. He is happily married to Tamara and they are raising a beautiful baby daughter, Sofia. In his free time, he likes to work on contributions for the open source projects he is using. He also has a personal blog about jBPM, Drools, and Decision Management (`http://marianbuenosayres.wordpress.com`). You can find him through the official jBPM IRC channel #jbpm at `http://webchat.freenode.net`, under the nickname `mariano` or `mariano84`.

Besides writing this book, he has previously collaborated in the review of several other books, including *jBPM5 Developer Guide, Mauricio Salatino and Esteban Aliverti, Packt Publishing*, and *A Practical Guide to jBPM5: JBoss Business Process Management Framework, Venkataganesh Thoppae*.

Acknowledgments

First of all, I would like to thank my family. I dedicate this book to Tamara, my wife, and Sofia, my daughter. Their support through all the book writing process is what kept me going and confident. They are the most important part of my life.

I would also like to thank the excellent team at Packt Publishing, whose guidance throughout the book writing process has been invaluable.

I would also like to thank all the people I worked with at Plugtree and the JBoss community, with whom and for whom I had to investigate so many new features of this beautiful framework — which helped me gather the knowledge to write this book. A special thank you to Mauricio Salatino and Diego Naya, founder of Plugtree, for believing in me, and thanks to all the companies that pushed us to investigate new features every day — Multi-Support, iHealth, the Sura Group, and many others who prefer no mention, but are pushing the edge of technology in so many ways.

About the Author

Mauricio Salatino (a.k.a. Salaboy) has been an active part of the Java and open source software community for more than 9 years. He got heavily involved in the JBoss jBPM and Drools projects as a community contributor 6 years ago. After publishing his first book about jBPM for Packt Publishing, he was recognized as a valuable member of both projects at the JBoss Community Awards 2011.

He has participated in international conferences such as Java One, Rules Fest, Jazoon, JudCon, JBoss In Bossa, and RuleML as the main speaker. He is now a Drools and jBPM Senior Software Developer at Red Hat/JBoss, fully dedicated to move these projects forward. He is currently in charge of developing the next generation Business Process Management Suite, along with contributing to the evolution of the Drools and jBPM community projects.

He is now based in London. In his free time, he passionately promotes the open source projects he is using, and is very active in the community forums on these projects. He also runs his personal blog (`http://salaboy.com`) about jBPM, Drools, and artificial intelligence.

I would like to thank Mariano for updating the book to the latest version of jBPM, which is an invaluable asset for the whole jBPM and Drools Community.

About the Author

Esteban Aliverti is an independent IT consultant and software developer with more than 8 years of experience in the field. He is a fervent open source promoter and developer with meaningful contributions to JBoss Drools and jBPM5 frameworks. After he got his software engineering degree in Argentina, he started working with local IT companies fulfilling different roles ranging from web developer to software architect. In 2009, while working for Plugtree, he was introduced to JBoss Drools and jBPM5 projects. Over the next 3 years, he became one of the lead consultants at Plugtree, providing services to its most important clients all around the world.

A former Professor of Java and object-oriented programming at Universidad de Mendoza, Argentina, he decided to continue with his passion for education outside the academic field by co-authoring jBPM5 Community Training and Drools 5 Community Training online courses. The urge to transmit his knowledge and experience led him to participate as speaker and co-speaker in several international conferences, such as Java One Brazil, RuleML, October Rule Fest, and various Drools and jBPM summits.

In JUDCon 2012 and 2013, he was recognized as a JBoss Community Leader during the JBoss Community Recognition Awards, in acknowledgement of his contributions to Drools framework.

Currently located in Germany, he works as an independent Drools/JBPM consultant and developer. During his free time, he enjoys contributing to Drools and jBPM projects and helping other people to embrace these technologies. In addition, he has a personal blog (http://ilesteban.wordpress.com), which he uses to publish his work and discoveries in his journey through the open source world.

About the Reviewers

Stefan Bunciak is a Quality Assurance Engineer for Red Hat JBoss Middleware, and is currently focusing his efforts on improving the quality of the SOA Governance solution within JBoss Fuse Service Works.

While trying to do his best as the Quality Assurance Engineer, he earned several professional certificates, including Red Hat Certified System Administrator (RHCSA), Red Hat Certified JBoss Administrator (RHCJA), and ISTQB Certified Tester (CTFL). Furthermore, he took part in the Business Process Modeling and Analysis course held by Prof. Dr. Mathias Weske to deepen his knowledge regarding the BPM discipline.

Although he is not an experienced writer, he has found some free time and published several articles, which can be found at `https://community.jboss.org/people/sbunciak`.

He currently lives in Brno, Czech Republic, where he also finished his Bachelor's and Master's degrees in Applied Informatics at Masaryk University.

Hassan Ebied has more than 9 years of experience in the field of software development, and has specialized in JEE applications, middleware integration, and SOA/EAI. He was introduced to BPM 3 years ago when he started using IBM BPM technologies starting from 7.5, 8.0, 8.5, IBM ILOG, JBoss jBPM, and Drools.

He has been working for well-known software companies in Egypt and the Gulf area, including RAYA Integration Services, Cairo; Diyar Middle East, Kuwait; and SAPiT, Cairo. Currently, he is working at SAPiT, a leading system integrator in the Gulf area, as a Senior BPM Specialist.

I would like to thank the team at Packt Publishing who gave me the opportunity and confidence to participate in the reviewing of this book. Also, a special thanks to my lovely wife Hala who always gives me smiles and pushes me forward.

Peter Johnson has over 34 years of enterprise computing experience. He has been working with Java for 16 years, and for the last 12 years has been heavily involved in Java performance tuning. He is a frequent speaker on Java performance topics at various conferences, including the Computer Measurement Group annual conference, JBoss World, and Linux World. He is a moderator for the build tools and JBoss forums at Java Ranch. He is also the co-author of the book *JBoss in Action, Manning Publications*, and has been a reviewer on numerous books on topics ranging from Java to Windows PowerShell.

Toshiya Kobayashi is a support engineer at Red Hat, Inc. He has over 10 years of experience in Java and open source software. Since joining Red Hat, he has been supporting various technologies such as JBoss AS, Seam, SOA platform, and Portal. He has been focusing on the BRMS/BPM suite for over three years while contributing to Drools, jBPM, and Designer, among others.

He is also a subleader of Japan JBoss User Group and is happy to encourage open source community activities.

Marcelo Daniel Martini is a BPM consultant. He is responsible for sales and technical analysis and provides advice on technologies and patterns to implement a BPM Middleware/SOA. He is associated with BPM/SOA technologies such as jBPM, Bonita, Intallio, ProcessMaker, Activiti, Bizagi, Lombardi IBM, TIBCO BPM, and Oracle BPM/SOA/OSB (Fusion Middleware) 11g (Decision Tables, BPEL, Business Rules, ADF Task Forms for Human tasks, Mediator services, and Adapter services). He has also worked on the BPEL component of Oracle SOA Suite 11g. He was the Network Administrator for the Oracle database of the Ministry of Economy and Production.

At Garbarino S.A. (http://www.garbarino.com/), he worked with jBPM6 Business Process Management (BPM), WebLogic, BAM, and Confluence. Also, he worked on Drools, CEP, BPEL, and Oracle projects. At Grupo OSDE (http://www.osde.com.ar/), he worked as the Drools Guvnor (Business Rules Manager) and on jBPM6 and CEP projects as well. He was also involved in the implementation of Biometric Electoral Register in Bolivia. He is also a Java architect. He has worked at NEC (http://ar.nec.com/) on Biometrics projects. He worked at Prefectura Nacional Argentina (http://www.prefecturanaval.gov.ar/) on migrating of systems to BPM processes.

I would like to thank my family for always being by my side.

Edem Morny is a passionate consultant and evangelist of enterprise Java technologies who has over 8 years of experience in the enterprise Java field. He spent much of his career working for Genkey, architecting and leading a team in building its multimodal, multialgorithm, and fully clustered biometric deduplication product. This product has become the reference point for deduplication services by many African governments including Ghana, Cameroon, and Mozambique. He is now the co-founder and CTO of Queauji Consulting, an enterprise systems integration consultancy in Ghana, specializing in the healthcare sector.

He currently lives in Accra, Ghana. He is married with one little boy. He has also been a reviewer of three other books by Packt Publishing:

- *JBoss Tools 3 Developer's Guide, Anghel Leonard*
- *JBoss AS 5 Development, Francesco Marchioni*
- *JSF 2.0 Cookbook, Anghel Leonard*

Antonio Mendoza Pérez is a software developer with over 8 years of experience in designing and implementing Java Enterprise applications. Always curious to find out and try new ways to build software, three years ago, he grew interested in BPM technologies — in particular jBPM, which he immediately adopted in his projects, together with Drools. From then on, he has been passionately following the Drools world and its evolution. He is also interested in Scala, Groovy, and other JVM programming languages.

You can get in touch with him at https://www.linkedin.com/in/antmendoza or through his blog at http://antmendoza.com.

I would like to thank Mauricio Salatino for his guidance while I was taking my first steps with jBPM, as well as Naiba for her support during this review.

www.PacktPub.com

Support files, eBooks, discount offers, and more

You might want to visit www.PacktPub.com for support files and downloads related to your book.

Did you know that Packt offers eBook versions of every book published, with PDF and ePub files available? You can upgrade to the eBook version at www.PacktPub.com and as a print book customer, you are entitled to a discount on the eBook copy. Get in touch with us at service@packtpub.com for more details.

At www.PacktPub.com, you can also read a collection of free technical articles, sign up for a range of free newsletters and receive exclusive discounts and offers on Packt books and eBooks.

http://PacktLib.PacktPub.com

Do you need instant solutions to your IT questions? PacktLib is Packt's online digital book library. Here, you can access, read and search across Packt's entire library of books.

Why subscribe?

- Fully searchable across every book published by Packt
- Copy and paste, print and bookmark content
- On demand and accessible via web browser

Free access for Packt account holders

If you have an account with Packt at www.PacktPub.com, you can use this to access PacktLib today and view nine entirely free books. Simply use your login credentials for immediate access.

Table of Contents

Preface

jBPM6 Developer Guide was written to provide a comprehensive guide that helps you understand the main principles used by the jBPM6 project to build smarter applications using the power of business processes. This book covers important topics such as the BPMN 2.0 specification, the WS-HT specification, domain-specific runtime configurations, integration patterns, and tooling descriptions. All these topics are covered with a technical perspective that will help developers to adopt these technologies. The book is also targeted at topics that are not usually covered by BPM systems, such as business rules, complex event processing and tooling extension capabilities, which are introduced to demonstrate the power of mixing different business knowledge descriptions into one smarter, adaptive platform.

What this book covers

Chapter 1, Why Do We Need Business Process Management?, introduces the BPM discipline. This chapter will provide the basis for the rest of the book, by providing an understanding of why and how the jBPM6 project has been designed, and the path its evolution will follow.

Chapter 2, BPM Systems' Structure, explores what the main pieces and components inside a Business Process Management system are, in depth. This chapter introduces the concept of BPM system as the natural follow-up of an understanding of the BPM discipline. The reader will find a deep and technical explanation about how a BPM system core can be built from scratch and how it will interact with the rest of the components in the BPM system infrastructure. This chapter also describes the intimate relationship between the Drools and jBPM projects, which is one of the key advantages of jBPM6 in comparison with all the other BPM systems, as well as existing methodologies where a BPM system connects with other systems.

Chapter 3, Using BPMN 2.0 to Model Business Scenarios, covers the main constructs used to model our business processes, guiding you through an example that illustrates the most useful modeling patterns. The BPMN 2.0 specification has become the de facto standard for modeling executable business processes since it was released in early 2011, and is recommended to any BPM implementation, even outside the scope of jBPM6.

Chapter 4, Understanding the KIE Workbench, takes a look into the tooling provided by the jBPM6 project, which will enable you to both define new processes and configure a runtime to execute those processes. The overall architecture of the tooling provided will be covered in this chapter as well.

Chapter 5, Creating a Process Project in the KIE Workbench, dives into the required steps to create a process definition with the existing tooling, as well as to test it and run it. The BPMN 2.0 specification will be put into practice as you create an executable process and a compiled project where the runtime specifications will be defined.

Chapter 6, Human Interactions, covers the Human task component inside jBPM6, in depth. A big feature of the BPM system is the capability to coordinate human and system interactions. It also describes how the existing tooling builds a user interface using the concepts of task lists and task forms, exposing the end users involved in the execution of human tasks, coming from multiple process definitions, to a common interface.

Chapter 7, Defining Your Environment with the Runtime Manager, covers the different strategies provided to configure an environment to run our processes. You will explore the configurations for connecting external systems, Human task components, persistence strategies and the relation a specific process execution will have with an environment, as well as methods to define their own custom runtime configuration.

Chapter 8, Implementing Persistence and Transactions, covers the shared mechanisms between the Drools and jBPM projects used to store information and define transaction boundaries. When we want to support processes that coordinate systems and people over long periods of time, we need to understand how the process information can be persisted.

Chapter 9, Integration with Other Knowledge Definitions, gives a brief introduction to the Drools rule engine. It is used to mix business processes with business rules, to define advanced and complex scenarios. We also cover Drools Fusion, and an added feature of the Drools rule engine to add the ability of temporal reasoning, allowing business processes to be monitored, improved, and covered by business scenarios that require temporal inferences.

Chapter 10, Integrating KIE Workbench with External Systems, describes the ways in which the provided tooling can be extended with extra features, along with a description of all the different extension points provided by the API and exposed by the tooling. A set of good practices is described in order to give you a comprehensive way to deal with different scenarios a BPMS will likely face.

Appendix, The UberFire Framework, goes into detail about the based utility framework used by the KIE Workbench to define its user interface. You will learn the structure and use of the framework, along with a demonstration that will enable the extension of any component in the workbench distribution you choose.

What you need for this book

This is a developer guide, so the thing you will find most useful when you read this book is a computer beside you, where you can try the examples and open, compile, and test the provided projects. The main idea behind the book is to get you up to speed in the development of applications or tooling that use jBPM6, and for this reason the book spends a lot of time with code examples and unit tests to run.

Good programming skills are required to easily understand the examples presented in this book. Most of the chapters complement the covered topics with a set of executable Maven projects. A basic understanding of Maven, Java, and JUnit is required.

Who this book is for

This book is intended for Java developers and architects who want to start developing applications using jBPM6, as well as start working on top of the provided tooling, either using or extending it. jBPM6 is a very flexible framework, but with this flexibility comes architectural and design decisions that we need to make when we start using it. This book offers a complete reference to all of the components distributed with jBPM 6.1.0.Beta3 community version, and it can be used as reference material to guide a team of developers in building efficient solutions using business processes and other knowledge definitions such as business rules and complex event processing.

After reading this book, you will have a good understanding of the jBPM6 architecture and components. jBPM6 is a Red Hat's lead open source community project and is fully supported through JBoss BPMS product. If you are interested in the BPMS product, you can find more details at `http://www.redhat.com/products/jbossenterprisemiddleware/business-process/`.

Conventions

In this book, you will find a number of styles of text that distinguish between different kinds of information. Here are some examples of these styles, and an explanation of their meaning.

Code words in text, database table names, folder names, filenames, file extensions, pathnames, dummy URLs, user input, and Twitter handles are shown as follows: "You can also run the server using the same command line by typing `mvn exec:exec` once the installation is done."

A block of code is set as follows:

```
public class RuleFlowProcessInstance implements ProcessInstance {
  public RuleFlowProcess getRuleFlowProcess() { ... }
  public int getState() { ... }
  public void setVariable(String name, Object value) { ... }
  public Collection<NodeInstance> getNodeInstances() { ... }
  public Object getVariable(String name) { ... }
}
```

When we wish to draw your attention to a particular part of a code block, the relevant lines or items are set in bold:

```
TaskService taskService = HumanTaskServiceFactory.
        newTaskServiceConfigurator().
        entityManagerFactory(emf).
        userGroupCallback(ugCallback).
        interceptor(priority, new UserLogInterceptor()).
        getTaskService();
```

Any command-line input or output is written as follows:

```
bin/standalone.sh --server-config=standalone-full.xml
```

New terms and **important words** are shown in bold. Words that you see on the screen, in menus or dialog boxes for example, appear in the text like this: "Once the **Finish** button is clicked on, we're directed to the project editor, where we can configure dependencies, KIE bases, KIE sessions, and all the project-relevant components."

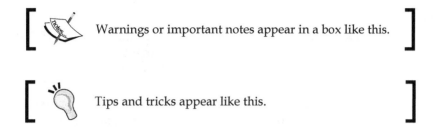

[Warnings or important notes appear in a box like this.]

[Tips and tricks appear like this.]

Reader feedback

Feedback from our readers is always welcome. Let us know what you think about this book—what you liked or may have disliked. Reader feedback is important for us to develop titles that you really get the most out of.

To send us general feedback, simply send an e-mail to feedback@packtpub.com, and mention the book title via the subject of your message.

If there is a topic that you have expertise in and you are interested in either writing or contributing to a book, see our author guide on www.packtpub.com/authors.

Customer support

Now that you are the proud owner of a Packt book, we have a number of things to help you to get the most from your purchase.

Downloading the example code

You can download the example code files for all Packt books you have purchased from your account at http://www.packtpub.com. If you purchased this book elsewhere, you can visit http://www.packtpub.com/support and register to have the files e-mailed directly to you.

Errata

Although we have taken every care to ensure the accuracy of our content, mistakes do happen. If you find a mistake in one of our books—maybe a mistake in the text or the code—we would be grateful if you would report this to us. By doing so, you can save other readers from frustration and help us improve subsequent versions of this book. If you find any errata, please report them by visiting `http://www.packtpub.com/submit-errata`, selecting your book, clicking on the **errata submission form** link, and entering the details of your errata. Once your errata are verified, your submission will be accepted and the errata will be uploaded on our website, or added to any list of existing errata, under the Errata section of that title. Any existing errata can be viewed by selecting your title from `http://www.packtpub.com/support`.

Piracy

Piracy of copyright material on the Internet is an ongoing problem across all media. At Packt, we take the protection of our copyright and licenses very seriously. If you come across any illegal copies of our works, in any form, on the Internet, please provide us with the location address or website name immediately so that we can pursue a remedy.

Please contact us at `copyright@packtpub.com` with a link to the suspected pirated material.

We appreciate your help in protecting our authors, and our ability to bring you valuable content.

Questions

You can contact us at `questions@packtpub.com` if you are having a problem with any aspect of the book, and we will do our best to address it.

1
Why Do We Need Business Process Management?

We software developers are used to embracing new technologies. Every day, we have to learn new versions of frameworks to make best use of the features available in them. We deal with the frustration of learning new APIs, integrating them in our project's architecture, and taking advantage of the all-new functionality that these new components provide us. We thrive on that. The software industry continuously pushes us into innovating how we design and architect our software solutions, sometimes to the point of not just creating a new framework, but a new paradigm to enhance communication and descriptiveness of the company's internal sequence of activities and software, which we need to understand as developers.

Business Process Management (**BPM**) is one of those paradigms whose scope goes further from the development arena and into all sorts of company realms. BPM provides visibility about a company's business processes, allowing us to improve and speed them up to increase profits and reduce costs, consequently improving the way the company works. It is a discipline with its own objectives, life cycle, and best practices, and one of its biggest added values is the common language it defines between all its participants—the business process.

You will find in this chapter the starting point to define these business processes, and how they help in building solutions that drive a company in a way that helps it to adapt faster to the business reality.

We will review this paradigm and how it enriches what we already know about building solutions, along with the technical topics to put them in practice into the latest jBPM version. To do so, we will cover both theoretical topics that would apply to understanding any **Business Process Management System** (**BPMS**) and the technical topics to build highly adaptable applications using jBPM6. Important concepts and definitions are highlighted throughout this book to help you solve new problems as they are found.

When you start embracing these new concepts, you'll find new ways of modeling situations, finding solutions, and building applications that will be of interest for many different people: the development team for integration purposes, the business analysts and managers for formalizing processes, the end users who will interact with the user interface, and pretty much anyone with an interest in the company processes. It is of great importance that you share this new knowledge with as many people in the organization as possible, because BPM is not just a development tool but a full company driver that will surely help your project and your company to be a success by establishing a common language between different areas of expertise.

BPM improves the quality and flexibility of the software solutions we build by helping the company to drive its business. BPM establishes a management strategy to establish an integral way of managing the company's activities, which allows different domains to concentrate on the efficiency of tasks in terms of time as well as costs. BPM allows a company to use an iterative cycle to continuously detect and improve both activities and processes as needed or desired by a company. Driving a successful BPM implementation requires a lot of learning, but we'll cover as much of that learning as possible in this book. I strongly recommend that you involve as many areas and roles as possible in your BPM implementations by taking advantage of the common language generated by the BPM methodology. Furthermore, sharing your experiences develops your professional skills and helps you to gather different perspectives and visions from the topics that you find relevant. So, let's get started!

The content of the book is divided into three different stages:

- Theoretical background
- Introduction, analysis, and explanations of standard specifications
- BPM APIs and common practices

Each stage focuses on different concepts.

Theoretical background

This stage will drive the language used when you discuss BPM-related topics. Important definitions that you will adopt will be explained, exemplified, and dissected. That makes this stage vital, as those definitions will relate to your everyday work and to the way you communicate with others in the project (and in the company). This is also the reason why it is important that the important aspects of BPM are discussed with your peers. You might constitute a new vocabulary out of them, and just like any vocabulary, it's important that it is shared by everyone.

Each definition will be scoped to a particular context. I will first explain each concept in a very generic way, as it helps you to understand the reason and purpose of the concept without including any reference to implementation or technical details. In more technical sections, I will map these concepts to more technical terms with concrete references to jBPM6.

Introduction, analysis, and explanations of standard specifications

This stage will (hopefully) drive your architecture and integration strategies. Standard specifications are created to define a common baseline to be shared and applied in new developments, which is based on the collaboration and experience of many groups and companies to aid in integration with other systems. If you decide to change implementations, standards could help you a lot in not having to rework migrations from one implementation to another.

This book introduces two main standards specifications, **Business Process Model and Notation** Version 2.0 (**BPMN 2.0**) and the Web Service Human Task specification. Both are used by jBPM6 and reflect good practices to create industry accepted and interoperable applications.

We won't go into the full details of the specifications in this book. We'll cover the details regarding where jBPM6 is not 100 percent compliant with the standard specification and how to deal with those cases. The standard specifications are not included for being size restrictive. Reading them, however, is very good to gain perspective on common practices adopted in a wide range of industries. We will provide links to them as we dive into them.

Technical details and common practices of jBPM6

This stage will ultimately drive your implementations by covering a complete list of the most important technical topics inside jBPM6, which will be discussed and demonstrated in practice.

We will begin with simple examples, and then the examples will gain complexity to reach real-life situations. All the source code used in the examples will be available to download and examine, but not all the lines of code will be explained. The technical sections of this book should be read with the source code available. The main idea is that you see the projects in your favorite IDE to practice just as if you were developing your own projects; this will help you to practice and get used to real development tools, projects, and errors.

This first chapter is focused on the whole conceptual background needed to get you started with jBPM6. Most of the concepts that will be introduced in the next section are related to the BPM discipline. These concepts are essential, and the clearer you understand them, the easier it will be to start with your first projects.

The conceptual background of BPM

In order to understand the concept that guides BPM, we must first begin by understanding all the concepts behind that name, and the first one we need to understand is the concept of **process**.

In the broadest sense, a process is *a series of steps or transformations to achieve a specific objective in a particular context*. Like any transformation, it needs to have something to transform and a well-defined desired output of the transformation.

For example, if we want to build a house, we need to follow a set of steps depending on the area of the house, the materials, any services available, and so on. The steps also depend on the outcome (house style) we want. Some of the steps can be done at the same time, while some need to wait for other steps to be finished.

The important thing is the coordination between those steps to perform the transformation in the way we intend to, and each step needs to be clear and concise. In short, for each transformation (process), we need to know all the steps required to achieve the required outcome (goal), which will be the desired result of a process. Usually, goals and objectives have the ultimate outcome of improving the revenue or production of a company, and can have multiple yet different end results, thereby improving the conditions of the business.

The knowledge of how to achieve the goal and the transformation steps are usually held by an expert in the context. I may probably have a basic idea about how to lift a few walls for a room, but for a real-life scenario, I may not be able to describe all the steps needed to make quality housing. If we really want to know about real-life processes, we need to talk to experts in that field. This expert knows how to deal with normal processes and also how to deal with specific or exceptional situations for a wide range of different houses and buildings.

Business processes

The word *business* associated to the process definition can seem ambiguous, but it is mostly due to how abstract the concept of business really is. From a developer-friendly perspective, we can think of business as a particular domain or context, or group of contexts. It could be easily exchanged in this case for domain, field, company, company unit, and any lingo that specifies a defined area of work. Business processes need to be evaluated, analyzed, designed, modeled, and validated by people who understand the domain where those processes belong. Since there are different business roles within a company, each should know a different perspective of the same process. Then, the business process becomes a common point of interaction and a common language between those roles. Activities, decisions, events, and many different components will define the structure of the way a process that is relative to a business needs to be conducted.

It is important to notice that the goal of business processes is tightly associated to the business goals, objectives, and strategies. With all these considerations in mind, we can arrive to the following definition:

Business processes are a sequence of business activities done by business users and business applications (company or third-party systems) to achieve a business goal for the purpose of a specific increase in value from the business' perspective.

We'll analyze this definition in detail by splitting it into its three main concepts and covering them thoroughly.

Sequence of business activities

An **activity** is a black box piece of work that contributes directly to achieving a business goal. We surely need to understand how the activity is performed. However, as we say, it is a black box, because from the process' perspective, the only things important are the inputs it needs and the outputs produced. The activity performed can be very simple or very complex, depending on the perspective of the process definition.

What is considered an activity in one process perspective can be composed of a group of low-level processes, which are in turn composed of a series of simpler activities. For example, a high-level process in a car factory can have an activity called "Build the Car's Engine", but from a lower-level perspective, activities could be detailed to the point of just telling a robotic arm to activate the weld for a second (one minuscule step in the car's engine preparation). In other words, a business process can be composed of multiple subprocesses.

Once you select a perspective or level for a particular process definition, you should stick to it for describing all activities regarding that specific process. You can call other lower-level processes from activities, so you can always go into more detail later. Besides, high-level strategic processes and low-level more technical processes will surely have different roles and experts behind them. A manager in a car factory might not be interested in having so much detail in their perspective, but an engineer would. Also, managers prefer to see the bigger picture, and tend to simplify their views to be able to cope with everything at once.

Usually, the low-level perspectives end up driving the operative end of the company, performing work such as the following:

- Handling customer information
- Documenting specific metadata
- Invoking service notifications

In the end, all processes are tied together by high-level perspective processes, which end up providing information for decision making, managing, and coordination. High-level processes usually aggregate information about the general performance, possible improvements, or any sort of relevant information for management. We will see examples of subprocesses, role assignment, and different activity type handling when we cover process writing in *Chapter 3, Using BPMN 2.0 to Model Business Scenarios*.

Naming our activities

The activity name is usually composed of the following:

- A verb
- A noun

Some examples of activity names are "Review Architectural Document", "Clean the Cutting Machine", "Analyze Client Risk", and so on.

It might seem a simple thing to put a name to an activity, but there are a few considerations to take beforehand. Remember that when you write a process, you are doing it from a particular perspective—whether it is a high level view of the whole company activity inside a process, or the flow of a very specific step performed by a company. Therefore, the activity name must make sense from that perspective. It wouldn't make much sense to name an activity "Rotate robotic arm elbow 45 degrees" in a high-level process, because its point of view should be much more abstract and wide.

Also, you should avoid any technical developer jargon in your activities' names. Remember that the process is thought to be a place for common language within a business or business unit, so the jargon used (if any) to write the process should be the jargon of that particular domain. It should be clearly understood by business users. In other words, try to avoid names such as the following:

- Call `InternalWebService->getMyData()`
- Execute batch command W-3302
- REST call to `http://my.domain:8080/rest/esoteric-service`

Also, try to avoid any terms that will make the process hard to read, like obfuscated IDs or out-of-scope terminology. Remember that depending on the process perspective, the people who will be interested in reading or updating such processes will be accustomed to different terminologies.

Business users and business applications

Business processes, at least when designed correctly, are not thought to be monolithic systems that cover everything, but coordination software between other systems (the business applications) and people (the business users). There are some differences in the way people and systems behave and also in the way they need to be coordinated.

Humans and systems behave differently

Human activities represent the human interactions in our processes. In the BPMN 2.0 specification, they are called User tasks. Every time we have a person involved in our business processes, we will have a human activity in our processes to represent such interaction.

When we think of human interactions in our business process execution, we think of having a person or group of people involved in a set of activities that will produce a specific result; the human response time to complete such activities takes minutes, or hours, or days. So, the process engine must be prepared to handle such activities in a way it can wait for long periods of time for the result of the task by providing asynchronous management of those tasks in runtime configurations.

Systems, on the other hand, usually represent automatic responses. Compared to human activities, external system activities take very small amounts of time—usually ranging from milliseconds for the fastest cases to minutes for the slowest automated activities. Companies generally have a set of external systems exposed through well-defined interfaces that solve very specific problems. When we need one of these services' information, we can just call external systems (through service calls, event handling, or simple scripting) and get the results into the process.

However, it is worth mentioning that systems may not provide automatic responses, or may take a long time to respond. Because of this, and for many other reasons we will mention later on, we should try to consider as many tasks in our process as asynchronous tasks.

Humans and systems – classification strategies

Systems can be classified based on their technical behavior as synchronous (the process engine will wait for the completion of a task, that is, a service invocation) or asynchronous (the system will continue its execution and wait for the external system to notify the process engine when the task is completed, that is, a thread-managed operation), while human interactions are intrinsically asynchronous. Also, systems can be classified, depending on their provider, as either internal or external third-party interactions.

Human interactions can be classified depending on the people involved in executing them. They can be performed by a specific role or group of roles within a company or domain, just one specific person, or maybe specified through a specific variable in the process. Examples of this classification would be the call center group of a company, customers, third-party users, and so on.

It's important to understand that these classifications are not important from the process engine perspective. All the engine will deal with is a name mapping of a particular group of activities to their implementation. The classification is useful mostly from the point of view of maintenance and documentation, which helps to know the ownership of each application/system in order to understand how the interaction will be made.

Achieving a business goal

The most important part of the business process definition is achieving a goal. It's the sole reason for the process' existence; without it, the process has no purpose at all. This should never be forgotten.

The business goal of a process shouldn't be disruptive or impossible to accomplish in any way in the selected business process perspective. Each business process definition must define a clear goal and all the activities must be defined in order to contribute to achieving said goal.

Mixing goals and perspectives is a common mistake that you need to avoid when you model your first business processes. For example, when defining the process of building a car in an automated factory, we might use the same process to define the steps a robotic arm should follow to make a simple weld, overcomplicating the process. When this happens, it's recommended to split the business process definition into multiple well-scoped processes for the sake of understandability and maintainability.

One way of achieving this difficult task is to create a brief textual description of the process' main responsibility, its ownership, and the concrete goal that it was designed to achieve. This brief description can be used to train new people to understand why the process is useful to the company. You will also end up with a self-documented process that can be used by the company to improve quality levels.

The BPM discipline

Now that we have defined what a business process is, we can start understanding how to manage the way processes interact with our organization. To do so, we will define six different stages that involve business process discovery, modeling, formalizing, execution, monitoring, and improvement. They constitute an iterative lifecycle for our business processes and the way they relate to their context. The following figure shows all the relevant participants and the cyclic nature of BPM:

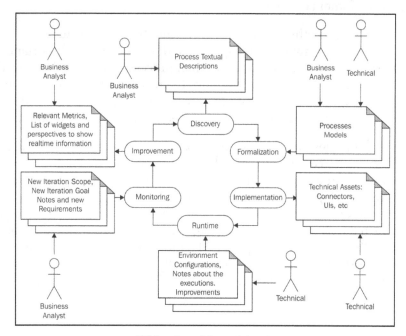

BPM cycle and its participants

The BPM discipline's scope and main goal is to improve the current business situation by planning iterations to solve well-defined problems, and it is not about coding Java or software development at all. You may be wondering how BPM achieves such a difficult task and also how it is related to jBPM6.

After the first three chapters of this book, the content will be really technical. However, it will be clearly shown how all these concepts solve real-life situations. We will see that the jBPM6 project structure, APIs, and designs are backed up by these concepts, and you will understand the importance of knowing them for future designs.

The following sections describe the stages proposed by the BPM disciplines. These stages highlight the most important points that need to be understood to start using BPM systems.

BPM stage 1 – discovering your business processes

Discovery of new processes is started most of the time by business analysts. It involves a certain level of **knowledge engineering**; a branch of requirement gathering involved in correctly merging different knowledge representation strategies, such as business rules, process definitions, and so on, with the knowledge from domain experts.

This stage has added weight when you're implementing the first iteration of the BPM cycle, which is choosing a starting point to demonstrate the importance of BPM for the business. I recommend choosing a small process to start, with a noncritical objective from the business perspective, since the results of the first iteration will surely teach you a lot of ways to do it better in the next iteration. It is important to take time to evaluate the learned lessons at the end of each of the iterations.

You'll notice that business analysts alone are not enough to perform this stage. Most companies that reach a certain level of maturity on BPM end up having a **Process Improvement department**, which involves technical people and a project leader solely dedicated to discovering and improving company business processes. They also include or collaborate with business experts, sponsors, and BPM champions (highly ranked people in the company, by title or merit, who are dedicated to encouraging the use of BPM throughout the company). Making BPM an enterprise-wide discipline is extremely important to make it work successfully; therefore, communication and acceptance of all areas of the company involved in BPM becomes a priority.

After identifying a goal to build a process around, this stage consists of performing interviews with business experts, representatives of operation, and anyone who is involved (or that should be involved) in the process. To achieve effective interviews, you have to prepare a questionnaire for each person/role involved in the process. Always target your questions to each role in the company. It is also advisable to have a wide set of questions to ask each interviewee as well as more specific questions, in case complex activities arise.

Some questions that I've found useful for these interviews are as follows:

- What is your role in process X?
- Which screens do you use to complete the activity X?
- Are you doing paper work? What kind of forms are you filling out?
- Is the activity related to the review of information sent by another person or system?
- Are you an expert of a specific topic? Are you the only one responsible for that activity? Are there more people trained for that specific activity?
- How many activities are you doing inside a specific business process?
- How many activities related to different business processes are you currently doing? (per day/week/month)
- Do you need to move information from one place to another by moving paper forms to different departments or using the postal service?
- Do you use e-mail/chat as a communication channel to send information to customers or to other business units?
- Do you interact directly with customers/clients face to face?
- Are you aware of the BPM practice and why the company wants to adopt it?
- Are you handling duplicate or unnecessary information?
- What are the well-known flaws of your activities?
- How do you deal with exceptional situations, missing pieces of information, or new cases?

If they answer that they do paper work, you should get a scanned version of all the forms that have to be filled out. If they are using different systems/screens/ applications, get those screenshots.

Always let interviewees know the goal of the process being analyzed and the purpose of improving the processes and how that would help them in their everyday work. This will increase collaboration on their side and reduce the stress associated with the fear of being scrutinized on work performance. You're not there to evaluate them, but to learn from them. Let them know that.

The information the interviews provide will help you understand what is being done to achieve the business goal, and it will result in a list of all the activities that the company executes related to that particular process.

Once you have all the different answers, you will be able to cross-reference them to determine the main path of the business process at hand. An example that could be the outcome of this first stage can be seen in the following figure:

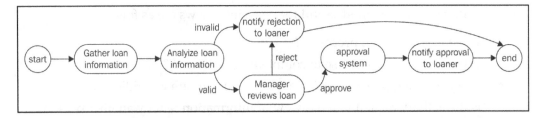

The preceding figure shows a brief graphical description of the relevant steps in approving a loan, but still doesn't adhere to any specific format. This is something to be dealt with in a later stage.

During this stage, you might also find new terms related to the activities in the process. Try to disambiguate those terms as much as possible by creating and updating a business dictionary with all the related terminology of the particular process.

Finally, find hidden activities related to company-wide processes (the most usual case is related to batch processes whose result end up impacting process activities). You'll need some expertise in the domain, which is why you need to check with domain experts to point out vocabulary inconsistencies, missing activities, and ambiguous terms, as well as to identify irrelevant business activities, duplicated activities, and so on.

BPM stage 2 – formalizing your new processes

When the business process, its owner, and the business goal have been identified, we can start working in a formal, unambiguous representation of the business process.

Formalizing processes is done using a predefined language. The purpose of the language is to be able to share the model with other people in a way that can only be understood in one way, as long as other people understand said language. There are many languages that have been designed over the last 20 years for this purpose; most of them are based on different graphical representations to help people quickly understand the activities needed to achieve the business goal.

When picking a language, you should always consider the ones that define the most widely accepted standard to make sure that most people can understand it. In 2014, the most widely accepted standard happens to be BPMN 2.0. We will learn the graphical representation and execution semantics of BPMN 2.0 in depth in *Chapter 3, Using BPMN 2.0 to Model Business Scenarios*. For the time being, let's just say that it provides a widely accepted formal language to represent processes that is not just implemented by jBPM6, but by many other process engines. So, even if you decide to use another engine, writing your processes in BPMN 2.0 would still be a good idea.

In this stage, business analysts trained in BPMN 2.0 will model the business processes. They should choose the level of accuracy of the process representation, depending on the time and information available for this stage. Since BPM is an iterative discipline, they can improve on that accuracy in later iterations.

This stage is also a very good point to start testing our processes through simulations. By determining the resources assigned to our process activities (people, time, and money), we can predict in a statistical way which activities would consume the most of each resource and plan ahead on assigning appropriate resources based on those simulations.

The resulting artifacts from this stage will be the formalized process with a graphical representation that can be shared and understood by different roles in the company.

BPM stage 3 – implementing your technical assets

In the third stage, the Development team works with the Business Analyst team to add all the technical details that will allow the process to run.

By now, we have a very important asset already implemented, that is, the business process' formal representation. This will act as common ground for exchange of ideas, improvement, formalized contract between areas, and also as documentation of what is being done. For that reason, it is important to keep it safe, versioned, and centralized. For this purpose, we usually set up a knowledge repository to store them.

Also, at this stage, the process definition needs to be enriched with all the information that its activities will handle and manipulate to achieve the business goal. There are different options to achieve this, and we'll discuss them in detail in the following sections.

The business entity model

We will select a model to work with, and our executable entity model will be created based on discovery stage results.

We usually have an inherited business model from legacy systems. When that's the case, you have three options:

- The first option is using the inherited model for your process activities. Its pros and cons are as follows:
    - ° **Pros**: It is fast to implement, especially if the developers of your organization already know the model.
    - ° **Cons**: Inherited models could carry an unnecessary complexity for the process' required level of data. Also, any change needed to be done to the process' internal model might impact a third-party project.
- The second option is storing external keys for the real entities inside your business process. The data will remain consistent and updated as long as it can be managed by a master data source from the process' engine point of view. Its pros and cons are follows:
    - ° **Pros**: You can reuse your old model and even its persistence, and only store a key to get the related information when needed.
    - ° **Cons**: If you store a key, you will need to query another data source every time the information is needed, and depending on the case, you might need to modify external information (with all the problems regarding permissions, communication, transactions, and so on). Depending on the amount of concurrent process executions, this could cause a performance issue.

- The third option is creating an understandable wrapper model that abstracts the legacy model, data sources, and communication strategies required by your business processes' model objects. Its pros and cons are follows:

  - **Pros**: You can map any outdated terms or concepts to a business process' relevant names and structures, and define underlying strategies to fetch information from external systems or to produce the needed data.

  - **Cons**: Writing and maintaining the integrity of the wrapper model will take time, and an expert on both models will have to worry about keeping everything in sync.

Once you define and know how to get and update information from your business model, you will need to bind each bit of information with the correspondent activity in your process. We usually do this with an expression language that allows us to express, in a declarative way, the information that we need without saying where it can be obtained. One example of this could be `#{ambulance.doctor.speciality}`.

This expression will be evaluated at runtime, and an internal mechanism will be used to retrieve the information.

Coordination and orchestration of activities

The business process provides us with a set of activities that need inputs and produce outputs. As technical developers, we will have to provide technological assets to provide such functionality, from creating form renderers for human interactions to creating connectors to external web services and transformations for external models to our entity model. In *Chapter 7, Defining Your Environment with the Runtime Manager,* we will analyze all the technical requirements to implement user interfaces, and in *Chapter 10, Integrating KIE Workbench with External Systems,* we will review all the relevant details about system-to-system interactions and the mechanisms that we need to know in order to keep everything simple.

Having a clear vision of the components that we need to implement and having a standardized and conceptually coherent way of interaction will make our life easier, and we will end up with simple applications that are easy to maintain.

By the time we finish this stage, our business processes will be executable. This will allow us to test, verify, validate, and simulate the process behavior. For the next iterations, this stage becomes unnecessary, and the only thing that changes between one implementation and another are the external systems' connectors as well as the technologies used to build frontends. All these topics will be covered in the jBPM6 technical sections where the technical details that need to be considered and best practices will be introduced. Also, in this stage, we can start showing the progress of our process definition in playbacks, so all parties involved in the process discovery and formalizing can see that the goals of the business processes are achieved.

BPM stage 4 – runtime

At runtime, we will put our business process and assets in a production environment. For the first iterations, it will probably be a production-like environment (that is, a full development environment).

This is the point where we start training users to understand how to interact with the activities of the business processes. For doing so, it's a best practice to use a unified approach to build **User Interfaces** (**UIs**), because it simplifies training (the user will not need to adapt to different components). We will see about unified user interfaces in *Chapter 6*, *Human Interactions*.

During the first iteration of this stage, the runtime should be restricted to a few simple processes and to a small well known group of users. When we have already tested the processes doing the real work in this situation, we will be ready to handle bigger processes, bigger groups of people, and more critical tasks and business goals.

This stage is when we actually start detecting how our processes behave in the real world. We can measure how the model allows users to have information; if they need extra information, we can see which tasks can have an improved performance and many other things that start providing us with invaluable information for the next iteration. Always take notes of that information, as it will be very important for future process-related improvement.

The first step is the most difficult. After we learn to take them, pretty soon walking becomes a simple thing. The same thing happens when sending our processes to a production environment. The experience you gain from doing so is very useful, and following this book, I hope you can do it with the least amount of problems possible.

BPM stage 5 – monitoring

Once we have finished the major steps of stage 4 and we have a stable enough runtime, we need to start concerning ourselves with the information that runtime gives us. Process execution can send many events to components that are external to the actual runtime. Those components can be fed to a dashboard-like tool to allow us to monitor process execution and actual performance metrics. This is a stage where the process simulation from stage 2 can be validated, and notes of the actual estimations should be taken for improvement of process simulations in the next iteration.

These dashboards are really important for key people who want to see snapshots of how the company is working in order to make the right decisions. As you can imagine, knowing the number of processes and activities that are completed per hour can be really helpful for planning, accepting new commitments of work from providers and customers, as well as measuring the company's growth rate. This is just one example of the things that you can do if you have the information available.

Monitoring is about real-time information analysis and display, but it should also be about flexibility. You might need to add new sources and types of metrics as fast as possible to measure them within the runtime. A related branch of studies called **Business Activity Monitoring (BAM)** defines best practices for doing so. Tools for BAM must be flexible enough to show information in such a dynamic manner. For example, a manager might want to see aggregated data from different sources when he asks for something like this:

> "*The average time of completion of one or a group of processes related to client X accounts in the last month.*"

We usually display this information in different widgets that are specially designed to show very simple values. These widgets provide an overview about what is happening in the company in just one screen where we can see multiple bar graphs, line graphs, and tables that let us quickly see what percentage of processes are in different stages throughout our process runtime environment.

The important thing about the monitoring stage is the externalization of information. These metrics can provide you with different perspectives to know which are the best places for improvement in your business processes and in your company altogether.

BPM stage 6 – improvements

Now, we will bring together all the things that we learn from the other stages and plan accordingly to better our business processes in our next iteration. By the time we reach this stage, we have our process runtime (and business relevant metrics) running to provide us with relevant information about the processes' execution. We might also have learned about exceptional situations in our processes that weren't considered at first and their ad hoc solutions. We now know how to simulate our processes better. We might also have new questions for our business experts from what we learned.

In this stage, we take care of business changes that need to be reflected in our business processes. All their improvements, along with the planning generated from the learned lessons, is used as an input for the next iterations — starting again from stage 1 and completing the BPM cycle.

BPM applications in the real world

Once we understand the basic elements of the BPM discipline, we need to apply it to a real-world scenario in order to learn from involvement and acquire experience. To do so, the best way to go is to use **Business Process Management System (BPMS)** as an aid in most of the BPM discipline stages.

A BPMS helps in the BPM discipline in the same way an **Enterprise Service Bus (ESB)** helps in defining a **service-oriented architecture (SOA)**. It provides a centralized environment to define, implement, and run business processes.

BPMS is a middleware component (a piece of software that allows us to create more software). It provides us with the tools to directly work on the specifics of our case, taking advantage of the already available functionality that is oriented to solve very specific tasks for each stage of the discipline. In the next section, we will see a list of things to take into account when we are evaluating a BPM system.

The BPMS check list

A BPM system must have a lot of different features to be a good asset for its users. For each individual stage of the cycle, you should find different tools or projects that you will need to evaluate before deciding to adopt them.

For the Discovery stage, a BPMS should provide you with a way to gather business knowledge. The tools that are most useful for this stage are questionnaire builders, interview recording software, and other means to store and analyze information from interviewees and other sources to understand how things work in the company. Most of the open source projects provide a modeling tool without giving us the appropriate information gathering and analysis tools. This usually confuses new adopters, because they start working without figuring out first what they need to model and solve. You should be aware of this and be prepared to spend some time asking questions and analyzing the results.

The Formalization stage needs tools to model your business processes. The best ones nowadays should all support the BPMN 2.0 language to write these processes. Most of these tools are targeted to business analysts whose only technical requirement is understanding of the BPMN 2.0 language, so be prepared to provide training for the people involved in writing the processes. During the first iterations, the first processes are usually defined by people who already know how to write the processes and the implications of modeling an executable business process, and they can even use that writing time to transmit their knowledge.

Another thing to notice about the quality of a process editor is how it integrates with external configurations and modeling information, such as entity models and specific business-centric activity descriptions. Make sure that you're able to do those things when you evaluate a process editor.

The Implementation and Runtime stages are the ones where the most tools are usually found. They constitute the main component of a BPMS, that is, they provide an execution environment for your processes. From the software point of view, these two stages are well covered by the existing open source projects in the market. It's important to understand that a BPMS should allow the technical people of the company to directly interact with the process engine so that they can customize and extend the provided generic behavior. During these stages, we will see a strong relation of BPM with SOA-based applications. BPM can become a very important component in relation to web services, as a coordinator, and as a consumer; it can even be exposed itself as a web service. In *Chapter 10, Integrating KIE Workbench with External Systems*, we will see how to expose existing tooling through web services.

In the Monitoring and Improvement stages, you should concentrate on three things; the API provided to extract information about process executions from the runtime, how simple it is to create a new indicator, and the dashboard's visual flexibility.

Most problems arise in the most decision-intensive stages, that is, stages 1, 5, and 6. There is no current standard methodology to discover business processes. Since they are nontechnical tasks, the maturity of the software related to these stages is usually not great. Even if you have automated questionnaire forms, dashboards, and improvement planning software, you still need to analyze the data by people and make decisions. Also, to make those decisions, you need to learn about the company to do those tasks correctly.

BPM APIs and common practices

From a developer's perspective, most BPMS provides a set of API's to easily plug and integrate your applications with the process engine (irrespective of the technology or language that you use in your company's applications). BPMS also provide a clear description about the information they store by default, and how to extend and customize that information for specific domain analysis. This mechanism is usually designed to be generic and extensible.

The main differences that you can usually find between process engines are as follows:

- How flexible the core is in adopting new custom services
- How well documented the engine is
- How often releases are updated
- What standards the project implements
- How well it integrates with other technologies and frameworks
- How much support it receives, either paid or from the open source community

These items are a good starting point to evaluate and compare different Process Engines' features. After that is done, the next step is to analyze the available tools for each stage.

Tooling usually is heavily evaluated during the first phase of comparison between different projects, especially in case of integration projects. For real-life full implementations, it is always preferable to adapt the tools for a particular usage—after modest to extensive modifications are made to them. Usually, the desired output is to integrate it with existing applications and within company proprietary frameworks.

From the process engine internal functionality perspective, it's easy to build tools and integrate them into your existing applications using the APIs provided. From the BPMS perspective, you should always check that the internal functionality from the process engine is easily exposed through a set of APIs, because the majority of closed source products don't expose the internal APIs to provide extension points, and this can make integration quite difficult to manage. BPM plays an important role in integration with other enterprise applications and providing service coordination. The more importance BPM gains for a company, the more it will be related to controlling different activities performed by many different applications in a company. The easier the said integration can be done, the better and less painful BPM adoption becomes.

To integrate tools, if it is in the interest of your company during evaluation time, you should check the following features:

- The amount of tooling available
- The number of features
- The flexibility of the results generated by the tooling
- The technology that the project uses to build the tooling
- The skills that you have over those frontend technologies
- The difficulty of extending or porting the tooling

Remember, you must be ready to change all project generic UIs/tools provided by the BPMS. You must know how they were built. A good measure of the tooling development quality is how easy it is to start extending the tooling projects.

BPM – adoption of standards

Last, but no less important, is the evaluation of how well the features of the selected BPMS relate to established standards. There are two standards you should check for current applications, the **Web Service Human Task (WS-HT)** standard and the BPMN 2.0 standard. The WS-HT standard defines two main features:

- A standard set of APIs (interfaces) to interact and manage human activities.
- A complete and flexible human activities life cycle. This life cycle defines the states through which a human interaction will transit during its life.

Also, the BPMN 2.0 standard defines a set of XML tags to describe business processes, their interactions with external systems, and their structures.

The biggest advantage of having a set of standard API's is that the better the different implementations adhere to those standards, the easier it is to decouple the definitions of processes from the engine's internal functionality — this allows for the possibility of migrating to another technology if you ever wish to. We will learn more about BPMN 2.0 and human interactions in *Chapter 3, Using BPMN 2.0 to Model Business Scenarios*, and *Chapter 6, Human Interactions*, respectively.

Summary

Now that we've covered all these conceptual topics, we are finally at a point where we can start applying them to real-life projects. All the presented concepts in this chapter will be quite necessary over the next chapters to help you understand how and why the tools are designed the way they are.

In the following chapters, we will analyze how to implement and use tools that are related to the BPM realm. We will learn about leveraging rule engines, complex event processing, and other tools with the process engine to be able to solve real world problems.

We'll start by explaining how BPM systems are structured to provide an automated way of handling the BPM discipline stages, and how those tools are used to develop applications to help your company do its job.

2
BPM Systems' Structure

Business Process Management (**BPM**) systems are pieces of software created with the sole purpose of guiding your processes through the BPM cycle. They were originally monolithic systems in charge of every aspect of a process, where they had to be heavily migrated from visual representations to executable definitions. They've come a long way from there, but we usually relate them to the same old picture in our heads when a system that runs all your business processes is mentioned. Nowadays, nothing is further from the truth.

Modern BPM Systems are not monolithic environments; they're coordination agents. If a task is finished, they will know what to do next. If a decision needs to be made regarding the next step, they manage it. If a group of tasks can be concurrent, they turn them into parallel tasks. If a process's execution is efficient, they will perform the processing 0.1 percent of the time in the process engine and 99.9 percent of the time on tasks in external systems. This is because they will have no heavy executions within, only derivations to other systems. Also, they will be able to do this from nothing but a specific diagram for each process and specific connectors to external components.

In order to empower us to do so, they need to provide us with a structure and a set of tools that we'll start defining to understand how BPM systems' internal mechanisms work, and specifically, how jBPM6 implements these tools.

Components of a BPMS

All big systems become manageable when we divide their complexities into
smaller pieces, which makes them easier to understand and implement.
BPM systems apply this by dividing each function in a different module and
interconnecting them within a special structure that (in the case of jBPM6) looks
something like the following figure:

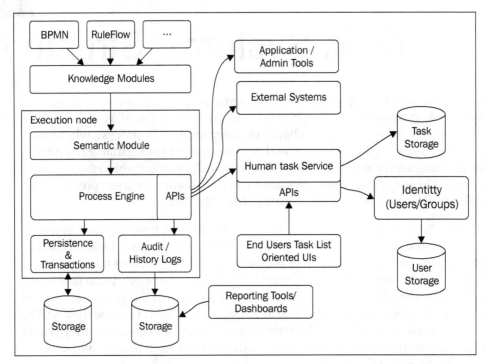

BPMS' internal structure

Each component in the preceding figure resolves one particular function inside the
BPMS architecture, and we'll see a detailed explanation on each one of them.

The execution node

The execution node, as seen from a black box perspective, is the component that
receives the process definitions (a description of each step that must be followed; from
here on, we'll just refer to them as processes). Then, it executes all the necessary steps
in the established way, keeping track of each step, variable, and decision that has to be
taken in each process's execution (we'll start calling these process instances).

The execution node along with its modules are shown in the following figure:

The execution node is composed of a set of low-level modules: the semantic module and the process engine.

The semantic module

The semantic module is in charge of defining each of the specific language semantics, that is, what each word means and how it will be translated to the internal structures that the process engine can execute. It consists of a series of parsers to understand different languages; of these, we'll concentrate on BPMN2 in *Chapter 3, Using BPMN 2.0 to Model Business Scenarios*.

It is flexible enough to allow you to extend and support multiple languages; it also allows the user to change the way already defined languages are to be interpreted for special use cases. It is a common component of most of the BPMSes out there, and in jBPM6, it allows you to add the extensions of the process interpretations to the module. This is so that you can add your own language parsers, and define your very own text-based process definition language or extend existing ones.

The process engine

The process engine is the module that is in charge of the actual execution of our business processes. It creates new process instances and keeps track of their state and their internal steps. Its job is to expose methods to inject process definitions and to create, start, and continue our process instances.

Understanding how the process engine works internally is a very important task for the people involved in BPM's stage 4, that is, runtime. This is where different configurations can be used to improve performance, integrate with other systems, provide fault tolerance, clustering, and many other functionalities.

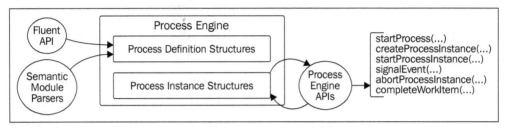

Process Engine structure

In the case of jBPM6, process definitions and process instances have similar structures but completely different objectives. Process definitions only show the steps it should follow and the internal structures of the process, keeping track of all the parameters it should have. Process instances, on the other hand, should carry all of the information of each process's execution, and have a strategy for handling each step of the process and keep track of all its actual internal values.

Process definition structures

These structures are static representations of our business processes. In *Chapter 3, Using BPMN 2.0 to Model Business Scenarios*, we will see how these representations can be written by technical people and different domain experts in detail; we do this using an XML standard called BPMN 2.0 for process definition and graphical representation.

However, from the process engine's internal perspective, these representations are far from the actual process structure that the engine is prepared to handle. In order for the engine to get those structures generated, it requires the previously described semantic module to transform those representations into the required object structure.

The following figure shows how this parsing process happens as well as the resultant structure:

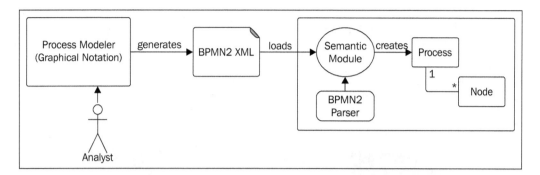

Using a **process modeler**, business analysts can draw business processes by dragging-and-dropping different activities from the modeler palette. For jBPM6, there is a web-based modeler designed to draw **Scalable Vector Graphics (SVG)** files; this is a type of image file that has the particularity of storing the image information using XML text, which is later transformed into valid BPMN2 files.

Note that both BPMN2 and jBPM6 are not tied up together. On one hand, the BPMN2 standard can be used by other process engine provides such as Activiti or Oracle BPM Suite. Also, because of the semantic module, jBPM6 could easily work with other parsers to virtually translate any form of textual representation of a process to its internal structures.

In the internal structures, we have a root component (called **Process** in our case, which is finally implemented in a class called `RuleFlowProcess`) that will contain all the steps that are represented inside the process definition.

From the jBPM6 perspective, you can manually create these structures using nothing but the objects provided by the engine. Inside the `jBPM6-Quickstart` project, you will find a code snippet doing exactly this in the `createProcessDefinition()` method of the `ProgrammedProcessExecutionTest` class:

```
//Process Definition
RuleFlowProcess process = new RuleFlowProcess();
process.setId("myProgramaticProcess");

//Start Task
```

```
StartNode startTask = new StartNode();
startTask.setId(1);

//Script Task
ActionNode scriptTask = new ActionNode();
scriptTask.setId(2);
DroolsAction action = new DroolsAction();
action.setMetaData("Action", new Action() {
    @Override
    public void execute(ProcessContext context) throws Exception {
        System.out.println("Executing the Action!!");
    }
});
scriptTask.setAction(action);

//End Task
EndNode endTask = new EndNode();
endTask.setId(3);

//Adding the connections to the nodes and the nodes to the processes
new ConnectionImpl(startTask, "DROOLS_DEFAULT",
        scriptTask, "DROOLS_DEFAULT");
new ConnectionImpl(scriptTask, "DROOLS_DEFAULT",
        endTask, "DROOLS_DEFAULT");
process.addNode(startTask);
process.addNode(scriptTask);
process.addNode(endTask);
```

Using this code, we can manually create the object structures to represent the process shown in the following figure:

This process contains three components: a start node, a script node, and an end node. In this case, this simple process is in charge of executing a simple action. The start and end tasks simply specify a sequence.

Even if this is a correct way to create a process definition, it is not the recommended one (unless you're making a low-level functionality test). Real-world, complex processes are better off being designed in a process modeler, with visual tools, and exported to standard representations such as BPMN 2.0. The output of both the cases is the same; a process object that will be understandable by the jBPM6 runtime. While we analyze how the process instance structures are created and how they are executed, this will do.

Process instance structures

Process instances represent the running processes and all the information being handled by them. Every time you want to start a process execution, the engine will create a process instance. Each particular instance will keep track of all the activities that are being created by its execution.

In jBPM6, the structure is very similar to that of the process definitions, with one root structure (the ProcessInstance object) in charge of keeping all the information and NodeInstance objects to keep track of live nodes. The following code shows a simplification of the methods of the ProcessInstance implementation:

```
public class RuleFlowProcessInstance implements ProcessInstance {
    public RuleFlowProcess getRuleFlowProcess() { ... }
    public long getId() { ... }
    public void start() { ... }
    public int getState() { ... }
    public void setVariable(String name, Object value) { ... }
    public Collection<NodeInstance> getNodeInstances() { ... }
    public Object getVariable(String name) { ... }
}
```

After its creation, the engine calls the start() method of ProcessInstance. This method seeks StartNode of the process and triggers it. Depending on the execution of the path and how different nodes connect between each other, other nodes will get triggered until they reach a safe state where the execution of the process is completed or awaiting external data.

You can access the internal parameters that the process instance has through the getVariable and setVariable methods. They provide local information from the particular process instance scope.

Node instance structures

jBPM6 uses a node-instance-based approach to determine what steps are being executed by the process instance. This means, for every active step in the process, a node instance object exists in the process instance. When the step is completed, the node instance is removed. This allows us to have a list of active steps in the process instance that are accessible by jBPM6 from the getNodeInstances method available from the NodeInstanceContainer interface. The following code shows a simplification of the methods of most of the node instance implementations:

```
public interface NodeInstance {
  public ProcessInstance getProcessInstance() { ... }
  public long getId() { ... }
  public long getNodeId() { ... }
  public void trigger(NodeInstance from, String type) { ... }
  public void cancel() { ... }
}
```

Here, you can see that node instance objects have methods to trigger the execution of a particular step or to cancel it from the outside. It also has an identifier for itself, the step definition, and the process instance it belongs to.

Finally, we can assert the internal status of the process instance by the getState method. Its implementation will return an integer value determined by constants in the ProcessInstance interface to any of the following states:

- STATE_PENDING: The process instance hasn't started yet
- STATE_ACTIVE: The process instance is running
- STATE_COMPLETED: The process instance has finished successfully
- STATE_ABORTED: The process instance has been forcefully finished
- STATE_SUSPENDED: The process instance is paused

Process instances are created based on the process definitions using a special ProcessInstanceFactory implementation. This implementation contains the logic on how to create and initialize process instances according to a particular process definition and environment configuration. Since this factory is internally used by the exposed runtime, let's start learning about the said runtime to get a better picture of using processes in jBPM6.

Components inside jBPM6

In order to be able to use jBPM6, we need to create a specific runtime in which it can execute processes. Since Version 6, this runtime configuration has changed from being simple programmatic components to add BPMN files to a knowledge runtime to a complete API to create, interpret, and monitor Maven-based projects that contain BPMN resources in their structures. Maven is a Java-based tool for project integration, that is, from compilation to deployment time. It's widely supported by many different products that need to connect with specific deployments of objects, and this is why jBPM6 has embraced Maven as an internal representation of its modules. In order to provide ourselves with a runtime, we now need to obtain BPMN process definitions, rule definitions, and a full umbrella of different knowledge definitions from established structures.

There are enough components that surround jBPM6; it would take multiple books to cover each one of them in detail. There are planning frameworks for planning problems, probabilistic components, integrations with persistence frameworks, and many more that appear every day. We obviously won't be able to cover all of them, but we'll try to cover the ones that are most related to BPM systems in the following sections of this chapter.

A specific runtime allows you to have a wide variety of knowledge definitions to work together in a single environment. The following diagram shows how the runtime is constructed in an abstract way to allow us to understand how this is possible:

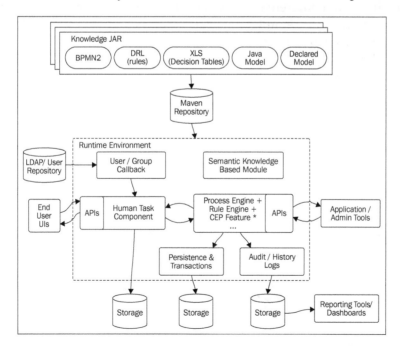

As you may notice, the **rule engine** (Drools, www.drools.org), the **process engine**, and **complex event processing** (**CEP**) features are merged to work together. This is very useful when it comes to defining processes; it's because the decision points that would make a very complex process definition are sometimes complemented by other knowledge representations such as business rules and decision tables. Having all the features running in a single environment allows the engine to communicate decisions made by rules or processes in a very direct way. Because of these features, it is important that we understand the knowledge-centric APIs to know how to interact with processes. The following section will cover the most important concepts so you can start using and understanding these APIs.

Transactions and persistence

Transactions and persistence of the runtime status of the process execution engine are two extremely important topics to cover. BPM systems usually integrate systems and people to achieve a common goal. Deciding the next step could take milliseconds, but executing each step could take a lot more time. Persistence and transaction mechanisms allow for resource release in the process engine environment, load distribution, and fault recovery mechanisms.

Persistence is not meant, at least as provided by default, to make sessions and processes easily searchable from external tools. It is mostly used to provide a recovery strategy for the content that sessions and processes need in order to be able to continue them from different threads or even different servers. The persistence mechanisms, therefore, are simple serializations of the minimal content that the runtime needs to carry on the execution in a different environment.

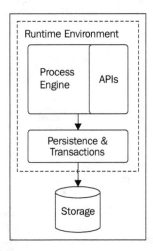

Persistence works by wrapping the KieSession object's methods in a transactional environment where KieSession and all its internal components can be persisted after every call that is made inside a transaction boundary defined by the application. This provides us with a mechanism to define the following:

- How to handle long-running processes
- How and when can we store information about the status of the process and the information that the process is handling
- How and when do we need to create, commit, or roll back the process engine transactions
- Which business exceptions can roll back or compensate the already executed business actions

All these topics and its configuration mechanisms will be discussed in detail in *Chapter 8, Implementing Persistence and Transactions*.

Persistence for a process's execution is thought to be a recovery point between different environments. It wasn't thought of as a tool that provides a history of the process's execution or much readable information from external tools, but just to store its current state. Completed process instances are deleted from the runtime's database to maintain it at a steady size. For the same reason, only running steps are stored, and everything with regards to the runtime is simply serialized to the database to make restoring the process instance as efficient as possible. To keep historical information about our process executions separately, we need to use the Audit/History logs.

Audit/History logs

To provide searchable historical data of the process executions, a specific component stores the changes of the different process instances, its steps, and its variables. This information is known as the history logs of the process engine. **Business Activity Monitoring (BAM)** tools and dashboards are some of the most common clients for the information generated by this component. They display different aggregations and compositions of that data to different people (developers and business analysts, among others). It is heavily used during state 5 (monitoring) of the BPM cycle.

Some common applications that can be created using these components are as follows:

- Real-time dashboards
- Data-mining or data-analysis tools

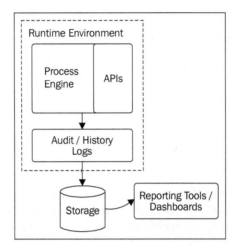

Real-time dashboards

The first line of analysis for the generated history logs are the real-time dashboards. They are usually composed of different widgets to display information from the last few hours to months of executions in our environment and present them in a way that assists users in making judgments about the environment's efficiency.

The jBPM6 BPM system provides a dashboard tool that we will start learning in *Chapter 4, Understanding the KIE Workbench*. In it, we can set different metrics and calculations that will define how the information will be aggregated and summarized for the end user. They provide tooling to make new indicators on the run and make a quick in-depth analysis of the historical information.

Data mining and data analysis tools

These kinds of tools provide a second level of analysis by allowing you to have huge amounts of information to be presented in a more detailed, cross-referenced way. Data mining and data analysis tools help us identify patterns, find hidden or hard-to-discover situations, and also improve the way information is being stored or generated.

Real-time dashboards are thought to typically query the data storage too often and do a lot of in-memory calculations in order to present summarized information. Data mining tools, on the other hand, are prepared to query huge amounts of information just once in an offline fashion. Usually, this sort of analysis requires a restructuring of the available information into different structures that are easier to query from data mining tools.

The KIE APIs

As of Version 6, both jBPM and Drools (the parent project of jBPM that establishes an inference engine and runtime for both rules and processes) have changed their umbrella name from Drools/jBPM to KIE.

KIE stands for **Knowledge Is Everything**; this change was made to encompass all the new components that keep on getting added to the Drools and jBPM family, such as **OptaPlanner** for planning problems or **Predictive Model Mark-up Language (PMML)**, an import functionality. It also uses the KIE name to group generic parts of the unified API, such as building, deploying, and loading knowledge-related projects.

The main aspect that you should pay attention to is that KIE runtimes work by taking the knowledge definitions not just from a group of knowledge files like previous versions did. They instead work by reading their knowledge definitions from the Maven-based JAR files (Maven: http://maven.apache.org) that could contain anything a JAR file could contain, from classes and configuration files to processes, rules, and much more. This means that building and loading applications can align with Maven and Maven repositories by adhering to a standardized way of managing code and configuration updates through JAR publications in specific repositories.

It also includes a declarative configuration in an XML file for KIE projects called kmodule.xml; for this configuration, we will create different components to define knowledge definitions and runtimes, along with the kbase and ksession tags. It must be located inside the META-INF folder. Here's an example of a kmodule.xml file:

```xml
<?xml version="1.0" encoding="UTF-8"?>
<kmodule xmlns="http://jboss.org/kie/6.0.0/ kmodule">
   <kbase name="namedKieBase">
      <ksession name="ksession1">
   </kbase>
</kmodule>
```

Before we get to understand this configuration, we need to cover what structures we will use to actually access the Maven dependencies that define our knowledge runtime. We will start with a few main concepts, as follows:

- KIE services
- The KIE module
- The KIE container
- The KIE base
- The KIE session

KIE services

In the KIE API, there are a lot of different services for the instantiation of components that could be implemented in different ways. Luckily, a helper method to access those instantiations is provided by the `KieServices` class, which serves as a simple starting point for the generation and access of the KIE components. It is accessible through the following method:

```
KieServices ks = KieServices.Factory.get();
```

This method will be used in the next pieces of code.

The KIE module

Any Maven dependency that contains a `kmodule.xml` file (like the one we showed at the beginning of this section) is considered a KIE module. They can be loaded from the classpath, dynamically from any knowledge resource, or can be built programmatically, shown as follows:

```
//Create a virtual file system for our generated project
KieFileSystem kfs = ks.newKieFileSystem();
//Write content in a maven project structure
kfs.write("src/main/resources/my-process.bpmn2",
        getFile("my-process.bpmn2"));
//Set a specific maven release ID for a pom.xml in the file system
kfs.generateAndWritePomXML("com.wordpress.marianbuenosayres",
  "test", "1.0-SNAPSHOT");
//Use a Kie Builder to generate a Kie Module
KieBuilder kbuilder = ks.newKieBuilder(kfs);

//build the content
kbuilder.buildAll();
KieModule kmodule = Kbuilder.getKieModule();
```

In the previous code, you first created a filesystem representation where you will write a specific Maven module. This is pretty much the same method you should use when creating a new project using maven, but here you'll use the KIE API to do it for you. You then add a BPMN2 file to it (whose content will be loaded from the `getFile (my-process.bpmn2)` invocation) and set the release ID of the project (composed of the group ID, artefact ID, and version). Afterwards, a `KieBuilder` instance is used to build a specific `KieModule` object from that filesystem representation.

The KIE container

The KIE container provides an accessory to utilize the KIE module. It will provide versioning and building through maven, and you can dynamically update the version of a KIE container to work with other KIE modules.

From inside the KIE container, we will have access to the knowledge definitions and runtimes defined for each KIE module:

```
KieContainer kcontainer = ks.newKieContainer(
kmodule.getReleaseId());
```

You can also get the container from the current project classpath:

```
KieContainer defaultKcontainer =
   ks.getKieClasspathContainer();
```

Then, you can get the default knowledge definitions and runtimes from the container:

```
//Getting default knowledge definitions from the container
KieBase kbase = Kcontainer.getKieBase();

//Creating knowledge runtimes directly from the container
KieSession ksession = Kcontainer.newKieSession();
```

The KIE base

A KIE base is a repository for a particular group of knowledge definitions. It will contain rules, processes, functions, and type models. They don't contain data. Runtime environments are created from `KieBase` and wrapped in the `KieSession` objects. They're represented in the `kmodule.xml` file by the `kbase` tag. Constructing a `KieBase` repository can be quite heavy, so if they're built programmatically, it's recommended to have them cached. They can be obtained from `KieContainer` by getting the default KIE base:

```
KieBase kbase = kcontainer.getKieBase();
```

Alternatively, we can get a specific `KieBase` repository by name:

```
KieBase kbase = kcontainer.getKieBase("namedKieBase");
```

The KIE session

In contrast to the `KieBase` objects, `KieSession` objects store and execute all the runtime data. They're represented in the `kmodule.xml` file by the `ksession` tag. They can be created from `KieBase` or, as we saw in the *The KIE container* section, from the `KieContainer` object directly. This object is the point of contact to start, signal, and complete process instances:

```
KieSession namedKsession = kcontainer.newKieSession("ksession1");
KieSession newKsession = kbase.newKieSession();
```

There is another flavor of `KieSession` called `StatelessKieSession` that can run isolated one-time-use-and-dispose executions, but since they don't support process executions, we will skip them in this book.

From the process's perspective, we are interested in the following methods that are exposed by the `KieSession` interface:

```
public ProcessInstance startProcess(String   processId);
public ProcessInstance startProcess(String   processId,
    Map<String, Object> params);
public void signalEvent(String type, Object event);
public void signalEvent(String type, Object event,
    Long processInstanceId);
```

We will use these methods (and other services implemented with these methods) to interact with our process instances at the runtime. You can see a quick example of these configurations in the `testKieAPIConfigurations` method of the `KieAPIProcessExecutionTest` class, as shown in the following code:

```
KieServices ks = KieServices.Factory.get();
KieFileSystem kfs = ks.newKieFileSystem();
Kfs.write("src/main/resources/my-process.bpmn2",
    getFile("my-process.bpmn2"));
kfs.generateAndWritePomXML(ks.newReleaseId(
    "com.wordpress.marianbuenosayres", "test", "1.0"));
```

So far, we have created a new filesystem to start writing our project programmatically. It will have one process (since it is a maven project, it should be located by default at src/main/resources); then, we set a group, artefact, and version for the POM file of the maven project. Once we've done this, we have to validate its content using a KieBuilder instance:

```
KieBuilder kbuilder = ks.newKieBuilder(kfs);
kbuilder.buildAll();

if (kbuilder.getResults().hasMessages(Level.ERROR)) {
  System.out.println("Errors compiling Kie Module");
  System.out.println(kbuilder.getResults().getMessages());
  throw new IllegalStateException("Errors compiling KieModule");
}
KieModule kmodule = kbuilder.getKieModule();
ks.getRepository().addKieModule(kmodule);
```

This will create a KieBuilder instance that will try to construct a KieModule object from a filesystem that contains maven files. If the building of the KieModule object encounters any errors, all messages related to the build will be printed through the system output, and an exception is thrown to stop the system from continuing with the load. Otherwise, we obtain the KieModule object from the KieBuilder instance and add it to the in-memory repository.

Once the module is added to the repository, we can use a KieContainer instance to obtain the knowledge definitions and knowledge runtimes that are defined in it:

```
KieContainer kcontainer = ks.newKieContainer(
  kmodule.getReleaseId());
KieBase kbase = kcontainer.getKieBase()
KieSession ksession = kbase.newKieSession();
```

We obtain the default KieBase object for the container and create a simple stateful session from the said KieBase; we could have also requested it directly from the container. Once we have a session, we can use it to start process instances:

```
ProcessInstance pI = Ksession.startProcess("myDesignedProcess");
```

Since the `my-process.bpmn2` file contained a process definition with the `myDesignedProcess` ID, we can use that ID to create a new process instance. We store its reference in the `pI` variable. Since it is a completely automated process with no external interactions or wait states, the process instance will be completed by the time the variable is assigned. So there is nothing more you can do with it.

Now that we understand the core of the process engine, we can continue looking at how other components around the process engine fit inside jBPM6.

External interactions

As said before, good process engines are not meant to be monolithic software that manage everything inside; instead, they are coordination frameworks for people and other systems. One key component to achieve such a behavior is to provide a connector strategy to configure and/or code external interactions between the process and other systems.

From the runtime point of view, each one of these external interaction instances are called Work items. Work items are a representation of a specific step in a process execution. They will store the input and output information for each interaction and its state (pending, active, completed, or aborted).

However, information about the actual occurrence of the external interaction invocation is not enough. We need a way to create our own external interaction code to determine what to do for each particular case. To handle these interactions, you need to implement the `WorkItemHandler` interface, which is used to manage external interactions with other systems by providing a way to invoke them from inside the process:

```
public interface WorkItemHandler {
    public void executeWorkItem(WorkItem i, WorkItemManager m);
    public void abortWorkItem(WorkItem I, WorkItemManager m);
}
```

We can later on bind different types of tasks to different `WorkItemHandler` implementations by registering them in the `KieSession` exposed manager:

```
KieSession ksession = KieServices.Factory.get().
    getKieClasspathContainer().newKieSession();
Ksession.getWorkItemManager().registerWorkItemHanlder(
    "mySpecificTask", new MySpecificWorkItemHandler());
```

Inside the `executeWorkItem` method, you can define the interaction with your external system. You can continue with the execution after the method by calling the following method:

```
m.completeWorkItem(i.getId(), i.getResults())
```

You can make the process stay in a continued state. This invocation is the one thing in `WorkItemHandler` that will notify the engine that the step has been completed. If you don't call this method, the process will pause the execution of the process instance and reach a safe state after executing the `executeWorkItem` method. For the process to continue on to the next step, someone needs to invoke that method from outside using the `KieSession` exposed manager:

```
Ksession.getWorkItemManager().completeWorkItem(...);
```

The other method in `WorkItemHandler`, called `abortWorkItem`, gets invoked when a specific work item that is waiting for someone to call the `completeWorkItem` method is suddenly stopped. It can be used to clean up any elements that might be waiting for an external interaction.

You can find an example of creating, registering, and using `WorkItemHandlers` in the `testExternalInterations` methods of the `ExternalInterationsProcess-ExecutionTest` class:

```
KieSession ksession = KieServices.Factory.get().
getKieClasspathContainer().newKieSession();
//My test implementations of WorkItemHandler
TestSyncWorkItemHandler handler1 = new TestSyncWorkItemHandler();
TestAsyncWorkItemHandler handler2 =
  new TestAsyncWorkItemHandler();
Ksession.getWorkItemManager().registerWorkItemHandler(
  "task1", handler1);
ksession.getWorkItemManager().registerWorkItemHandler(
  "task2", handler2);
```

In the previous code block, we created a session from the default knowledge base of the classpath container. We also created two variables, `handler1` and `handler2`, that hold special implementations of the `WorkItemHandler` interface created exclusively for this exercise. The first one stores the amount of invocations it gets and carries on with the process execution, as shown in the following code:

```
public class TestSyncWorkItemHandler implements WorkItemHandler {

    private int invocationCount = 0;
```

```
    public void executeWorkItem(WorkItem item,
      WorkItemManager manager) {
      this.invocationCount++;
      manager.completeWorkItem(item.getId(), null);
    }

    public void abortWorkItem(WorkItem item,
      WorkItemManager manager) {
    }

    public int getInvocationCount() {
      return invocationCount;
    }
  }
```

The second one stores the work item that invoked it, but doesn't complete itself. So, it leaves the process instance in a wait state, as shown in the following code:

```
  public class TestAsyncWorkItemHandler implements WorkItemHandler {

    private WorkItem item;

    public void executeWorkItem(WorkItem item,
      WorkItemManager manager) {
      this.item = item;
    }

    public void abortWorkItem(WorkItem item,
      WorkItemManager manager) {
    }

    public WorkItem getItem() {
      WorkItem retval = item;
      item = null;
      return retval;
    }
  }
```

Notice that the handler will only return each work item once. After that, all invocations of the getItem method will return null until executeWorkItem is called again by the process engine.

Have these implementations of `WorkItemHandler` registered in the session when we execute a process composed of a call that is firstly identified by `task1` and secondly by `task2`; the execution will stop in the second task and wait for signals to carry on:

```
ProcessInstance pI = ksession.startProcess(
  "myExternalInteractionsProcess");
Assert.assetEquals(ProcessInstance.STATE_ACTIVE, pI.getState());
Assert.assertEquals(1, handler1.getInvocationCount());
WorkItem item = handler2.getItem();
Assert.assertNotNull(item);
```

Now that we have the reference to the work item, we can use it to tell the session to carry on with the process's execution:

```
Ksession.getWorkItemManager().completeWorkItem(item.getId(), null);
```

We will cover a lot more about using work item handlers later on in this book. However, one of the provided `WorkItem` handlers has one particular importance: the external system it communicates with allows you to interact with human beings. It is registered in the exposed manager with the key `Human Task`. We will fully cover the configuration of this handler in *Chapter 7, Defining Your Environment with the Runtime Manager*, along with the runtime manager in detail. Let's first discuss the system behind it and its components.

The Human task component

The Human task component (also referred to as a task service) is, from the process engine's perspective, a service just like any other to which each process instance coordinates deferred calls (that is, when the task service is invoked, the process reaches a wait state until the service says it can continue).

The particularity of this service is what it is prepared to do. It allows you to manage tasks that reflect any sort of human interaction. The process engine interacts with it when a process instance reaches a User task to notify the service of new tasks that different people in a domain will have to execute. After that, it is the responsibility of the Human task component to make sure that all tasks fall into the right hands.

To do so, it will need to interact with three other components:

* The User/Group callback to get access to the company's users
* A persistence to store the internal state of tasks

• End user UIs to show information related to tasks that each user must do, and forms to allow them to do so

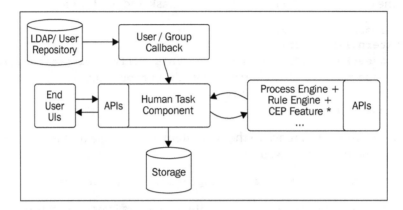

The task service exposes a set of APIs that obey a specific life cycle. We will proceed to explain both.

Human tasks – life cycle

In the preceding diagram, the Human task component box represents the core of the human task service. It provides methods to create tasks, assign them, start them, complete them, and much more. We'll learn more about the different stages in a human task's life cycle in *Chapter 6, Human Interactions*. At the moment though, it will provide different statuses for our tasks, depending on their assignment, who can work on them, and whether they've already been started, claimed, skipped, or completed. All these statuses are based on an industry-based, strong standard called **Web Service Human Task (WS-HT)**. It provides core definitions to structure our tasks and define their stages.

Human tasks – APIs

The Human task component exposes a set of APIs that are also based on the WS-HT standard specification, which is defined in the `https://incubator.apache.org/hise/WS-HumanTask_v1.pdf`. The API's responsibility is to provide us with a way to handle human tasks from the user interfaces in a task-list-oriented way. Those APIs are also used by the process engine to create tasks and register themselves for listening to changes on each task (specifically, completion, failure, or skipping of the tasks that the process engine created).

It is important to understand at this point that the Human task component itself doesn't need to understand anything about processes. It merely provides a framework to work with human tasks. It is the process engine that will depend on this component if it has processes with human tasks defined in them.

User UIs will use the APIs provided by the task service to provide task lists with relevant tasks for different groups and users and also to populate and complete forms that represent tasks performed by people.

The User/Group callback

The Human task component will assign tasks to different groups and users depending on the potential users, groups, and administrators defined for each task. Those groups and users need to be defined within some specific security context. In order to provide such understanding to the Human task component regardless of the way your domain validates users and groups, the API provides a UserGroupCallback interface. The User/Group callback is a component in jBPM6 to abstract the way your company stores and accesses your business users. This will allow us to write our process definition's human tasks by already assigning specific user and group IDs, knowing that later on the end user UIs will be able to map the logged-in user's ID to obtain all the tasks assigned to him or her and his or her groups. The User/Group callback is an interface that defines the following three methods:

```
public interface UserGroupCallback {
  boolean existsUser(String userId);
  boolean existsGroup(String groupId);
  List<String> getGroupsForUser(String userId,
    List<String> groupIds,List<String> allExistingGroupIds);
}
```

With this simple interface, the Human task component can easily understand how to manage user assignment for all different tasks. We'll learn more about the different implementations of the User/Group callback (and how to plug them in) in *Chapter 6, Human Interactions*.

The BPMS ecosystem

BPM systems can be very useful as enterprise-wide development tools. However, they are usually just one system among many others that piece together the enterprise architecture of a company. We will cover some of the most common or most related components to BPM systems in this section. We'll cover what they are and how they relate to BPM systems. I strongly recommend that you learn more about the ones you feel would be most useful for your particular case. Their use will allow you to build more robust and scalable applications with preexisting solutions.

BPM and service-oriented architecture

SOA has been around for quite some time now. It is a software design principle based on creating discrete pieces of software that expose an application's functionality as services to other systems. It promotes the creation of highly decoupled and self-contained units of functionalities called services. They can live alone without external requirements, and they expose well-defined interfaces to access a specific functionality.

When you create a new application, you can use the previously exposed services. This will allow pieces of software to be decoupled, easily maintained and reused, and exchanged in an easier way than if they were embedded in an existing application.

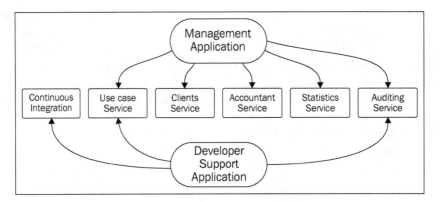

As you can see in the preceding figure, we can create applications by composing and reusing different sets of services. Each service provides a specific functionality that each application uses. In this example, we can see how both the use case service and Auditing service are being used by two different applications.

BPM systems relate to service-oriented architectures by either BPM systems exposing services (that can be called by other applications to handle the creation of the process and signaling) or by handling service executions with processes. Since services are to be considered as external interactions, we can create `WorkItemHandlers` to invoke different kinds of services.

Service orchestration

So far, we've mentioned processes that call services as a way to relate BPMS and SOA. However, we need to differentiate that from a separate concept called service orchestration and **Web Services Business Process Execution Language (WS-BPEL)**. WS-BPEL is an orchestration language for services that are exposed using web services. It was only meant to work with web services to manage the sequence in which they are to be called for a specific purpose. BPM systems go beyond that to create a process that can orchestrate many different things, one of which can be web services.

When we talk about BPM systems guiding services, we usually mean a business process that, during its execution, will call one or more web services to obtain or change specific results.

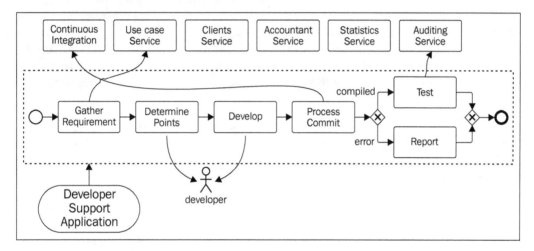

When we talk about service orchestration, however, it usually means the far more narrow-scoped concept of providing a sequence for web services alone. In this book, we will only cover topics related to BPM systems and not these kinds of service orchestrations.

Enterprise Service Bus

Enterprise Service Bus (ESB) is another SOA-related technology that is meant to provide a common point for a service's publication, discovery, and (from an infrastructure point of view) coordination of services. It hides the low-level complexity of connecting to different services while providing a centralized infrastructure for them. It is highly recommended that you use an ESB as part of an SOA implementation because it simplifies integration problems and centralizes the monitoring of services.

ESBs and BPM systems are not exclusive tools; they are quite the opposite. Using ESBs simplifies connectivity issues when dealing with external interactions in business processes; they do so by providing a common place for service discovery. Also, BPM systems can be integrated as services exposed in ESBs.

Most ESBs provide an integration with jBPM6 by means of two different frameworks: Spring (`http://www.spring.io`), a framework for component integration and initialization, and Camel (`http://camel.apache.org`), a framework for service interconnection through endpoint declarations. Both (Spring and Camel) are supported by most of the latest ESB tools, and the KIE projects provide two projects to expose `KieSessions` through both the aforementioned frameworks: `kie-spring` and `kie-camel`.

The full picture could be a combination of process interactions (for services and human tasks) and the BPM system and service interactions wrapped with the ESB; this allows different system providers to just worry about writing new services, new processes, or new versions of both.

The business process flows will describe how the work is being done in the company and not the technical details required for sending information from one place to another. This is later provided by the actual implementation of `WorkItemHandlers` in the runtime configuration; this is possible thanks to the semantics proposed by business process modeling languages such as BPMN2, which will be introduced in *Chapter 3, Using BPMN 2.0 to Model Business Scenarios*.

Business experts appear in this scenario as users of the BPM systems in the roles of business process creators, editors, and auditors. Meanwhile, other roles don't need to interact with the processes nor the services, but only with the tasks assigned to them. In a scenario like this, it is the process's responsibility (and not the responsibility of specific applications) to access the services and exchange information with them through Service tasks, a component we will see in detail in *Chapter 3, Using BPMN 2.0 to Model Business Scenarios*.

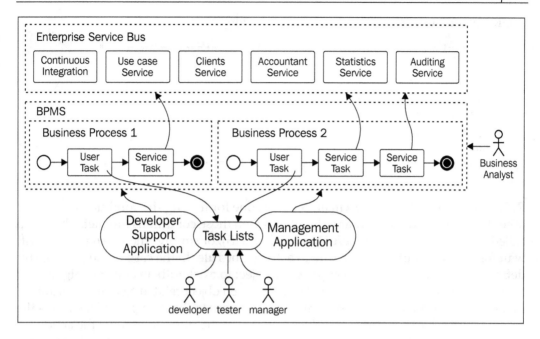

Rule engines

Business processes are good to express a sequence of activities in a visually simple way. However, sometimes, specially when we want to express complex business logic for specific decisions, writing business process can become too complex and cryptic; also, depending on the number of decisions that are taken, they could make our processes look like a labyrinth. To implement complex business logic inside activities or the business logic surrounding all the processes, we can use a declarative expression language that writes those decisions as business rules.

The Drools rule engine, which will be introduced in detail in *Chapter 9, Integration with Other Knowledge Definitions*, allows us to define business rules using the **Drools Rule Language** (**DRL**). DRL is an expressive declarative language to define business situations and a way to interact with them. There are mappings that can be created by transforming from natural language to DRL in order to make them user friendly to read and write by business analysts.

A DRL-based business rule looks like the following:

```
rule "Driver License only for apt applicants over 18 y.o."
when
  $a: Applicant(age > 18)
  $md: MedicalRevision(
    applicant == $a,
status == "Approved")
  then
  startProcess("driverLicenceProcess", $a);
   end
```

Rules are described using two main sections: one for finding the conditions and the other for the consequences that will follow when those conditions are met. The first is called a conditional section, **Left-Hand Side (LHS)**, or simply "the when part". It will wait for all the conditions to be true to activate the rule. In the case of the previously defined rule, it will wait for an `Applicant` object to exist with an age over eighteen. When found, it will search for a `MedicalRevision` object related to that applicant that has been approved. Once both are found, it goes to the then part of the rule — the consequence section or **Right-Hand Side (RHS)** of the rule — to execute the actions associated with that condition. In this case, it will call a previously defined function to start a specific process for that applicant.

This rule is very simple, but in an environment where many rules exist, each rule distinguishes a very specific decision of the business logic. Together, very complex decisions can be made using highly decoupled rules. The rule engine will be in charge of matching all of these rules against the current state of the world in the most efficient way possible. Rule engines were specially designed to evaluate a huge number of rules at the same time without any impact on performance.

BPM systems have an intimate relationship with business rule engines to determine decisions at specific points of process executions and to govern process executions themselves. In the following section, we'll see different ways in which BPM systems and rule engines integrate.

Classic BPM system and rule engine integration

BPM systems rely on rule engines to take complex decisions based on business logic expressed in a declarative way. For most BPM systems, this rule engine execution was handled through external calls to the rule engine that resided outside the BPM systems (sometimes in a completely different server). Doing it like that involved a lot of work. BPM systems had to gather information to send to the rule engine and prepare it for transmission.

Then, when the rule engines were executed, the results would have to be retransmitted to the BPM system as well. This could become more complicated if you also wanted to invoke your BPM system from inside your business rules. This is because in that case, you would also have to implement external calls to the BPM system from inside the rule engine. The more the communication between components, the higher the risk of communication problems between runtimes.

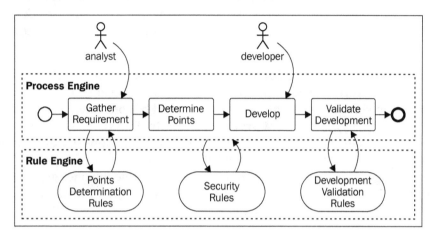

Due to this communication overload, just a small percentage of the rule engine's capabilities were usually used. Most interactions were intended to be stateless to facilitate testing, and therefore only small, well-scoped problems were solved at a time by the rule engine.

For jBPM6, integration with the Drools rule engine happens seamlessly. The process engine *is* in fact a rule engine as they are both running on the same environment. This allows you to handle complex stateful scenarios with ease using rules, from simple validations to handling process activity monitoring and decision management based on rules. Every process instance that is running in the same KIE session will share the same rule-based memory, state, and data, and have special rules to determine situations that cross-reference many different process instances. This would be impossible to do in a stateless environment where each process instance would be completely isolated from other executions. With those functionalities running for us, we can create smarter and more flexible processes that at the same time are easier to read, thanks to being able to take all complex decisions using rules. This means that we need to only worry about the sequence of activities from the process's perspective.

Event-driven architecture and complex event processing

Event-driven architecture (**EDA**) allows developers to construct highly decoupled systems composed of single function components that interact through events and manage complex situations by aggregation of more components in the architecture. It is another way of building scalable applications that are different from SOA, but both methodologies complement each other depending on the desired result and the path of the growth of our systems.

The components proposed by EDA are divided in four different elements: event producers, event processing agents, event consumers, and event channels. Event producers are in charge of generating events that will be consumed, composed, aggregated, and analyzed by **event processing agents** (**EPAs**). EPAs can also generate high-level events based on composition or aggregations of other events. The resulting object is called a complex event. Event consumers will usually consume these generated events, but they can also consume the ones generated by the producers. Event channels merely represent communication structures to send data between producers, consumers, and EPAs.

To relate it to our BPM systems, we could consider the process engine, an event producer, which will produce a new event every time a process is created or completed. An event consumer in this scenario would be a process-monitoring dashboard that handles warnings when the process engine is performing in a non-sustainable way. One or more event-processing agents would be in charge of monitoring when specific scenarios that could indicate such behavior present themselves. One of such cases could be the process creation to completion ratio given by all the events produced in the last few hours. When it exceeds a particular threshold, we should send alerts to the dashboard.

It is important to notice the decoupled nature of event-driven architectures. Event producers, consumers, and processing agents don't need to know about the existence of each other. They all work and are able to exist separately, without any other dependency than the possibly shared event definitions.

The Drools rule engine allows you to create rules that perform complex event processing, therefore producing event-processing agents. Since jBPM6 is seamlessly integrated with Drools, if we chose both technologies to construct our EDA, the event channel could simply be the internal memory of `KieSession` (called the working memory).

More examples on this topic will be provided in *Chapter 9, Integration with Other Knowledge Definitions*.

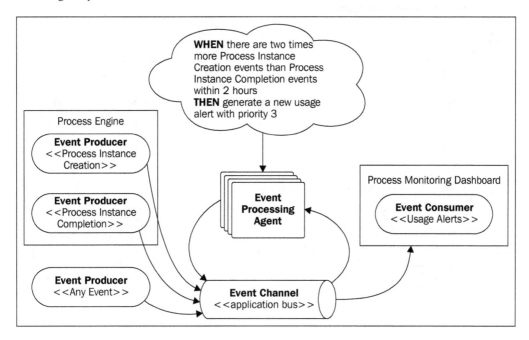

The biggest added value of the EDA infrastructure is the concept of event-processing agents. When they generate complex events from different sources, they usually do it by using a complex event-processing framework, such as the Drools rule engine to handle different stream of events and define filters and conditions.

We can leverage the power of an event-processing agent to influence our business process's execution, create new process instances based on the aggregation and correlation of events that come from different sources, or even notify external applications or users about the completion of a business process under a set of specific circumstances. In *Chapter 9, Integration with Other Knowledge Definitions*, we will see how we can use the Drools rule engine (and particularly a set of APIs called Drools Fusion) to integrate complex event-processing features with our BPM systems.

In the next figure, we see a combination of process engine and event-processing agents from the perspective of a particular process; combined, they can model very complex business scenarios.

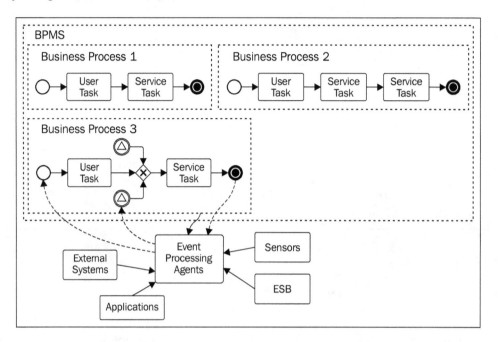

Predictive analytics and decision management

Predictive analytics is a highly recurring concept that surrounds decision management systems. It is based on analyzing the information exposed by knowledge-based services and finding missing cases, detecting projections in the values of variables, and expanding the universe of information by cross-referencing other sources of information.

In order to analyze this information to obtain such insights, events from different sources (including process executions from BPM systems), that is, from real-time production environments, are fed into a simulation environment. Here, queries are raised and data analysis conducted to test different scenarios to see which ones have a better coverage of all the cases.

The information obtained is later used to feed new knowledge definitions to production environments. This cycle is known as the decision analysis cycle.

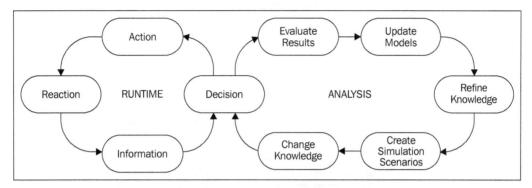

Decision analysis cycle, encompassing both runtime and analysis

BPM systems assist in decision management by providing a way to define business processes that are both very visual and faster to update than other system implementations. Of all the possible forms of quickly representing and adapting knowledge, business processes are the most descriptive way to provide a sequence of steps. They provide a great added value to the decision management software by allowing them to inject new process definitions to increase the number of decisions that can be taken or handled.

At the same time, decision management provides a great added value to BPM systems by providing feedback for a new process's discovery and analysis tools to detect cases not yet covered by processes, allowing process quality to be improved.

The analytics of production data is a very powerful tool that can be used in three different stages of the BPM cycle. In stage 5 (monitoring), it is involved in collecting information from runtime environments to create a data source for future investigation. In stage 6 (improvements), analytics is heavily involved in finding new cases not previously covered by the existing runtime. Finally, for stage 1 (discovery), simulation environments play a fundamental part in understanding the impact of new processes or modifications to existing processes in the real-time existing production environment.

At the moment, there aren't any tools inside the KIE suite to create these decision analytics directly, but new features are added constantly to the existing suite. So, I wouldn't be surprised if by the time this book is published, some form of tooling to do this analysis is introduced to the suite as a new experimental feature, probably as an add-on to be adopted in the future.

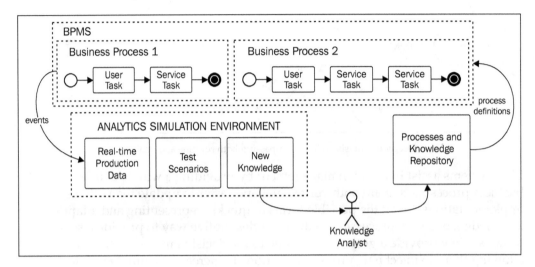

As you can see in the preceding figure, events from the BPM system can be fed to the decision software analysis tools, and the acquired information can be used to define new business processes or improve existing ones. Thanks to the simulation tools, new processes can be tested with existing data to see whether they will meet the discovered scenarios.

There is a lot more content regarding decision management software, and unfortunately we can't fit it all in this book. The tooling provided by jBPM6 can be connected to decision management in one way or another, and during the course of this book, whenever we start explaining each tool in detail, we will mention how it can connect to the decision management software. For the moment, let's just explain that it provides a methodology to provide fast and continuous improvement of knowledge definitions in order to drive smarter actions in all our systems (including our BPM systems).

Summary

In this chapter, we have covered all the components that create a BPM system and also how the said components are implemented for jBPM6. We've started learning APIs that use the said components. In further chapters, we will go deeper into the configuration and coding details to fully cover the components discussed in this chapter.

There are a lot of architectures and design components that can be mixed with BPM systems. We will continue by solving problems with the described tools and concepts to learn where to apply them and mention good connection points to other architectures or concepts. Learning more about technologies that BPM systems relate to will help you enrich your design and implementations, by providing you with a whole set of middleware solutions.

To download the source code used in this and the following chapters, go to `http://github.com/marianbuenosayres/jBPM6-Developer-Guide`. You will find a folder for each chapter that contains the source code that we see in each code section.

In the next chapter, we will discuss in detail how to write and use BPMN2 files to define our business processes, and explore more examples regarding process executions.

3
Using BPMN 2.0 to Model Business Scenarios

After learning about the BPM discipline, we understand that we need to have a formal language to express our business processes. This language will help us in defining a well-established sequence for the decisions our organization makes. We want to make sure such definitions are as powerful as possible, so we want the formal language to be extensible. We also want the freedom to choose our BPM system regardless of our definitions as much as possible, so we want the formal language to follow widely accepted standards. For all these reasons, in this chapter we focus on BPMN 2.0, a standard, flexible language that is supported by jBPM6 and many other providers as the current de facto language for executable business processes.

We will introduce a real-life use case to demonstrate best practices and design strategies based on managing requirements in a Sprint Development use case, where we will perform the following operations:

- Introduce the BPMN 2.0 standard specification
- Model different elements of our business processes
- Create an example to run our processes

We will be covering most of the most common constructs required to model and build real-life processes. You might already have a particular use case, so if you do, try to use such constructs and best practices for your particular scenario. The concepts we'll learn in this chapter apply for virtually any domain.

Introduction to BPMN 2.0

The idea behind BPMN Version 2.0 is to provide a standard way to both represent the visual structure of a business process and its execution semantic, all in the same file, while also providing a mapping between both. This way, the gap between business analysts drawing a new business process and the business process actually running in an execution environment is significantly reduced. This also provides a common ground for technical people and business people to share ideas. The purpose of this chapter, and of the BPMN standard, is to make process diagrams (such as the following diagram), something that can be easily read and understood by different groups of people:

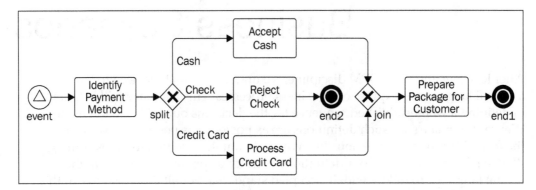

The standard was formally released in January 2011, and it is a result of the collaboration between companies such as Oracle, IBM, Red Hat, Intalio, and many others within the **Object Management Group (OMG)**. They combine almost 20 years of business process standardization experience in this standard. This specification (Version 2.0) is divided into four sections that allow different vendors to comply with one or more of the following compliance types:

- Process modeling
- Process execution
- Collaboration modeling
- Choreography modeling

In this book, we will cover only process modeling and process execution because jBPM6 focuses only on those areas.

Process modeling compliance

Process modeling only needs to worry about the visual representation of the business process to comply with that part of the BPMN 2.0 standard. This usually provides graphical tools to draw/model business processes and collaboration diagrams. The specification defines two types of business processes:

- Non-executable
- Executable

Modeling tools only need to model non-executable processes, but they can also add all the details necessary to make the process definitions they create executable in different environments.

Non-executable processes are something to still take into account. In a sense, all processes start as non-executable processes until all the details necessary for their proper execution are added in a BPMS environment. Non-executable processes can also be very useful for documentation, sketching, and as common ground to discuss the internal processes of an organization.

If we want to model executable processes, the specification creates a subcategory (such as a subclass) of this compliance type called **Common Executable Conformance**, covering the minimum requirements for an execution environment for executable business processes. These requirements are as follows:

- The data types and data models that will be related with our business processes must be XML schemas
- The default service interfaces must be WSDL service definitions
- The default data access language must be **XML Path Language** (**XPATH**), a query language used to select nodes from an XML

Of course, different vendors can decide how to cover these requirements — by changing technology stacks on different points or adding new possible implementations. It is a good point of comparison between vendors to see what features each vendor implements and how they implement them.

BPMN 2.0 elements

Now, we will explain all the different components that the BPMN 2.0 standard defines for process modeling and execution. We will also mention how jBPM6 adheres to this standard. For the full specification of BPMN Version 2.0, you can visit http://www.omg.org/spec/BPMN/2.0.

In the next section, we will use those concepts to define example processes that will help us fully understand how all the concepts work together.

The specification divides elements in the process definition as follows:

- Flow elements
- Connecting elements
- Data
- Swimlanes
- Artifacts

Flow elements

Flow elements are one of the most important elements, as they are in charge of defining behavior. The specification defines three types of different flow elements: events, activities, and gateways. Each is in charge of very different kinds of steps, and therefore all very necessary to define a complete business process.

Events

Events represent a capture of a particular occurrence that interests the process. They are usually caused by an external cause or trigger. They're represented with a circle and, depending on the type of the border and its contents, the behavior that events expect to trigger. In the following diagram, we see an example of different BPMN events with types and subtypes:

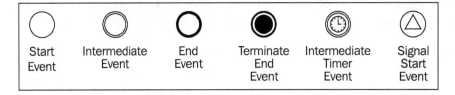

There are three main types of events:

- **Start events**: These events are drawn with a single, thin border line. They represent an external interaction that causes the beginning of a business process instance.

- **Intermediate events**: These events are drawn with double, thin border line. They are in charge of catching external events or throwing events, even outside the process instance scope. They can influence the flow of the process, but they cannot start it nor end it.

- **End events**: These events represent the end of a process instance or the end of an execution path inside a process instance. It is always sent and never received from outside the process instance scope.

For each main type of event (start event, intermediate event, and end event), there are many subtypes defined by the specification. For example, the last three events in the previous diagram are specific subtypes. The terminate end event marks that all the active execution paths in the process instance must finish, as long as one path reaches said node. The intermediate timer event will wait for a given amount of time before continuing with the execution flow. Finally, the start signal event will start a new process instance when an external signal of a specific kind is sent to the runtime environment. There are many more; but for the first examples we'll see, these will suffice. Support for a wide variety of all three main types of events is provided by jBPM6.

Activities

Activities define a piece of work that is being done inside the process scope. They could be atomic or nonatomic activities, depending on whether they can be further divided into more activities or not. For such purposes, the standard defines three different types of activities: tasks, subprocesses, and call activities. These are represented as boxes in the following diagram:

As seen in the preceding diagram, a rounded rectangle defines a task, which can have different subtypes. An icon on the top-left corner can define different types of atomic activities, such as User tasks (a human should provide a specific input in these kind of tasks), a Script task (when a particular piece of script needs to be executed), a generic task (it will have no icon and is thought to be defined in runtime), or many more.

When the rounded rectangle has a particular sign on the bottom, the activity is considered as a subprocess, which means that it can be decomposed into different activities. Depending on the sign, it can mean that the round rectangle will contain many subactivities that are just not relevant to the current process definition's scope. This can be executed once (when it is a plus sign) or many times (when three parallel lines are on the bottom). Usually, these subactivities are embedded inside the subprocess activity box.

Finally, if we want to invoke a process definition defined outside the scope of the current process, we use call activities. This encourages reutilization and transfers the control of the execution to the activity being called. Call activities are defined by a thicker border line, like the third rectangle from left in the previous diagram.

All of these types of activities, tasks, subprocesses, and call activities are supported by the jBPM6 process designer at runtime.

Gateways

Gateways control the divergence and convergence of sequence flows in a process. They are represented by a rhombus, and the drawing inside the rhombus determines the different types. The following diagram shows examples of different BPMN gateways:

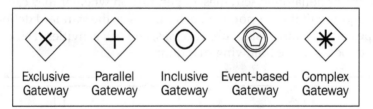

BPMN2 gateways have one outgoing connection and many incoming connections (when a gateway is diverging), or many outgoing connections and one incoming connection (when a gateway is diverging). The most commonly used gateways are as follows:

- **Exclusive (or XOR-based) gateway**: This is marked with an **X** sign and it allows only one outgoing execution path to be executed, depending on conditions defined in the outgoing flows. When converging, it carries on whichever path reached it, because it expects one flow to be executing only.

- **Parallel (or AND-based) gateway**: This is marked with a plus sign and allows us to define concurrent paths. When diverging, it creates a new execution path for each outgoing connection; when converging, it waits for all connections to finish and carry on with one execution path.

- **Inclusive (or OR-based) gateway**: This is a less restrictive version of the exclusive gateway. It allows one or more paths to continue when diverging, depending on conditions defined in the outgoing flows. When converging, it should wait for all active paths to finish before continuing with a single execution path.

- **Event-based gateway**: This defines a branching point in the process where we should wait for one of many different events before continuing with the process execution. Event-based gateways allow the process to make a decision on which path to follow based on the event received first.

- **Complex gateway**: This allows us to define a more complex condition, where 1 to *n* branches should be able to continue. When joining branches, we can also decide whether to wait for one or more execution paths before continuing with the next activity of the process.

Complex gateways are the only ones not supported by jBPM6. Also, for converging gateways, only exclusive and parallel gateways are supported.

Connecting elements

To define the sequence between flow objects, we use sequence flows. They are represented as arrows, and the specification defines three types of sequence flows to specify different behaviors to propagate the execution. The following diagram shows different sequence flows:

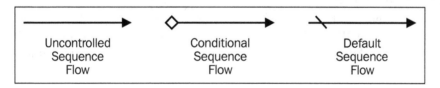

The different sequence flows are defined as follows:

- **Uncontrolled sequence flow**: This is the most common sequence flow. It represents a connection between two flow objects, with an origin and a destination.

- **Conditional sequence flow**: This evaluates an expression to determine whether it should continue to the next flow object or not. The expression is evaluated at runtime when the process is being executed, usually involving a check on a process variable.

- **Default sequence flow**: This is used in inclusive/exclusive/complex gateways. It determines the flow that will be selected if no other path matches the specific criteria.

Sequence flows are the standard way of providing a sequence in business processes, and they are fully supported by jBPM6.

Finally, the relationship between these data components, the process, and its flow objects is done using message flows. They represent an association between a data object and a flow object. The specification mandates that message flows don't affect the process execution flow, and they only provide a way to share information between a source and a target. The specification also allows transformations to be applied by using expressions, as shown in the following diagram:

Data elements

Data elements represent information that will be manipulated by the process instance during its execution. BPMN 2.0 allows us to define this information graphically and to specify where the data will be used. Data objects can be divided into the following:

- Data objects
- Data inputs and data outputs
- Data stores
- Properties (no visual representation)

Data objects are the most basic representation of a piece of information used in a process. They can be added to processes and subprocesses and can be associated with their life cycle. That means, when our processes are instantiated, we can instantiate our data objects as well. We can mark data objects to be a single instance or a collection, as shown in the following diagram:

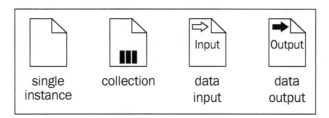

The other two types in the preceding diagram are also data objects, but they are called **data inputs** and **data outputs**. They map specifically to inputs or outputs of a specific activity.

Data stores are used to interact with information outside the scope of the process. They represent external sources of information that are not instanced by the process, but that the process execution can access nonetheless, that is, a database. The following diagram shows the **Data Store**:

Properties include data objects, but those that have no visual representation. They are pieces of information that can be associated with processes and flow objects. Depending on where the properties are defined, some parts of the process can or cannot access said properties. Process properties can be made accessible to all the activities inside the said process. Activity properties can only be accessed inside the same activity.

Data stores and data objects are supported by the jBPM6 parser, but no runtime configuration is provided for them. Data objects are mapped in jBPM6 as process variables. Activities' inputs, outputs, and process variables, are usually represented as properties, mainly because jBPM6 doesn't support message flows to correlate specific data objects to inputs or outputs of a specific component.

Swimlanes

Swimlanes are defined to organize and categorize the activities that belong to a process. Using swimlanes, we can denote responsibility from a role or a business unit to a set of activities. Most of the time, they are used to improve process readability.

From the jBPM6 implementation, swimlanes are used to define a particular group of User tasks (see the *Task types in jBPM6* section later in this chapter) that should be performed by the same user. In the following example, **Task 3** has to be performed by the same user who executed **Task 2**:

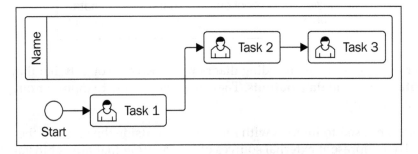

Artifacts

Artifact elements add additional information to diagrams. They're used to improve documentation aspects and the specification defines two types of artifacts: **Groups** and **Text annotations**.

Groups are used to encapsulate a group of tasks together by any sort of criteria. They don't affect the flow of the process. Text annotations allow us to add notes to our process diagrams, such as comments inside our process, as shown in the following diagram:

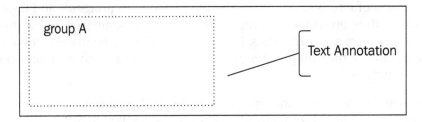

Since they don't affect process execution, jBPM6 skips them from its internal parsing.

Task types in jBPM6

As we previously mentioned, one of the most important types of flow objects is the activity. Each activity will represent a task related to our business scenario. The specification provides a set of specific tasks that can be used to define different behaviors. This section covers the most commonly used tasks that we need to know in order to start modeling our business scenario. The task types shown in the following diagram will be described in this section:

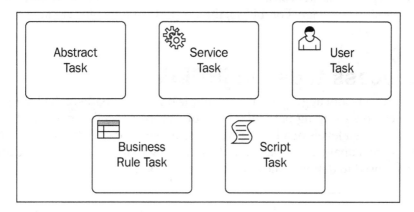

The tasks in the preceding diagram are defined as follows:

- **Abstract task**: This is the base type of all the other tasks in BPMN 2.0. According to the specification, this task is abstract and we should never use it in our processes. However, jBPM6 uses it as an extension point to introduce new task definitions. We will see how this is achieved in more detail in *Chapter 5, Creating a Process Project in the KIE Workbench*.

- **Service task**: This allows us to represent interactions with external automated systems. Each time our business process needs to interact with a service or procedure, we will use a service task. The service task element defines an attribute called implementation, which is used to specify the underlying implementation of the service that we are calling.

- **User task**: This represents a human interaction. Each time we want to represent a person doing an activity, we use a User task to model this situation. Because User tasks represent a human interaction, we need to provide a way to assist the performer during this interaction. The jBPM6-based BRMS provides a task list-oriented user interface that assists each user during these interactions. We will take a close look at this approach in *Chapter 6, Human Interactions*.

- **Business Rule task**: This allows us to interact with a **Business Rule Engine** (**BRE**) to do some business logic evaluation. The interaction with the BRE usually involves sending information to the Engine, which will be evaluated by a set of business rules and a result will be returned. In the case of jBPM6, integration with a business rule engine is already part of the process engine, so this integration becomes simple.

- **Script task**: This allows us to execute a script that can be specified in various languages. A script basically represents a set of actions that we can code using a scripting language. For jBPM6, the supported languages are Java and MVEL (`http://mvel.codehaus.org`).

Subprocess types in jBPM6

Activities can represent aggregations of multiple other flow paths, called subprocesses. The reason behind grouping particular parts of a process together could be hiding or grouping additional levels of a business process in detail or specifying a completely different way to manage those paths. In the following diagram, we can see different icons that are used to define some of these subprocess types:

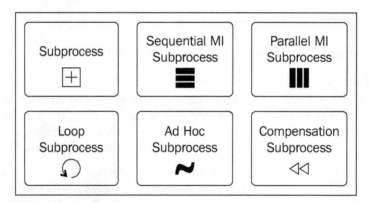

A basic subprocess (in its collapsed view) will be marked by a plus sign at the bottom. This is just to define that there is a different process definition inside this box. This type alone gives us a lot of power, because it lets us define a process definition hierarchy to define from the most atomic activities of our company to the general company drivers, all with different levels of processes.

Alongside the basic subprocess, there are other types of subprocesses. The most common ones are as follows:

- **Multiple instance (MI) subprocesses**: They define a subprocess that should be instantiated and executed multiple times from the external process instance. It comes in two flavors: **Parallel** (marked by three vertical lines at the bottom) and **Sequential** (marked by three horizontal lines instead). The iteration is done over a collection-based process variable in the external process instance. Both types are supported by jBPM6, but they are both treated as sequential.

- **Ad-hoc subprocesses**: This type of subprocesses is peculiar as it only contains activities, and there is no sequence defined. Every activity included in the subprocess can be executed in any order as long as specified completion conditions are fulfilled. Actually, the internal activities of an ad hoc subprocess might not even have to be executed at all to fulfill said conditions, making the whole subprocess optional. They are represented with a tilde (~) marker at the bottom and are supported by jBPM6 through the dynamic node utilities:

```
//We need to start with a KieSession:
KieSession ksession = ...
//We start a specific process instance:
ProcessInstance pI = ksession.startProcess(
"dynamic-process");
    //If the first node we wait at is an ad hoc subprocess,
    //the following code will return a node for it:
    DynamicNodeInstance node = (DynamicNodeInstance)
      ((WorkflowProcessInstance) pI).
      getNodeInstances().iterator().next();
DynamicUtils.addDynamicWorkItem(node, ksession,
"Human Task", null);
```

In the previous example, we used the `DynamicUtils` class to generate an execution of one of the tasks in the ad hoc process called `"dynamic-process"`.

- **Loop subprocesses**: Similar to multiple instance subprocesses, the loop subprocesses will repeat themselves over and over again in sequence until a condition is met that stops the loop. The main difference with multiple instance subprocesses is that this type of subprocess is not dependent on a collection-based variable, but only on a specific finish condition. It is not supported by jBPM6.

- **Compensation subprocesses**: This is a specialized version that only happens when a specific kind of event called compensation is triggered. Compensation events are thrown when a process has done something that it shouldn't, but still has a chance of completing successfully. Compensation subprocesses are related to undoing steps that were already successfully completed, because their results and possibly side effects are no longer needed and need to be reversed. They are supported by jBPM6.

The subprocess types explained here are also usable in common activities. I've decided to explain them as subprocesses because that's where most of them make more sense. You can have a multiple instance User task activity defined, and it would still be perfectly standard.

Event subtypes

Events, as we saw earlier in this chapter, trigger or capture situations of special interest to our process, depending on their type (start, end, or intermediate catch or throw). Depending on what the situation is, we need to define specific subtypes of events that define different situations. There are too many subtypes to explain them all in this book. In the following diagram, we see a few of the most commonly used event subtypes:

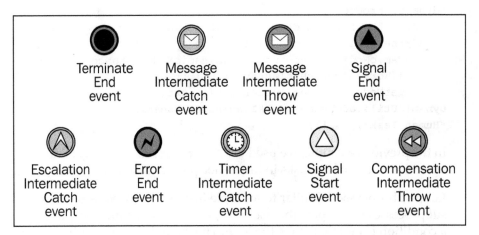

Among the subtypes that we can distinguish in the previous diagram, the following events are present:

- **Signal events**: These events are used to send and receive signals. Signals are generic, simple forms of communication. They can be sent between activities and even be shared between different process definitions. They don't have a specific recipient, so any other component in the same runtime can receive a signal by just defining that they are listening. The jBPM6 API can send signals to a process from outside its scope using the `signalEvent` method:

```
KieSession ksession = ...;
ksession.signalEvent("signalName", null);
```

- **Timer events**: These events are triggered by a defined timer. They must have exactly one element of the type `timeDate` (to determine the specific date at which the event should be triggered), `timeDuration` (to specify after how much time it should trigger the event), or `timeCycle` (to specify intervals at which the event should repeatedly fire). All three are supported by jBPM6.

- **Message events**: They are similar to a signal event, except they are directed to a single receiver. It has an attribute called `messageRef` that defines a message to be sent. From the jBPM6 perspective, however, it can be received by any number of listeners, and handles itself through the `signalEvent` method as well. The code is as follows:

```
KieSession ksession = ...;
ksession.signalEvent("Message-messageRefName", null);
```

- **Error events**: These events are prepared to handle specific errors that occur in a process execution. They can be used as end events to terminate a flow indicating an error occurred or used to catch specific errors. They can even be used to start a subprocess.

- **Compensation events**: These events are used to compensate for errors that occurred in the flow of a process. If you find yourself in a situation that shouldn't be happening, you can trigger a compensation event to notify the specific compensation handler (a catching compensation event) that an action should be taken to amend the execution somehow.

- **Escalation events**: These events are similar in implementation to compensation events. They mark a situation that cannot be handled anymore by the current process execution. The only difference with escalation events is that some higher scope of process execution (that is, a parent process) should handle the specific situation that fired the escalation event. That is why they can only use start and throw escalation events inside subprocesses.

- **Terminate events**: Processes can have multiple flows running in the same process definitions. The process instance is not considered completed until all active execution flows reach an end event. Terminate events are used to avoid this, since process instances are completed as soon as any of the execution paths of a process reach a terminate end event.

There are a few more that aren't covered by jBPM6 much or very widely used, so we skipped them from this book. We encourage you to look into the specification if you're interested in other types of events.

Boundary events

Boundary events are a very practical combination of two flow objects, activities, and events. When you assign an intermediate catch event to the border of an activity box, you determine events specific for that activity only. They are very useful for controlling the flow of tasks and subprocesses alike. The following diagram shows a few examples:

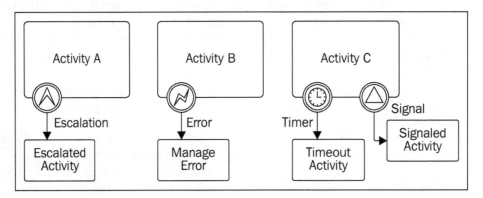

As the preceding diagram shows, you can capture escalations, errors, signals, and many other types of events being sent from an activity and divert flow accordingly. You can even have multiple boundary events on a single activity box. In the case of the preceding diagram, depending on whether **Activity C** sends a signal before or after a specific amount of time passes since the activity started, the flow might be diverted to two different steps.

The activity can still have a regular outgoing flow. For the first case in the preceding diagram, if no escalation is sent from **Activity A**, the process could continue through a sequence flow attached to the activity box directly.

Boundary events are a good way to manage alternate flows. Like all other components that add complexity to our processes, we must make sure that we don't make the process too complicated to be easily maintained.

BPMN 2.0

Now that we had a brief overview of the different elements that compose the BPMN 2.0 specification, we can start seeing how they can be combined to define our own business processes. To do so, we have a couple of scenarios to analyze where we will see the different modeling options we have to execute them. We will also take a look at the XML generated by the modeler tool.

Modeling business scenarios with BPMN 2.0

Translating our business scenarios into business processes that are modeled with BPMN 2.0 is a very sensitive task. Modeling our business processes using the correct elements sounds simple, but we really need to understand the technical implications that our decisions at the modeling stage will have when we want to execute our process definitions. So let's get started with a real example.

We will use the development life cycle, a case we are familiar with, as an example for the first scenario we will be covering. The business goal of this process is to manage the release management cycle in the most efficient way. We will start in the simplest way possible, and then increasingly add complexity to make it more complete:

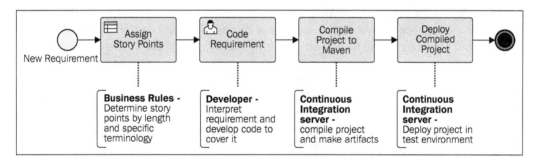

This process, shown in the previous diagram, describes the standard activities defined for a project development (or, at least, its happy path) from the moment the development starts to the moment the requirement is done and deployed. As you may know, the activities inside this process will be executed each time a new requirement arrives at the development group. As you can see, we will consider that the process ends when the requirement is deployed in a test environment.

As you can see in the process diagram, the first flow object that will be executed is a start event. This start event will contain information about the requirement specification that we will use to understand the context and complete the following activities accordingly. Once we receive the start event, we will use the information to execute a Business Rule task that will be in charge of assigning story points depending on the length of the requirement specification and whether or not it contains specific keywords that will be used to define its complexity. Once the story points are assigned, we will notify a developer in order to start working on the requirement. The developer will be in charge of coding the specified requirement. Once the coding is done, a continuous integration system has to compile the project where the development was done and then another activity has to use a similar system to deploy the project in a test environment.

This is a very simple representation of the proposed business scenario, but we need to start from somewhere. We need to be sure that we gather the correct information about the activities that are being executed. We need to be sure that we represent the activities that really matter from the development area's perspective. Modeling these scenarios is not about how the process will be executed but about which activities are relevant for modeling within the business processes. We will use this simple representation as a kick-start process to represent the situation more accurately.

At this point, we can create a brief description of the resources that our business processes are using. Also, we can see that the process requires the interaction of one human role: the developer. We are interacting with the rule engine to carry out the story point assignment; this means that we will need to have a set of business rules that evaluate the requirement and the development area's context in order to assign story points. We are also sending notifications to the continuous integration system using a connector to the **Continuous Integration** (**CI**) server that is being used in order to know when to build and deploy components. Using this information, we can easily define the business requirements in terms of resources and system interactions. After defining these requirements, when the processes get executed we can quickly define the metrics to understand how the process works in its context.

We will be able to analyze whether we will need to hire more developers, or whether we need to improve our continuous integration system to accept more requests because too many requirements are being developed too quickly.

The second version of our process could look like what is shown in the following diagram:

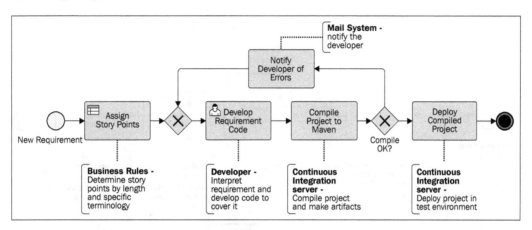

As we can see from the preceding diagram, we are adding two exclusive gateways. One of them, marked with the **Compile OK?** name, will evaluate whether the compilation was successful or not. Based on the evaluation from the compilation activity, we will continue with the happy path if the path of execution has no errors or exceptions, and produces the expected successful output. If errors are found, it will send a notification to the developer that corrections need to be made, go back to the other exclusive gateway (the one that converges) and continue into the same path two steps behind. We need to evaluate whether this gateway will add unnecessary complexity to our model or whether it will help us to better reflect what is happening. Once again, we need to be able to decouple how we are representing the business scenario and the technical implications that our model will have when we want to run it. We will see that these kinds of exceptional paths can also be solved technically without adding more flow objects to our business processes diagram. We need to find the right balance between the technical decisions and what the process diagram represents for the business scenario.

A third option for our business process could be the following:

This third option includes three intermediate catching events. Two of them are boundary events (they're attached to the border of an activity to capture such events from inside the activity) and are error boundary events. They change the way the process was working by going through the notification path if the compilation or the deployment throws an error.

Also, a signal event is being captured in the bottom part in order to notify the developer when a particular requirement is cancelled and then terminate the process instance. We are assuming that we will receive an external stimulus that notifies us if the requirement is cancelled. The notification can contain information about this cancellation event, for example, the reason for the cancellation. The **Notify Developer of Requirements change** activity for the mail system will be created only at that point. Once again, we need to properly identify whether this addition adds too much complexity to the process diagram.

A good practice is to validate each of these improvements with the business users who are executing activities. As a rule of thumb, we need to keep the process diagram as clean and simple as possible.

Technical perspective

Once we understand each scenario, we can start thinking about the technical implications that our models will have. We can start analyzing which technical details we need to add in order to automate our business processes. In this section, we will start analyzing the technical assets that will be generated when we model our business process diagram in a BPMN2 tool that allows us to export the model as an XML file.

Let's start modeling the first version of the sprint management scenario.

Sprint management technical overview

As we have the initial description of our business process, we can go ahead and model it inside our business process designer tool. If we do that in jBPM6 web designer (which will be introduced in *Chapter 5, Creating a Process Project in the KIE Workbench*) or in any other BPMN2 tool, we will get something like the following diagram:

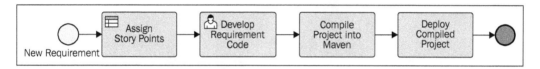

This process definition only contains the activities and flow objects as we described them previously. We haven't added any technical detail or data mappings yet. We first need to work on the completion of the model and reach a state where we are satisfied with what the process represents, in this case, for the development area.

If we analyze the XML generated by this simple model, we will see how each task is being represented inside the XML file. You can find it in the code section in the `chapter-03/BPMN2-scenarios/src/main/resources/sprintManagement-V1.bpmn2` file. The code is as follows:

```
<bpmn2:definitions ...>

  <bpmn2:process id="sprintManagementV1" name="Sprint Management"
isExecutable="true">
    <bpmn2:startEvent id="_1" name="New Requirement">
      <bpmn2:outgoing>_1_2</bpmn2:outgoing>
    </bpmn2:startEvent>
    <bpmn2:businessRuleTask id="_2" name="Assign Story Points">
      <bpmn2:incoming>_1_2</bpmn2:incoming>
```

```
        <bpmn2:outgoing>_2_3</bpmn2:outgoing>
      </bpmn2:businessRuleTask>
      <bpmn2:userTask id="_3" name="Develop Requirement Code">
        <bpmn2:incoming>_2_3</bpmn2:incoming>
        <bpmn2:outgoing>_3_4</bpmn2:outgoing>
      </bpmn2:userTask>
      <bpmn2:task id="_4" drools:taskName="compiler"
name="Compile Project into Maven">
        <bpmn2:incoming>_3_4</bpmn2:incoming>
        <bpmn2:outgoing>_4_5</bpmn2:outgoing>
      </bpmn2:task>
      <bpmn2:task id="_5" drools:taskName="deployer"
name="Deploy Compiled Project">
        <bpmn2:incoming>_4_5</bpmn2:incoming>
        <bpmn2:outgoing>_5_6</bpmn2:outgoing>
      </bpmn2:task>
      <bpmn2:endEvent id="_6" name="">
        <bpmn2:incoming>_5_6</bpmn2:incoming>
      </bpmn2:endEvent>

      <bpmn2:sequenceFlow id="_1_2" sourceRef="_1" targetRef="_2"/>
      <bpmn2:sequenceFlow id="_2_3" sourceRef="_2" targetRef="_3"/>
      <bpmn2:sequenceFlow id="_3_4" sourceRef="_3" targetRef="_4"/>
      <bpmn2:sequenceFlow id="_4_5" sourceRef="_4" targetRef="_5"/>
      <bpmn2:sequenceFlow id="_5_6" sourceRef="_5" targetRef="_6"/>
    </bpmn2:process>

</bpmn2:definitions>
```

After cleaning up the XML code a little bit to remove autogenerated IDs (from something such as `_F3AE87C3-F49B-4F0D-A2AA-E2F015188093` to `_1`) and removing the graphical layout and extra information, we get a clean description of the activities contained inside our process.

We can clearly see that the XML file structure begins with a `<bpmn2:definitions>` tag. This tag is in charge of containing our process definitions. This tag includes numerous references to OMG BPMN 2 schemas and namespaces that I have omitted. These schemas will be used to validate that our BPMN2 file is compliant with the BPMN2 specification, along with all the extensions (provided by a specific jBPM6 namespace) to provide vendor specific components to the XML file. I've cleaned up some global definitions and simulation information that can be included outside of the process definitions because we don't need them right now. Inside the `definitions` tag we will include our process definition tags.

The <bpmn2:process> tag requires us to assign an ID to the process; depending on the tooling, it will either let us create an executable process or not. In this case, the isExecutable attribute is set to true by the tooling by default.

Once we are inside the process tag, we can start defining our flow objects. Keep in mind that sometimes we may find that our activities are defined out of order inside the XML file. We don't need to worry about this, but it's good to understand how the activities are correlated. For this example, I've ordered the XML file so we can easily identify the activity sequence.

The first flow object that we found inside our process is <bpmn2:startEvent>. This is a very simple tag that represents the start event in our process. Notice that within the startEvent tag, we will find a referent to the outgoing sequence flow that will be in charge of propagating the execution to the businessRuleTask tag.

The <bpmn2:businessRuleTask> tag represents the interaction with the rule engine. As you may notice, inside this tag, there is no reference at all to how this interaction will happen or what information needs to be sent to the rule engine to be evaluated. As you can see, this tag also allows us to assign a name to this activity, which is Assign Story Points in this case.

The next activity in the process is the <bpmn2:userTask> tag, which contains the attribute name set to Develop Requirement Code. Until this point, we are only saying that there will be a human interaction. However, the process definition doesn't include any reference to any role in charge of performing the task or to any information that needs to be exchanged in order to complete the activity. We will need to include all this information in order to have a fully executable process.

The <bpmn2:task> tag represents the interaction with an external system (external from the process engine perspective). In this case, the tasks named Compile Project into Maven and Deploy Compiled Project will be in charge of contacting a specific service that the development area uses to compile and deploy assets automatically. This generic task will identify the specific external system connection by an attribute called drools:taskName, which will define a key to register a software component to handle the external system communication later on at runtime.

Next, the <bpmn2:endEvent> tag is defined. It represents the end of our business process.

Finally, we find all the sequence flows; they join all the activities in a sequence. Note that each sequenceFlow element specifies its id, sourceRef, and targetRef values.

So far, we have a very basic XML representation of our activities. Now, it's not just a diagram. We have a formalized description of the activities that we have included in our process and that can be used by technical people to add all the details needed to execute this process.

Once we reach this state, a business analyst can start adding information about data that will flow throughout the activities. Technical roles will be in charge of adding the information about the external systems that will be contacted.

Version 2 of this process will include an **XOR Exclusive Diverging gateway** that will be in charge of analyzing whether a compilation was successful. If not, a notification will be sent to the developer that created the code and an **XOR Exclusive Converging gateway** will create a new User task to develop the required code, as shown in the following diagram:

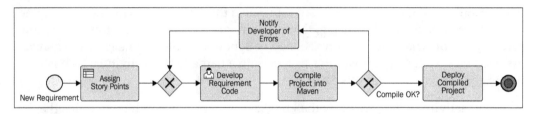

The following XML snippet from the `chapter-03/BPMN2-scenarios/src/main/resources/sprintManagement-V1.bpmn2` file shows:

```
<bpmn2:exclusiveGateway id="_8" name="Compile OK?"
gatewayDirection="Diverging">
    <bpmn2:incoming>_4_8</bpmn2:incoming>
    <bpmn2:outgoing>_8_5</bpmn2:outgoing>
    <bpmn2:outgoing>_8_9</bpmn2:outgoing>
</bpmn2:exclusiveGateway>
<bpmn2:exclusiveGateway id="_7" name=""
gatewayDirection="Converging">
    <bpmn2:incoming>_9_7</bpmn2:incoming>
    <bpmn2:incoming>_2_7</bpmn2:incoming>
    <bpmn2:outgoing>_7_3</bpmn2:outgoing>
</bpmn2:exclusiveGateway>
```

As you can see, two outgoing sequence flows are referenced from the diverging flow object, and two incoming sequence flows are referenced from the converging flow object.

Version 3 of the process includes an intermediate signal catch event definition, which is used to wait for an external notification. This notification will be generated if the requirement development is cancelled. It also has two error boundary event definitions that will be used when compilation or deployment throws an error. All these components are shown in the following diagram:

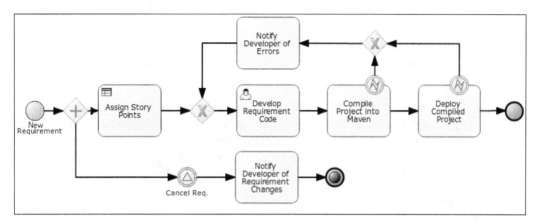

The intermediate signal catch event is represented by the following XML snippet:

```
<bpmn2:intermediateCatchEvent id="_D" name="Cancel
  Req.">
  <bpmn2:outgoing>_D_E</bpmn2:outgoing>
  <bpmn2:signalEventDefinition id="_D1"
    signalRef="reqCancelled"/>
</bpmn2:intermediateCatchEvent>
```

As you can see, this event flow object doesn't have any information about the event type; it just has a reference name for the signal name. It doesn't have the information that this event will contain (and that needs to be propagated to the process context) either.

One of the error boundary events is represented by the following XML snippet:

```
<bpmn2:boundaryEvent id="_A" name="" attachedToRef="_4">
  <bpmn2:outgoing>_A_C</bpmn2:outgoing>
  <bpmn2:errorEventDefinition id="_A1"
  errorRef="java.lang.RuntimeException"/>
</bpmn2:boundaryEvent>
```

As you can see, this event is attached to another component (in this case, the compile task) to receive events from it. It holds a reference to the error type that will be handled through this particular connection.

Adding simple process data

In this section, we will add more information to our process diagram so that we are able to execute it. We will need to specify the information that will be required by the process to start, the information that will be required and generated by the human interactions, and the information that will be sent to the external services that will be used by the process.

We will use the first and simplest version of the process to easily understand how we can technically define the information exchange that will be required to accomplish the process' business goal.

This information will be provided to the start event and will represent the information sent by the product managers to the system. Because this information needs to be stored inside our process, we will define what we call process variables. These process variables (or process properties) are defined within the `<bpmn2:process>` tag, but outside any other task, as it is shown in the following code:

```
<bpmn2:property id="project"
itemSubjectRef="_projectItem"/>
<bpmn2:property id="reqDescription"
 itemSubjectRef="_reqDescriptionItem"/>
<bpmn2:property id="storyPoints"
itemSubjectRef="_storyPointsItem"/>
<bpmn2:property id="developerId"
itemSubjectRef="_developerIdItem"/>
<bpmn2:property id="compiled"
itemSubjectRef="_compiledItem"/>
<bpmn2:property id="deployed"
itemSubjectRef="_deployedItem"/>
```

These process variables (called `project`, `reqDescription`, `storyPoints`, `developerId`, `compiled`, and `deployed`) represent the information that will be carried out by the process activities. We need to define all the information that we want to handle at the process level. These properties will not have any visual representation in our diagram, but we can usually define them in our modeling tool within the **Properties** panel.

Note that a process variable is composed of an `id` and an `itemSubjectRef` reference. The `id` parameter represents the name of the variable. We will use the value of `id` to reference the process variable in different activities in our process. The `itemSubjectRef` parameter is used to reference a type of information that was externally defined. Since BPMN2 is language-independent, we cannot make direct references to Java types.

For this reason, we use the following item definitions:

```
<bpmn2:itemDefinition id="_projectItem"
structureRef="String"/>
<bpmn2:itemDefinition id="_reqDescriptionItem"
structureRef="String"/>
<bpmn2:itemDefinition id="_storyPointsItem"
structureRef="Integer"/>
<bpmn2:itemDefinition id="_developerIdItem"
structureRef="String"/>
<bpmn2:itemDefinition id="_compiledItem"
structureRef="Boolean"/>
<bpmn2:itemDefinition id="_deployedItem"
structureRef="Boolean"/>
```

These item definition tags can be understood as type imports in Java. We are defining a name for all the items of type `String`, `Boolean`, or `Integer` in this case. We are using basic types for our first executable version, but these item definitions can be of any type as long as you provide a full class name.

With these two steps, defining the `itemDefinition` parameters and our process variables, we have defined placeholders for information. Now when we start our process, we can fill some of these buckets that will be accessible for all the activities inside our process. Let's analyze what exactly we have defined. The process will maintain the following information:

- The project name
- The requirement description
- The story points (integer value)
- The developer ID
- Requirement compiled (true/false)
- Requirement deployed (true/false)

Some of these variables will be filled when the process starts. The project name and the requirement description will be provided when a new instance of the process needs to be created. The rest of the activities in the process will generate all the other information.

After the execution of the first activity in our process, the rule engine will fill the process variable called story points. We will see how this happens later on.

The userTask instance in our process, called Develop Requirement Code, will require us to map information from the process scope to the userTask scope. We will be narrowing down the process information to just the information required by this task to work. This userTask instance will be in charge of creating the required code.

For this simple example, and to get the first version of this process working, we will execute the data assignments inside the userTask object. To see the complete mapping, open the process definition called sprintManagement-V1.bpmn2 and look for userTask. It can be found in the chapter-03/BPMN2-scenarios/src/main/resources folder of the code section. The code is as follows:

```
<bpmn2:userTask id="_5" name="Develop Requirement Code">
    ...
</bpmn2:userTask>
```

To understand — without all the visual clutter — what is going on inside the variable mappings, let's analyze the following XML structure:

```
<bpmn2:userTask id="_3" name="Develop Requirement Code">
  <bpmn2:incoming>_2_3</bpmn2:incoming>
  <bpmn2:outgoing>_3_4</bpmn2:outgoing>
  <bpmn2:ioSpecification id="_3a">
    <bpmn2:dataInput id="_3_requirementInput" name="requirement"/>
    <bpmn2:dataInput id="_3_complexityInput" name="complexity"/>
    <bpmn2:dataOutput id="_3_ActorIdOutput" name="ActorId"/>
    <bpmn2:inputSet id="_3b">
      <bpmn2:dataInputRefs>
        _3_requirementInput
      </bpmn2:dataInputRefs>
      <bpmn2:dataInputRefs>
        _3_complexityInput
      </bpmn2:dataInputRefs>
    </bpmn2:inputSet>
    <bpmn2:outputSet id="_3c">
      <bpmn2:dataOutputRefs>
        _3_ActorIdOutput
      </bpmn2:dataOutputRefs>
    </bpmn2:outputSet>
  </bpmn2:ioSpecification>
  <bpmn2:dataInputAssociation id="_3d">
    <bpmn2:sourceRef>reqDescription</bpmn2:sourceRef>
    <bpmn2:targetRef>_3_requirementInput</bpmn2:targetRef>
  </bpmn2:dataInputAssociation>
  <bpmn2:dataInputAssociation id="_3e">
```

```
        <bpmn2:sourceRef>storyPoints</bpmn2:sourceRef>
        <bpmn2:targetRef>_3_complexityInput</bpmn2:targetRef>
    </bpmn2:dataInputAssociation>
    <bpmn2:dataOutputAssociation id="_3f">
        <bpmn2:sourceRef>_3_ActorIdOutput</bpmn2:sourceRef>
        <bpmn2:targetRef>developerId</bpmn2:targetRef>
    </bpmn2:dataOutputAssociation>
</bpmn2:userTask>
```

Inside the `<bpmn2:ioSpecification>` tag, we will define the information that will be injected and generated inside our flow object. Using the `bpmn2:dataInput` and `bpmn2:dataOutput` tags, we define the variables that will be available in the activity context. From a business perspective, we can say that the `bpmn2:ioSpecification` tag represents the information that will be required to execute the interaction. If we are talking about a User task, this information will be probably displayed to the user so that he or she can work with it. If it is an external system, it will probably be used as parameters to invoke them.

The `bpmn2:inputSet` and `bpmn2:outputSet` tags represent the list of variables that will be expected inside the activity context. This looks redundant, but don't worry: most of the time, all of this XML code will be generated automatically by the tooling. We, as developers, just need to know its structure.

The `bpmn2:dataInputAssociation` and `bpmn2:dataOutputAssociation` tags are where the magic happens. In this section, we will map the information from our process scope to the activity internal variables and vice versa. In this case, the `bpmn2:dataInputAssociation` tag is copying the information from the process variable called `reqDescription` to the task input called `_3_requirementInput`. Note that the information will be copied and not moved. Inside the flow object, we will be able to modify this information without affecting the process scope information. If we want to modify or add more information to our process scope variables, we need to create a `bpmn2:dataOutputAssociation` tag that will be in charge of copying information from inside the activity scope to the process scope. In this case, we are copying the content of the `_3_ActorIdOutput` variable in the activity scope to a variable called `developerId` in the process scope. This action will override the value of the `developerId` variable with the content generated inside the activity object.

When we want to map information for an abstract task (or any other task type), we use the same XML structures and rules. You can take a look at the complete process and how all the variables are mapped by looking at the file called `sprintManagement-V1.bpmn2`.

The following diagram shows where the data is generated or moved:

The data inputs are omitted in all the activities and only the necessary information is copied for each task. At this point, don't worry if you feel a little bit confused by all the XML elements we have to use in order to define a business process. Most of the times, these processes are designed using a visual tool. We will cover one of these tools in *Chapter 5, Creating a Process Project in the KIE Workbench*, and it will introduce a step-by-step tutorial on how we can model this process (all three different versions) in it.

Summary

In this chapter, we learned the basic flow objects that we can use to model our process diagrams. We have also covered an introduction on how to add the initial technical details required to define information needed by our process definition's data interchange. This interchange is a requirement of every business situation, and hopefully this introduction has given you an insight on how BPMN2 covers the many necessities that BPM systems have.

The next two chapters will introduce the tooling provided by jBPM6 to model and execute our business processes. Knowing the tooling that the project provides will not only help us to get a complete overview of how we can implement the BPM discipline, but also provide you with many ideas for applying them to your own business domains.

4
Understanding the KIE Workbench

By now, you hopefully have a clear understanding of the BPM system structure, the language that we will use to define our business processes, and we already had a sneak preview of the jBPM6 project APIs and how BPMN 2.0 is used to describe processes.

Now, it is time to take a look at the tooling provided by the jBPM6 project. The jBPM6 tooling projects contain both a platform to integrate multiple forms of knowledge (information), as well as functionality to extend and run said commands. This knowledge can be in the form of processes, rules, decision tables, and so on. Because of that, it has been encapsulated under the concept of **Knowledge Is Everything** (**KIE**) and exposed in a workbench-like web interface called the **KIE Workbench**.

A **workbench**, in this context, means a piece of software that allows both file management and application functionalities. In this sense, the KIE Workbench provides knowledge asset file management (to design processes, data models, and other knowledge components) and process and rule runtimes. It also allows us to configure external communications (a topic we will cover in detail in *Chapter 10, Integrating KIE Workbench with External Systems*). In this chapter, we will study the tools provided by this workbench and their relationship with jBPM6.

This chapter starts by describing the tools provided by the workbench and describes how to implement your own domain-specific tooling from scratch, keeping in mind the important concepts to have on a full workbench. After we understand the tooling components, we will discuss how to extend the already provided workbench to add our own extra components.

In this chapter, we will cover the following topics:

- How to set up the environment to start working with jBPM6
- The workbench description and how to start working with processes in it
- The workbench internal architecture

What you need to start a jBPM6 environment

Before we start with the descriptions of each specific component, I would like to mention that in order to install and use the workbench, we need to have the basic knowledge of how to work with Java and Maven. The installation procedure is very simple, but we need to have a set of tools previously installed in our environment to be able to install and run the KIE workbench. The prerequisites are the following:

- JDK 6 or higher, which can be found at `http://www.oracle.com/technetwork/java/javase/downloads/index.html`
- Apache Ant 1.9.x, which can be found at `http://ant.apache.org/bindownload.cgi`
- Apache Maven 3.1.x, which can be found at `http://maven.apache.org/download.cgi`
- `<JAVA_HOME>/bin`, `<M2_HOME>/bin`, and `<ANT_HOME>/bin` added to the PATH system variable

Once we have these tools installed and ready to be used, we can run the KIE Workbench installer that you can find in the code section under the name `kie-wb-installer`. This section will cover the following topics:

- Installing the KIE Workbench
- What you will need to create the jBPM6 business processes
- What you will need to run the jBPM6 business processes

Running the KIE Workbench installer

KIE Workbench installation is quite simple. All components are part of a single WAR file, with very few customized configurations needed outside of it. The required steps are as follows:

1. Download the WAR file of the workbench and an application server.
2. Install the application server and place the WAR file in the `standalone/deployments` folder.
3. Add users to the application server configuration.

So we created a special Maven project to do those steps for us, by just invoking `mvn clean install` from the `chapter-04/kie-wb-installer` folder of the code section of this book. You can also run the server using the same command line by typing `mvn exec:exec` once the installation is done.

If you prefer to download it and install it manually, all you have to do is look for the WAR file published in `http://repository.jboss.org/nexus` under the `org.kie:kie-wb-distribution-wars:6.1.0.Beta3:jboss-as7` release ID and add it to a JBoss Application Server 7.1 installation. You can download JBoss Application Server from `www.jboss.org`. After you have installed the JBoss Application Server following the instructions on the site, all you have to do is put the WAR file in the `standalone/deployments` folder, change its name to `kie-wb.war`, and start the server with the following command:

```
bin/standalone.sh --server-config=standalone-full.xml
```

One good thing about this installer is that it will need all the prerequisites we listed in the previous section. So, it is also a test that all prerequisites are properly installed.

Installation could take a while to finish (it will download approximately 500 MB from the JBoss Maven repository), but once it is finished and the application server is running, you will be able to access the workbench from the URL `http://localhost:8080/kie-wb`, and log in typing the user `mariano` and password `mypass`. This username and password can be changed by using the `bin/add-user.sh` command from the JBoss Application Server and creating a user with an admin role for the Application realm. Once logged in, you will see the following page:

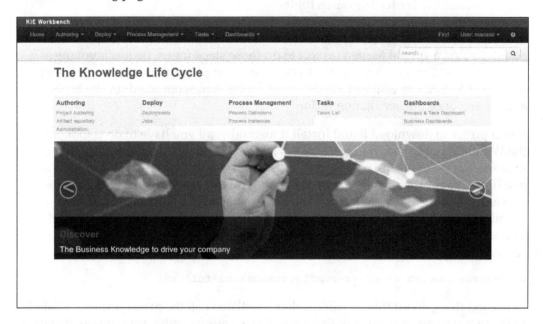

Notice the top navigation bar (the one in black). We will be using it to access all the functionality of the KIE Workbench. We have different functions to manage process-related project authoring and deployment tasks, process runtime, tasks assigned to a user, and even dashboards about the execution of our environment. We will be explaining the ones more related to running the process in the next few sections.

What you will need to create the jBPM6 business processes

One set of tools that we will need is the one related to creating new processes that we can execute later on. To do so, we need a new set of high-level tools (editors, validation tools, and different types of connectors) as well as low-level functionality (such as filesystem management and publication services for the runtime to grab finished components). The tools most related to process generation are as follows:

- **Workbench utilities**: In order to define special configurations that our business processes will need to be executed in the way we want, we need special utilities that will allow us to define the execution configuration that the runtime will have to use, such as external connectors for invoking other systems, special listeners to expose information about our processes to monitoring tools, and strategies to define the isolation level of processes. All these components will be discussed throughout this book as we get to each specific component.

- **A process designer**: This is the tool you will use to create executable processes. It could go from a simple notepad application to directly write XML-based BPMN files, and even to a full visual diagram tool to visually edit all the contents of your process. Luckily for us, the jBPM6 process designer is closer to the latter option.

- **Knowledge asset editors**: In order to create all of the process runtime elements that define our domain, most of the time, business processes alone won't be enough to define all the runtime. We will need data modelers to generate the data components that will be used by the processes, rule editors for complex decisions, or work item definitions to extend the possible types of tasks that a process could use.

Workbench utilities

The KIE Workbench provides a series of utilities that allow us to create a detached communication between the process definition and the process execution. In order to do so, it provides a very specific structure that will look quite familiar to developers. Let's first explore how the process definitions (and other types of knowledge assets) are grouped in the KIE Workbench.

The Workbench groups process in Maven-based projects. Each Maven project is an individual, self-sufficient unit containing information about the know-how to compile, deploy, run, and test itself and can declare dependencies to other modules in their `pom.xml` file. Each project is part of a repository, and each repository belongs to an organizational unit. The end picture for this structure looks something like what is shown in the following diagram:

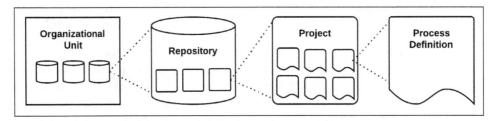

The configurations we will be most interested in tweaking when using the KIE Workbench to define our projects are the ones directly associated with our project. To edit those properties, we must go to the perspective available by clicking on the navigation bar option **Authoring | Project Authoring**. There, we can create a new project (clicking on **Project**) in a particular repository by selecting the option from the second menu bar, the one under the black menu bar, called **New Item**. A project creation wizard will guide us in configuring a Maven release ID for the project. Have a look at the following screenshot:

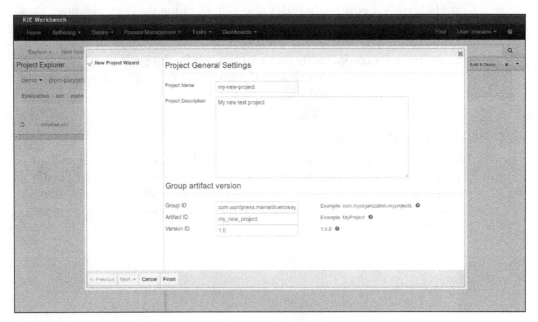

Once the **Finish** button is clicked on, we're directed to the project editor, where we can configure dependencies, KIE Bases, KIE Sessions, and all the project-relevant components. The project editor groups all responsibilities to define dependencies, for project runtime configurations, and to allow the user to build and deploy the project in a Maven repository.

The same options are available when selecting an already existing project by clicking on the **Tools | Project Editor** option that appears under the navigation bar in the **Project Authoring** perspective, as shown in the following screenshot:

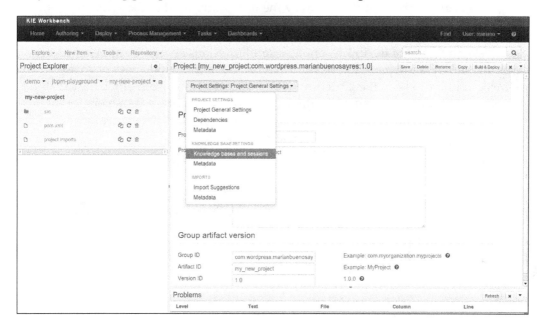

In the preceding screenshot, we can see that we have different types of settings for our project. We are mostly interested in the **Knowledge bases and sessions** item of the settings list box, because it will allow us to configure where and how the business processes that we will define will end up exposed to the runtime.

Each Maven project that we define in the KIE Workbench encloses a particular configuration for one or more types of runtime. Each runtime definition will have its own KIE Bases, KIE Sessions, and special configurations for each one to work in the way we expect them.

Keep track of how to get to the knowledge settings of our project for now, because we will use it later. But first, before we configure how to expose our process definitions, we need first to learn how to define them. To do so, let's take a look at the jBPM6 Process Designer.

Process designer

The process designer is started whenever we choose to create a business process (by selecting the **New Item** | **Business Process** option in the project authoring perspective), or open one that we previously created from the **Project Explorer** view (the one on the left-hand side of the **Project Authoring** perspective). It should be a tool flexible enough to allow users to create their own specific types of extensions to the BPMN2 standard, but strict enough to allow the generated process definition to still comply with the standard. That way, the generated process will be able to run the process runtime with jBPM6 the way the user wants, and at the same time, it will be able to run in any other type of process runtime that is compliant with BPMN2.

To achieve this level of flexibility, enough configurations should be allowed so that every implementation parameterization can be added to the business processes being defined. In order to keep the structure of the process in a tidy but efficient way, the process designer provides an attribute panel to define specific parameters for all the components in the diagram, from a specific sequence flow to the process itself.

In the following screenshot, we see a brief glimpse of the process designer UI present in the Workbench:

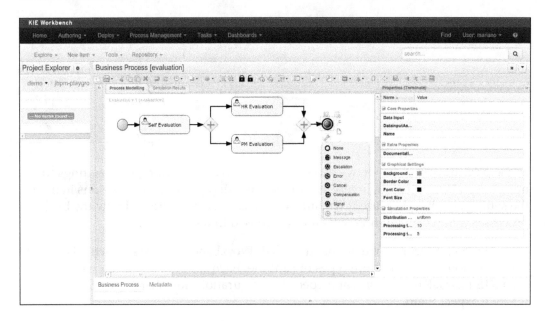

In the preceding screenshot, we can see a few of the characteristics available for the designer. We can see the diagram definition, the properties of a selected node (the terminate event) in the panel to the right-hand side corner of the editor, and we can see that we can change the type of the selected node as well. At the top of the editor, we can see a series of icons with many different functions: save, cut, copy, paste, delete, undo, redo, and a few others that we will cover in more detail in the next few chapters. This section is called the **action bar** of the process designer. We can also see other sections, such as the **Metadata** tab, at the bottom, where we can put specific information about our knowledge asset, such as version history and item description. Also, the canvas has tabulation at the top, dividing the **Process Modelling** view from another called **Simulation Results**, which will be explained in detail in *Chapter 5, Creating a Process Project in the KIE Workbench*.

There are more attributes to the process designer that, at this moment, are going to distract us from getting a full perspective of the Workbench, which is why we will leave the full induction to the designer for *Chapter 5, Creating a Process Project in the KIE Workbench*.

Other knowledge asset editors

In order to be able to create executable processes, we will end up needing more than just the process definitions. Process definitions will be dependent, at least in runtime, of a specific data model, handlers for specific tasks, and even rules to make complex decisions at particular points. In order to be able to run such complex processes we will need a way to define all these components along with the business processes. The KIE Workbench provides us with many different editors that cover all these necessities.

All types of knowledge definitions that we will need to create will be accessible later on from the **Project Explorer** view on the right-hand side of the project authoring perspective, and can be created from the display view after clicking on the **New Item** option. Each type of knowledge asset has a different structure, and due to size restrictions in the book, we won't be able to explain every single one. However, we will cover the ones most related to process definitions and runtimes.

The first things that a growing process definition will need are **work item definitions**. Work item definitions are specific mappings added to abstract tasks in BPMN2 in order to determine some form of special behavior that a given task should have. They have predefined inputs and outputs that suggest a way of communicating with the task, a given name to map it to a specific implementation, and (for the purpose of diagramming) they have a display name and an (optional) icon. In the KIE Workbench, work item definitions are written in a special scripting language called **MVEL** (`http://mvel.codehaus.org`), and the given editor provides a few helper buttons to create the needed script faster, as shown in the following screenshot:

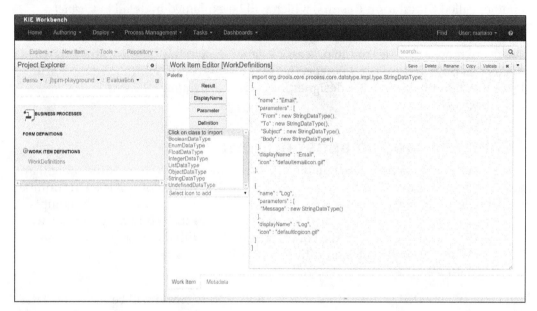

But work item definitions are just the beginning of the needed components. Also, depending on the type of tasks we use from the BPMN2 standard, we might need to create rules for Business Rule tasks, or classes to be used for data objects. The KIE Workbench provides a way to define both types of assets, through the different rule editors and the data modeler, as shown in the following screenshot:

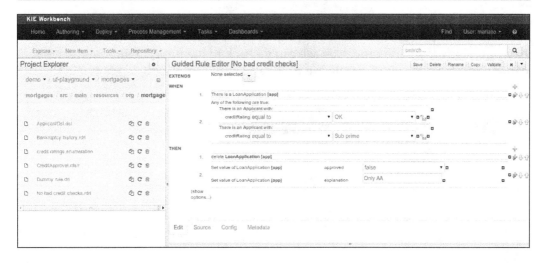

In the preceding screenshot, we see a business rule opened from the **Guided Rule Editor** window, which allows us to define a rule in natural language. It will be based on a Java-based model, created with the data modeler shown in the following screenshot:

Finally, we need a way to define all configurations to the runtime that will be specific for a particular process definition or group of process definitions. Now that we have seen how to define processes, we can go back to the project editor and see the configuration behind the **Knowledge bases and sessions** option, as shown in the following screenshot:

In the view shown in the preceding screenshot, we can define different KIE bases for our project. We can make one of them the default one and decide which packages to include inside them. The packages will represent the different folders that we create in our project and where we might add processes, work item definitions, rules, or anything else. In this way, we can have multiple KIE bases in one project with different process definitions working inside each one.

Each KIE base will have a series of KIE sessions associated, and we will be able to configure them to work in multiple ways. We will see the different configurations for KIE sessions when we see the interaction of processes and other knowledge definition types in *Chapter 9, Integration with Other Knowledge Definitions*.

This is the point where the process definition environment ends and the process runtime begins. The next step is to click on the **Build & Deploy** button in the project editor to make the project and all its configurations available for the runtime. I understand that you would have preferred to start defining your own processes, but don't despair. We will start doing so as soon as we start with *Chapter 5, Creating a Process Project in the KIE Workbench*. For now, we need to concentrate on understanding how all components are interconnected.

Process defining components only need to worry about the process until it is deployed in a Maven repository. Later on, each process runtime should be concerned with having the corresponding version of a Maven dependency running inside.

What you will need to run the jBPM6 business processes

Now, that we have the workbench running, we need to understand how its execution components are used. There are many components inside the runtime part of the workbench, ranging from dashboard indicators to asynchronous task management tools, but the ones we will focus on (and about which we will be going into the most detail) are the ones needed to get process executions running. In order for process instances to be able to interact with people, the workbench needs the following tools:

- **User configuration**: This tool is used to define roles and authentication (to which you can add users with the JBoss command line `add-user.sh` or `add-user.bat`)
- **Process Runtime**: This tool is used to execute processes
- **Process UI**: This tool is used to interact with the executions
- **Human Task List**: This tool is used to see assigned and potential human tasks
- **Human Task Forms**: This tool is used to perform said human tasks

Process runtime

The process runtime is the internal configuration that the workbench must provide to create and execute process instances. In order to do so, it must provide external system connectors to connect to other systems and human tasks. This configuration should be something that can be easily extended over time.

The KIE Workbench provides this extension capacity through the project authoring perspective, which allows us to manage all our knowledge through KIE modules. Once we have all the business processes and other knowledge assets we need in our project, we can open the **Tools | Project Editor** option from the second navigation bar in the project authoring perspective. This would open the editor shown in the following screenshot:

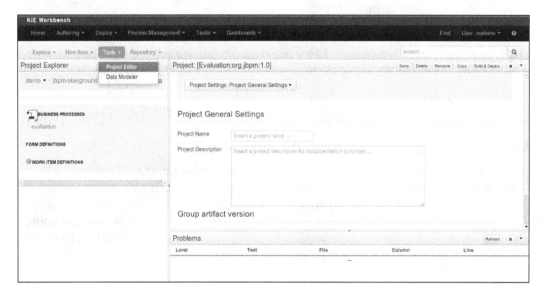

In the preceding screenshot, we selected the **Evaluation** project in the **Project Explorer** view, by clicking first on the jbpm-playground repository and then in the **Evaluation** project. Once in the project editor (which will open once you select the **Evaluation** project), we click on the **Build & Deploy** button to actually compile the project content and publish it on an internal Maven repository.

Once a project is deployed, it becomes a component in the engine that feeds process definitions that can be executed to our environment. We call this engine configuration the **process runtime**. In a sense, the process runtime is just a preconfigured environment for jBPM6 to execute processes already connected to all external systems and humans.

A process runtime should be configurable, that is, we should be able to include all the different configurations to make sure the environment is going to run the process definitions in the way we want. To do so, we can edit the kmodule.xml file of the projects we are creating. To do so, we need to select the **Project Settings: Project General Settings** to see a drop-down menu and select **Knowledge Base Settings** inside the **Project Editor** tool. The following screenshot shows the **Knowledge Base Settings** editor:

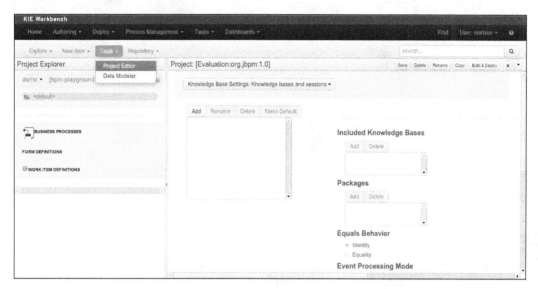

The process runtime can be configured in this editor to have special external connectors and can be later on exposed to many other servers using the runtime engine and runtime manager interfaces, which are discussed in detail in *Chapter 7, Defining Your Environment with the Runtime Manager*.

Process UI

Having the process runtime allows our processes to be able to execute in the backend of our workbench. In order to interact with said workbench directly, we need a special UI to access all the methods involved in process execution. For that, the KIE Workbench provides a few entries in the **Process Management** navigation bar option. We'll discuss each one of them.

Only when we have successfully deployed a KIE module, can we see its process definitions in the **Process Definitions List** perspective (found inside the **Process Management** navigation bar option). In the following case, we see the process definitions available in the demo/jbpm-playground-Evaluation project. The following screenshot shows the **Process Definitions** perspective in the KIE Workbench:

In the list shown in the preceding screenshot, we can see an icon (the magnifying glass icon) to see the process details (its human tasks, the users and the roles assigned to them, the process ID, and so on) and another icon (the play button icon) to start the process (which will provide a previously defined form to fill the data necessary to begin the process). When we press the play icon, it will show us the following form to start a process instance of the **Evaluation** process. After completing the form and pressing the large play button, we will have created a new process instance as shown in the following screenshot:

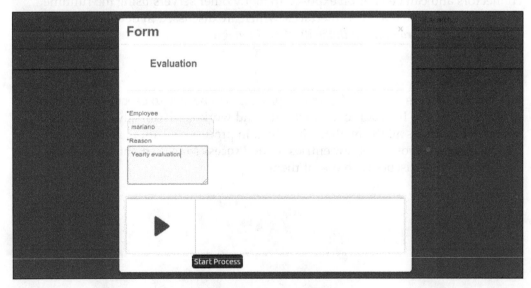

This interface allows us to see the different process definitions available to start them, but we still need an interface to see the currently running process instances and its internal state. For that, there is another option in the **Process Management** navigation bar option, called **Process Instances**. In the following screenshot, we can see the task initiated by completing the form in the preceding screenshot:

The UI allows us to filter process instances by their state, see their details, send signals to them, or abort them. But this is mostly an administrative topic to handle process systems. End users would mostly interact with the tasks assigned to them, or their roles. To do so, the workbench needs a way to show:

- A collection of all the different human tasks with which a user can interact
- A particular form to interact with each one of the said human tasks

For that purpose, the workbench provides us with task lists and task form interfaces.

Task lists

It is important that all asynchronous tasks (that the process runtime is waiting to be completed) have a way to be managed from external tools. The case of human tasks is special, because they won't be handled by an automatic external system, but by people who need a UI to interact with said tasks. For that purpose, the workbench provides a way to see tasks that are either owned by the current user or could be assigned to the current user in the form of lists. On this view, we can perform a series of different actions on each task: claim them, release them, and start them, which are all explained in detail in *Chapter 6, Human Interactions*. Task lists can be generic, but for some special cases, we might want to make them more specific to show special data of certain types of tasks.

In the following screenshot, which can be accessed using the main toolbar option **Tasks | Tasks List**, we will find several views for task lists dedicated to personal tasks:

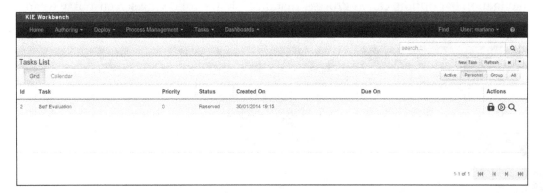

 To see tasks assigned to your user, created from the **Evaluation** process definition, you will need to complete the Employee field of the start process form with your user ID. Otherwise, the task will be assigned to some other user that you will have to log in with in order to see the **Self Evaluation** task assigned to him or her.

And when we click on the play button in one of those tasks, we go ahead to the next important UI point for human tasks, the **Task Forms** option.

Task forms

Task forms can be generic, based on task input and output information (elements described in *Chapter 3, Using BPMN 2.0 to Model Business Scenarios*), but should be dependent on each specific task to provide the most interaction help to the end user, because sometimes input/output information is not enough to infer the expected user interaction. Once a task is started, we can click on it to see its details, and we can have access in the workbench to the specific task form by clicking on the **Work** button. Have a look at the following screenshot:

From the view shown in the preceding screenshot, we can save the progress of the task, release it to the group, and complete it. Some generic abilities enabled for all tasks involve attaching documents and adding comments. Both are provided in the task details as well at a click on the **Attachments** or **Comments** buttons. At this point, if you go back to the **Process Instances** view, you will see that the process instance is in another stage because you completed the specific task.

Using these components, we will have enough user interfaces to work with any process we might encounter. We will use this chapter as a guide to start creating the managing processes in *Chapter 5, Creating a Process Project in the KIE Workbench*.

All these components are bonded together in the KIE Workbench thanks to a particular framework called **UberFire** that allows us to have a configurable and extensible workbench environment. We will dedicate *Appendix, The UberFire Framework*, to discussing its structure and use, which will become useful if you wish to extend the jBPM6 provided tooling for your own personal customization. This is an advanced topic, but will give you a full control over how to use the KIE Workbench to fit it best to your company.

Summary

The KIE Workbench provides a wide variety of functionalities, from process definition to process execution and any other functionality you can find useful related to the BPM discipline. It also allows a very simple way to extend itself, in order to add even more functionality to it. There is so much to show for it that we had to skip the least relevant topics. Still, we hope you learned how to use and configure the KIE Workbench to get the most out of it.

We went out of topic from jBPM6 a bit, but the added value these applications and their extension points provide to the BPM discipline is so large that I hope you find the detour worth your while.

In the next chapter, we will learn how to write our own business processes using the KIE Workbench process designer.

5
Creating a Process Project in the KIE Workbench

Even if jBPM6 uses BPMN 2.0, an XML-based standard, to define its processes, it's just not practical to write such files with a simple text editor. We need a way to define our process in a user-friendly environment that will aid both technical and non-technical people who know about the specifics of the steps involved in a process to define a process definition.

The BPMN 2.0 specification not only defines the behavior syntax for our processes, but also the look and feel for the process diagrams as well. This chapter will show you a step-by-step approach to learn how to use the jBPM6 Web Process Designer that lives inside the KIE Workbench to define BPMN 2.0 files using a diagram-writing UI. In this chapter, we will learn:

- To define our processes
- To test our processes with simulations
- To extend the BPMN 2.0 model to add our own types of tasks

An IDE to our knowledge

The main purpose of BPMN 2.0 is to provide business process representations that can be understood without the need for technical skills. Its concepts are not technical at all. There are abstract representations for when tasks need to be performed, decisions should be taken, and information needs to flow from one point to another—not tied to any technical implementation at the business process definition level.

The implementation, however, handles specific technical concepts that allow BPMN 2.0 to define connections to specific components in order to make it run on defined runtimes. These connections have several complex parts intrinsic to a technical implementation that require a deep understanding of IT. BPMN 2.0 needs to provide a way to work with these two perspectives, and this is why jBPM6 adds specific extensions provided by the tooling to configure all the specific components needed to define and run our process inside the jBPM6 runtime.

In this way, we can say that the graphical representation of the diagram is a business perspective of the process designer, while the specifics of configuring its properties and validating the process rely on a more technical profile.

A variety of process designers

When we start using jBPM6, one of the most confusing things is the fact that we have three different process designers to choose from. For those who are new to jBPM6 or who have used previous versions of it, it can be very confusing. Let's take a look at all the available options.

The BPMN 2.0 Eclipse editor

This is a graphical modeling tool for the creation and editing of processes in BPMN 2.0 (shown in the following screenshot), distributed as a plugin in the Eclipse IDE. If you wish to edit your BPMN 2.0 files from your own IDE, it is perhaps the best alternative to do so. Have a look at the following screenshot:

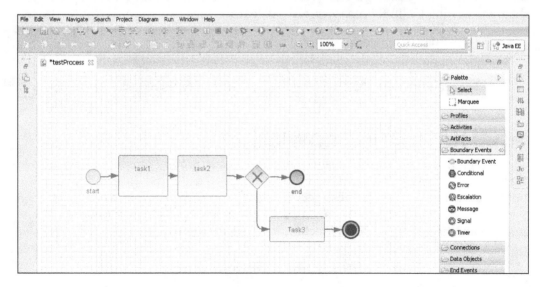

It has extended support for the BPMN 2.0 specification and for some jBPM6-specific characteristics. However, it is not fully integrated to jBPM6 runtime configurations, so some of the components that we might create with this editor might not be supported by the runtime afterwards. It is recommended to be used as a portable tool for IDEs to see process definitions exported from other designers (something we will see in more detail later in this chapter), but not for creating them from scratch.

The Web Process Designer

The jBPM6 Web Process Designer is an adaptation and almost complete reconstruction of an open source web editor capable of creating a full BPMN 2.0 diagram called **Oryx**. This project has been adapted, reconfigured, extended, and adapted again to the new web-based workbench applications provided for jBPM6 distribution into a completely new tool, and is now called the jBPM6 Web Process Designer. It is embedded in the workbench structures of UberFire and works as another editor for projects in the KIE Workbench, as shown in the following screenshot:

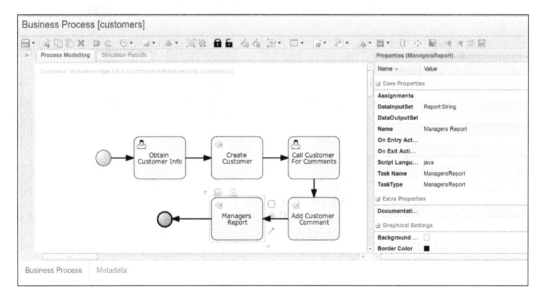

Today, the Web Process Designer is the official process editor that comes with the KIE Workbench. This designer is heavily maintained at the moment, with new features and bug fixes being implemented on a regular basis to keep track with all the jBPM6 changes. Because it is the designing tool most aligned with jBPM6 features, for the rest of this chapter, we are going to cover the usage of this editor.

The jBPM Eclipse plugin

The jBPM Eclipse plugin was the first plugin supplied with the early versions of jBPM5. This plugin was a straightforward migration from the already existing Drools Flow Eclipse plugin. When Drools Flow was rebranded into jBPM5, the decision was to stop supporting the **RuleFlow** (**RF**) proprietary language for process definitions and embrace the new BPMN 2.0 standard instead. This editor is now officially discontinued. No new features have been introduced in it for a long time. You can still use this editor to create really simple processes, but its usage is strongly discouraged.

Interacting with the Web Process Designer

The KIE Workbench comes with the latest stable version of the Web Process Designer. After the JBoss instance is launched (see *Chapter 4, Understanding the KIE Workbench*), we will have to access the process designer by going to the **Authoring** | **Project Authoring** perspective and interact with an existing project to work with its process definitions (and other types of knowledge).

In this section, we are going to explain how to create, modify, and delete processes in the KIE Workbench. After these three operations are explained, we will be ready to cover the different features provided by the Web Process Designer in detail as well as how we can use them to define some of the processes that have already been covered in previous chapters of this book.

Creating new processes

In *Chapter 4, Understanding the KIE Workbench*, we had a glimpse of how to list the processes residing in a project folder. We used the playground repositories and project already provided by the KIE Workbench by default as a demo. But of course, before we can list the processes of a project, we need to create them. If we want to create a new process, we need to go to the **New Item** action toolbar option of the **Project Authoring** perspective and select the **Business Process** option.

Before the new process is created, we need to provide some information using the pop-up window that is opened, shown in the following screenshot. It will provide us with a textbox for selecting a name for our process. It is also going to give us a **Virtual File System** (**VFS**) path for the folder where the process will be created.

 The KIE Workbench will store all knowledge assets we create in a VFS, which for the current version is implemented in Git repositories.

Please enter the resource name when this screen pops up.

The name we choose for the business process must be unique among all the assets in the same folder, as it's going to be used by the KIE Workbench to internally identify the process. Once we have selected a suitable name, `sprintManagement`, for our first process definition, we can create the new process by clicking on the **Ok** button. This will create an empty process definition and invoke the Web Process Designer so that we can start working.

Implementing our first process

Now that we know how to create and access our processes in the KIE Workbench, it's time to create a new process using the Web Process Designer. The process we are going to implement is the sprint management process introduced in *Chapter 3, Using BPMN 2.0 to Model Business Scenarios*. We are going to use this process to learn not only about its specific implementation, but also to cover the different features present in the process editor.

In the previous section, we created the `sprintManagement` process. The KIE Workbench will now display the Web Process Designer tool, and we can start using it. But before we start implementing the process, let's do a quick revision of the different sections we have in the Web Process Designer as well as its features.

The Web Process Designer sections

The Web Process Designer's UI contains four main sections: a **toolbar** at the top, **Shape Repository** as an accordion panel on the left-hand side, an **editing canvas** at the center, and a **Properties** panel as an accordion panel on the right-hand side of the editor. Let's analyze the main purpose of each one of these sections.

The toolbar

The toolbar is the topmost part of the designer panel; it contains different options to allow us quick access to most of the features present in it as well as other useful options regarding the layout of the process and its elements. The toolbar also has some other important features that we are going to cover in this chapter, such as importing process definitions or running simulations. So, feel free to play around with what's in the toolbar until you get used to the options that you have and where they are.

The Shape Repository panel

The **Shape Repository** collapsible panel contains the palette of BPMN 2.0 elements used to construct business processes. In this palette, you will find all of the BPMN 2.0 elements (described in *Chapter 3, Using BPMN 2.0 to Model Business Scenarios*) grouped according to their type. Sometimes, having all of the available elements in the palette is not the best thing. After you have designed a couple of processes, you will notice that most of the time you are using only a subset of these elements. This is why in the **Shape Repository** panel, there are two different library sets: **Full** and **Simple**. You can switch from one perspective to the other by using the drop-down list present at the top of the **Shape Repository** panel. There is also a third option called **RuleFlow**, used to create files with the legacy description language for process definitions in jBPM6, but it is an outdated format that no longer has support in the project, so we will skip it in this book.

At the bottom section of the **Shape Repository** panel, we'll find the **Workflow Patterns** panel with some predefined process flow structures to help you design your own processes faster and in a standardized manner.

The editing canvas

The editing canvas is perhaps the most important part of the Web Process Designer. It is where we are going to design our processes using the elements present in the **Shape Repository** panel.

When we drag-and-drop an element from the **Shape Repository** panel into the editing canvas, the element is added; we can change its position by simply dragging-and-dropping it around the canvas. Each element in the canvas has a context menu that we can access by clicking on the element. Using this menu (shown in the next screenshot with all the different icons that will appear around a task when we click on it), we can do different things such as creating new linked elements without using **Shape Repository**, changing the type of the element, accessing the process dictionary, editing its associated task form (if we are in a User task), or seeing the portion of BPMN 2.0 generated by the element. Have a look at the following screenshot:

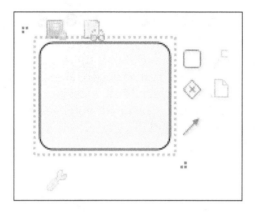

By default, the editing canvas comes with a preloaded Start Event, so you could start writing a process without the need to access **Shape Repository** at all. Some elements, such as **sequence flows**, have dockings that you can use to bind those elements to some other shape in the editing canvas.

In the upper-left corner of the editing canvas, we can see the process name, version, and ID. In the north, south, east, and west areas of the editing canvas, we can find little yellow arrows that will only appear when we move the mouse over their region. We can use these arrows to increase or decrease the total area of the editing canvas.

The Properties panel

When a BPMN 2.0 element is selected in the editing canvas, its properties are displayed in the right-hand side collapsible panel of the Web Process Designer. This **Properties** panel is very synced up with the properties supported by jBPM6, and to the greatest extent, to the core BPMN 2.0 specification.

Not all the elements have the same properties set, which is why the **Properties** panel adapts its content to the element currently selected in the editing canvas. If multiple elements are selected in the editing canvas, only the properties that the selected elements have in common will be displayed. In that case, changing the value of a property will modify the property value in all of the selected elements.

Properties can be of different data types: String, Boolean, complex, and so on. Depending on the type of the property being modified, the **Properties** panel can display different editors, such as a text area, a checkbox, a pop-up form, and so on.

Sprint management process design

Now that we have a better understanding of the tool, we can create a definition of the sprint management process introduced in *Chapter 3, Using BPMN 2.0 to Model Business Scenarios*. To explain the biggest variety of elements, we will use the third version of the process we defined, which is the most complex. Please refer to *Chapter 3, Using BPMN 2.0 to Model Business Scenarios*, if you need to refresh any information about what the process definition contains. The idea is to know how to create the diagram shown in the following figure:

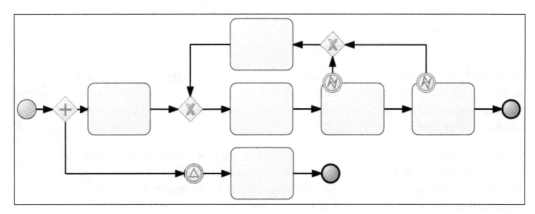

We'll continue working on the sprintManagement process definition. We will move the cursor over the predefined start node and select the **Task** option from its contextual menu (which should be the small rectangle with the rounded corners). This option will add a new task that is connected to the Start Event node in the editing canvas. We can repeat these steps, adding gateways (rhomboids) and sequence flows (arrows) when needed, by clicking on the rhomboid and rectangle icons on the context menu we previously described and by clicking-and-dragging on the arrow icon to create sequence flows connecting existing objects. Finally, we can create an End event node by clicking on the circle icon of the context menu with the thicker border.

When getting to the point where we need catching events and boundary events, we can search for them in **Shape Repository** by clicking on the left-hand side accordion panel, selecting from the different menus available (**Tasks**, **Gateways**, **Intermediate Catch Events**, and so on), and dragging-and-dropping a specific element into the editing canvas. We can drop the boundary events on the border of each task (you will see that the border of the task becomes green to indicate you can drop the catching event as a boundary event). Later on, selecting those intermediate events will allow us to continue adding components from their respective contextual menus of each element in the editing canvas.

Configuring the process properties

We will start our process definition configuration by populating the mandatory attributes of the process itself. To do this, we have to click on the background of the editing canvas and go to the **Properties** panel, located at the right-hand side of the designer in an accordion panel. Each process definition has the following jBPM6-related properties:

Property	Description
AdHoc	This Boolean property identifies whether this process is ad hoc or not. Ad hoc processes are special processes where the internal nodes don't have to be connected to each other, and the flow between the nodes is handled by an external component (either rules or specific user interactions). In our case, we will leave it as it is by default (false).
Executable	The BPMN 2.0 specification defines two types of processes—executable and nonexecutable. Of course, because the main idea of the process designer is to create executable BPMN 2.0 processes, the value of this property is true by default.
Globals	Using this property, we can define Drools global variables to share information amongst processes as well as among global services that can be later invoked inside the process.
	When we want to edit the value of this property, a drop-down menu appears, and when we try to open it, there will be a pop up containing an editor for global variables.
ID	This property identifies the ID attribute of the generated \<process> BPMN 2.0 element. The ID of the process must be unique inside a KIE base, as it is used at runtime to identify a process definition.
Imports	Just as in Java, when we're dealing with a process definition, we need to import all the different classes we want to use in our process.
Variable Definitions	This property defines the variables available in the process. Variables are important for maintaining internal values, sharing information between nodes, and getting some kind of result from the process execution.

Now that we have a clear idea of the properties a process has, we can see some extra details about some of them.

For example, the ID of the process has quite an important role. As it will identify the process definition inside a KIE base, we are going to depend on it to start a process or to define a Call Activity node (reusable subprocess). In our case, we will set the ID for this process as `sprintManagement-V1`.

Finally, we need to define the process variables required by this definition by editing the **Variable Definitions** property of our process. When we click on the list box display of the property value, an editor will show us the dialog box as shown in the following screenshot, where we can add, remove, and define the name and type of our process variables. In the process we are designing, we need six variables: `project`, `reqDescription`, and `developerId` of type **String**; `compiled` and `deployed` of type **Boolean**; and `storyPoints` of type **Integer**. The final result should be as shown in the following screenshot:

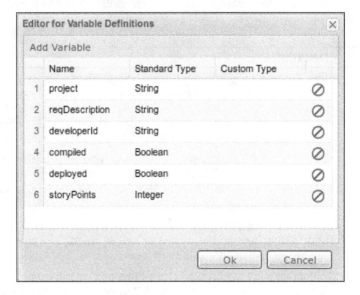

Once we have the process configured, we need to review each of the nodes it has in order to configure their properties.

Configuring the event nodes

The Start Event node represents the beginning of the process. From all the different Start Event types that we can use, we will use the None Start Event node, because in jBPM6, you have to use this type of Start Event when your process is going to be explicitly started using its ID, as the following line of code does:

```
Ksession.startProcess("id.of.the.process");
```

The properties present in this node relevant to the jBPM6 runtime are as follows:

Property	Description
DataOutput	This property defines all the output variables of the node. Each variable has a type (Java class) and a name.
	Specifically, in the case of the None Start Event node, this property has no meaning. The property exists for this node because it is used by other Start Event subtypes (that is, Signal Start Event, where it is used to hold a reference to the Signal event and the information it contains).
DataOutputAssociations	This is the way we assign data from the different DataOutput variables to process variables. The type of DataOutput must be assignable to the process variable type. This property is present in each node that has a DataOutput property.
	The editor will have to create DataOutput. Associations require a dedicated section, as it is probably the most complex property editor in the process designer. We are going to learn how to use it later in this chapter.

Given that this None Start Event node doesn't have any properties that affect its behavior during execution, we are not going to modify any of them.

After the Start Event node is invoked, a process execution will be started. During the process execution, we might capture two other types of events, **Signal Intermediate Catch** events (the circle with a triangle inside it at the bottom of the diagram) and **Error Boundary** events (the two circles with the lightning-like icon, located at the border of two of the tasks we defined).

Intermediate Signal Event nodes have to wait for an event to arrive in order to continue their execution. Events can be broadcast from another process or from the Java application. Using them allows us to create more maintainable and robust processes. The properties we can configure a Signal Intermediate Catch event are as follows:

Property	Description
DataOutput	Just like the DataOutput property explained for start nodes, this property is used to specify the output variables in this node. In jBPM6, the only output variable you can define is *event*. This variable will contain the event object.
DataOutputAssociations	Just like Start events, we have this property to map the output variable of this event to a process variable.
SignalRef	This is the key name of the event type that the node is waiting for. It is just a string that must be used when you want to signal the event.

In our scenario, the event we are going to be waiting for is the manual cancellation of the requirement, which is why we need to change the SignalRef property to reqCancelled. To do so, we select the event and then click on the **Properties** panel, where we will see the properties of the event selected. In this case, we don't want to know anything else from the event, so we are not going to define any DataOutput or DataOutputAssociations property in this node. The only other change we are going to make to this node is to add a meaningful name to it so that users reviewing this process can easily understand what event the node is waiting for. The value we are going to set for the Name property is: Req. Cancelled.

The Error Boundary events that we defined for two of our tasks show that we want to handle exceptions being thrown inside the execution of said tasks as part of the sequence of steps in this process. Just like the Signal events, they have DataOutput and DataOutputAssociations to capture the event being sent. In them, you define a single variable with any name that you can map to a process variable to keep the exception as a variable in subsequent nodes. For our case, we are not going to configure those properties.

The one property we are going to configure is the ErrorRef property. In it, you must write the fully qualified name of the exception you expect to capture. In jBPM6, it must be a single specific type (not a generic super class of the exception, but the actual exception), and it must have a fully qualified name even if you added the exception type to the Imports property in the process properties. For our case, we will type java.lang.RuntimeException in said property.

The last event nodes that we will configure in our process are the End Event nodes, which represent the end of the execution path on the process. We can configure them for many different purposes, but in our case, we will use only a type that will terminate the complete process instance (the **Terminating End** event), regardless of how many pending execution paths may still exist for both execution paths that diverge from the first parallel gateway.

Configuring the task nodes

The task nodes in BPMN 2.0 are where concrete actions take place. The steps that are required to achieve our process' goal are going to be defined using task nodes.

The BPMN 2.0 specification provides eight task types (Abstract task, Service task, Send task, Receive task, User task, Manual task, Business Rule task, and Script task), and jBPM6 supports all of them.

We will focus on the valid set of properties that affect each of the different tasks supported by jBPM6, but we are not going to cover the detailed behavior of the tasks at runtime.

In the Web Process Designer, all of the different types of tasks are implemented by just one element in the **Shape Repository** panel — **Task**. The TaskType property of each node is going to specify its concrete type. An empty value for TaskType (the default value in the Web Process Designer) identifies an abstract task.

Each task type has a different set of attributes that we can use to configure it. The Web Process Designer will automatically show only the valid attributes for each specific task type. The following table explains the valid properties for each type:

Abstract task	
Property	**Description**
Name	The name for the task that will be shown in the box.
DataInputSet	The input variables of the node.
DataOutputSet	The output variables of the node.
Assignments	The assignments between the process variables and the input and output variables of the node.
On Entry Actions	A piece of Java code that is invoked before the node gets executed. All of the process variables are available in this piece of code. This is an extension of BPMN 2.0 provided by jBPM6, and not part of the standard.
On Exit Actions	A piece of Java code that is invoked after the node gets executed. All of the process variables are available in this piece of code. This is an extension of BPMN 2.0 provided by jBPM6, and not part of the standard.

Abstract tasks are used by jBPM6 as an extension point for plugging in our business-related logic. `DataInputSet`, `DataOutputSet`, `Assignments`, `On Entry Action`, and `On Exit Action` are the properties common to all other types of tasks and have the same behavior for all of them. We will omit them in the next tables and concentrate exclusively on the extra properties that each task type has:

Business Rule task	
Property	**Description**
`Ruleflow Group`	This property is used to specify the group of rules that must be executed when the process execution reaches this node.

In jBPM6, the Drools rule engine performs rule execution. These two frameworks, jBPM6 and Drools, are so well integrated that the switch from one engine to the other is seamless for the user. Actually, the switch has never existed since both engines share the same core.

The following table shows the Send task's special properties:

Send task	
Property	**Description**
`MessageRef`	The name of the message being sent.

`DataInputSet` is especially important for the Send task, as it will map the message to be sent from the process variable.

The following table shows the Receive task's special properties:

Receive task	
Property	**Description**
`MessageRef`	The name of the message for which the node is waiting.

`DataOutputSet` is especially important for the Receive task, as it will map the message received.

The following table shows the Script task's special properties:

Script task	
Property	**Description**
Script	This property defines the piece of code we want executed when the process execution reaches this node. Inside this piece of code, we have access to all of the process variables and the special variable kcontext.
Script Language	This defines the language used in the Script property. This language could be Java or MVEL, which is a scripting language that runs on top of the JVM.

Business users do not commonly use Script tasks, but they are really helpful for technical people. By adding Script tasks to a process, we can easily modify the behavior of our processes without modifying any Java class. We can use this type of task to add logs, messages, or to perform data transformation tasks in our processes. As a rule of thumb, Script tasks shouldn't contain business logic inside them. Abstract tasks, Human tasks, and Service tasks are better places to implement this kind of logic. Let's start with the Service tasks as shown in the following table:

Service task	
Property	**Description**
Service Interface	If the jBPM6 predefined handler for this task type is used (ServiceTaskHandler), this property should be the fully qualified name of the class we want to use as a service; and each time this task is executed, a new instance will be created through reflection.
Service Operation	This property identifies the name of the method we want to invoke in the Interface object.

User tasks are the ones that should be performed by humans:

User task	
Property	**Description**
Actors	A comma-separated list of actor IDs or an expression of the form #{<expression>} that evaluates to a string object. In the default Human task implementations of jBPM6, this property defines the possible owners of a task.
Groups	A comma separated list of group IDs or an expression of the form #{<expression>} that evaluates to a string object. In the default Human task implementations of jBPM6, this property defines the actor's groups that can own this task.

User task

Property	Description
Task Name	This is the name of the user task. In the default Human task implementations of jBPM6, this property defines the task name that should be displayed to the user.
Comment	In the default Human task implementations of jBPM6, this property defines a comment for the task.
Priority	In the default Human task implementations of jBPM6, this property defines the priority of the task.
Skippable	In the default Human task implementations of jBPM6, this property defines whether this task can be skipped or not.
Notifications	In the default Human task implementations of jBPM6, this property defines a set of time rules for sending specific e-mail notifications to other users or groups when a task has not been started or completed within a specific amount of time.
Reassignment	In the default Human task implementations of jBPM6, this property defines a set of time rules for automatically reassigning this task to another user or group when a task has not been started or completed within a specific amount of time.

The properties of the User task are tightly related to the default Human task implementation of jBPM6. This implementation is going to be introduced and explained in *Chapter 6, Human Interactions*.

Manual tasks have the same attributes explained for an Abstract task. The variables you can define in the DataInputSet and DataOutputSet properties depend on the handlers you register for Send, Receive, User, and Manual tasks. We have discussed work item handlers in *Chapter 2, BPM Systems' Structure*. User tasks will have work item handlers defined with the key Human Task, Manual tasks with the key Manual Task, Send tasks with the key Send Task, and Receive tasks with the key Receive Task—all configurable from the runtime configuration of the different WorkItemHandler implementations, which we have seen in *Chapter 2, BPM Systems' Structure*.

Going back to our process, we have six different tasks to define—one Business Rule task (assign story points), one User task (develop requirement code), and four Abstract tasks (notify developer of errors, notify developer of requirement changes, compile project to Maven, and deploy compiled project). Let's now configure this process definition to achieve the goal defined in *Chapter 3, Using BPMN 2.0 to Model Business Scenarios*.

For the first task, the first thing we need to do is change its `TaskType` property to a Business rule. A little icon similar to a table will appear in the node. We then need to change the `Ruleflow Group` property. This property defines the group of rules to be executed when this node is reached. The value we need for this property is `assign-story-points`. Finally, we will assign "story points" to the `Name` property.

Regarding the second task, we need to configure it as a User task using its `TaskType` property. A small icon of a person will appear in the node. The `Name` and `Task Name` properties for this task should be set to "Develop Requirement Code". For the `Groups` property, we will use "developers"; this represents the possible users that could own this task (the ones that belong to the developers group).

Now, it's time to configure the input and output variables for this task. As you may recall from the original definition in *Chapter 3, Using BPMN 2.0 to Model Business Scenarios*, this task has two input variables: `complexity` of type **Integer** and `requirement` of type **String**. With the `DataInputSet` property editor, we can define these input variables to look like the following screenshot:

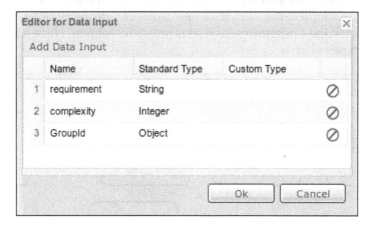

The GroupId input is automatically generated by the editor when you fill the Groups property in the **Properties** panel for a User task. A similar thing is done for the Actors property with the ActorId input and output. We will use this to our advantage and define ActorId as a data output to obtain the actual user that performed the User task, as shown in the following screenshot:

Once we have defined all of our input and output variables, we need to make assignments between the process variables (or fixed values) and the input variables of the task as well as assignments between the output variables of the task and the process variables. This operation is performed in the editor available for the Assignments property of the task. Using this editor, try to create the configuration as shown in the next screenshot. You will find the **From Object** fields and the **To Object** fields that provide you with selectable options. To see all the options needed, you will need to complete the Variable Definitions property of the process, as we have seen in the *Configuring the process properties* section. Have a look at the following screenshot:

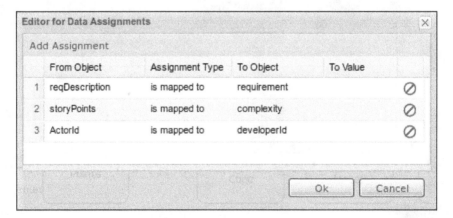

Before we continue, let's explore this editor in greater detail. An assignment is composed of three columns: **From Object**, **Assignment Type**, and either **To Object** or **To Value**.

For input assignments — which means the value we want to assign to one of the input variables of the task — we have to decide whether we want to assign a fixed value to it or if we want to map a process variable to it.

In the case of a fixed value, in the **From Object** column, we have to select the input variable that we want to assign from the drop-down list that contains all of the data input and output variables and process variables. The **Assignment Type** value required to assign a fixed value to a variable is is equal to. The third part of the assignment when we are assigning fixed values to an input variable is defined in the **To Value** column, where we have to enter the value we want to assign to the input variable. If what we want to do is map an existing process variable into one of the input variables of the task, we need to select the process variable first in the **From Object** column. Then, we have to select is mapped to for the next column, and finally, we have to select the task's input variable that we want to be assigned in the **To Object** column.

For output assignments, in the **From Object** column, we have to select the output variable we want as the source of the assignation. In the **Assignment Type** column, is mapped to is the only valid value, as we can't map an output variable to a fixed value. Because we can't use is equal to as the **Assignment Type** column, the only column we can use for the third part of the assignment is the **To Object** column, where we have to select the process variable we want to use as the target of the assignment.

The Service tasks

All the other tasks in our process are Abstract tasks. We'll learn how jBPM6 uses these tasks as an extension point after we see another editor later in this chapter, so for the moment, we will only configure them as Script tasks, selecting that option in their Task Type property. For the properties of these tasks, we will edit the Script property and just write a simple piece of code to see whether the node is executed:

```
System.out.println(kcontext.getNodeInstance().getNodeName());
```

This will print out the node name through system output when the node is reached. This can be done quite fast if you select all the tasks where you want to edit the same property. The **Properties** panel will show only common properties between those tasks and allow you to change their values at the same time. Skip adding the boundary events until we explain custom task types.

Configuring gateway nodes

In the case of gateways, there are not too many properties we can configure. The behavior of a gateway is determined by its type, which we have implicitly defined by selecting the specific gateway we want to use—XOR, also known as exclusive.

The Web Process Designer supports four types of gateway nodes, **exclusive (XOR)**, **parallel (AND)**, **inclusive (OR)**, and event-based gateway nodes, and the properties they can have are as follows:

Property	Description
Name	This property shows the name of the gateway. It is only used to display a label in the node.
Default gate	For exclusive and inclusive gateways only, this property allows us to select the default **sequence flow** that will be executed if all of the other outgoing sequence flows of the gateway evaluate to false.

We are not going to set the value of any of those properties for our gateways, because they are there just to provide converging points, not to diverge flows. Configuring diverging flows from a gateway is done inside the sequence flows.

Configuring sequence flow elements

Sequence flows are the elements used to connect the Activities, Events, and Gateways in our processes. Only the following two sequence flows' properties have an impact on the jBPM6 engine:

Property	Description
Condition expression	For sequence flow elements coming from a diverging inclusive gateway or a diverging exclusive gateway, this property defines the condition that needs to be evaluated. Depending on its result, the execution will either continue through this flow or not. Inside the condition expression code, we can access all of the variables defined in our process.
	The process designer provides a guided editor to write conditions based on process instance variable evaluations, but if you wish to write something more complex, it has a **Script** tab where you can write more complex scripts in a sentence of the following form:

```
return <expression resolving to Boolean>;
```

Property	Description
Condition expression language	Three different languages are allowed in the condition expression property: Java, MVEL, and Drools. We can use this property to specify the language we want to use.
	If Java or MVEL is selected, the condition expression must be valid Java code or MVEL script, respectively. Other than the process variables, a special variable with the name `kcontext` can be used to get extra information about the process instance.
	If we use Drools as the condition expression language, the syntax we have to use in the condition expression is Drools' DRL. Basically, we have to define a constraint using DRL that will evaluate to true or false.

As we are not using any diverging inclusive or exclusive gateway in the process that we are designing, there is no need to modify either of these properties in any of the sequence flows we have.

Accessing existing processes

Before we can open an existing process in the KIE Workbench, we first need to find it. In the KIE Workbench, there are two different ways to search for an existing process: through the **Project Explorer** section in the **Project Authoring** perspective's left-hand side or through the **Search...** textbox on the right-hand side of the action toolbar.

The **Project Explorer** will give us (by default) an accordion-based view of all possible assets, split by asset type. Processes will reside in the **Business Processes** tab. We can change this by clicking on the gear button next to the **Project Explorer** title and selecting the **Repository View** option to see all files with their extension type and to browse subfolders.

If you're not sure where you stored the process you're searching for, you can use the **Search...** textbox to search by the name or part of the process name. A list with links to different matches will appear in the editor panel. Each one will have an **Open** button that we can use to open the desired process in the Web Process Designer.

Modifying and deleting existing processes

Once we have a process opened in the Web Process Designer, we can start working on it. For the rest of this chapter, we are going to cover the most important options and features to do this editing. When we want to save the changes we have made in a process, we have to use the disk icon that appears on the topmost bar of the process designer panel, and we can select **Save** to store changes, **Enable autosave** to continuously store any changes we make, or **Delete** to remove the process from the project (shown in the following screenshot):

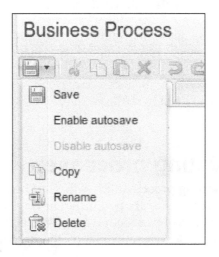

 Clicking on **Delete** removes the asset from the project, but older versions will still be stored in the internal Git repository and can be recovered through Git external tools. The KIE Workbench exposes all Git repositories at port 9418 by default.

Testing the process definitions

By now we should have a process definition ready to be executed in the jBPM6 engine if we've correctly followed all of the steps so far. We should save the process by clicking on the **Save** button at the top-left corner of the designer screen and clicking on the **Save** option when the drop-down menu appears. We have two ways to test our processes: running process simulations in the designer or writing a unit test in Java code.

Process simulations

The **Properties** panel provides different sets of properties for different situations. By now, we are familiar with the core properties (the ones shown by default), but there are also extra properties for the least common core properties, graphics properties for color selections, and another set for statistical analysis of process models over time, the **simulation properties**. On these properties, we will define statistical information for our processes, tasks, and flows, which will later on allow us to determine the costs of our process executions, possible bottlenecks, statistical distribution, and likeliness of each path to execute.

We won't be able to get into the details of all of the simulation properties, but we will mention that they allow us to configure how much time each task can take with properties that will be determined by the statistical distribution of each task. Also, for diverging flows, they will allow us to determine the probability of following each different path. After that configuration is done for each task, we can execute simulations by clicking on the simulations icon shown in the following screenshot, and by configuring two parameters—the number of instances that will be simulated to run, and at an interval of time (specified by a number and a time unit).

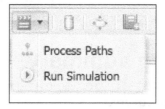

The results of the simulations will be then shown in the **Simulations** tab, located in the top-left corner of the editing canvas. Simulation results include graphics and tables, with probabilities of each path, associated costs for each task, and resource utilization and idle times.

Unit testing the process definition

If we look for a project called `process-examples` inside the `chapter-05` folder, we'll see that it contains a test file called `SprintManagementV1Test.java`. It uses a file called `sprintManagementV1.bpmn2` that contains the definition of the process. So, basically, the test will execute the process definition to check that everything is working as expected. If you want, you can take a look at the source code of the test. We will now look at the important parts of the `SprintManagementV1Test` class, where we test how the process we just defined executes in the following code:

```
KieSession ksession = createKieSession();
TestAsyncWorkItemHanlder h1 = new TestAsyncWorkItemHandler();
```

```
TestAsyncWorkItemHanlder h2 = new TestAsyncWorkItemHandler();
TestAsyncWorkItemHanlder h3 = new TestAsyncWorkItemHandler();
ksession.getWorkItemManager().registerWorkItemHandler(
    "Human Task", h1);
ksession.getWorkItemManager().registerWorkItemHandler(
    "compiler", h2);
ksession.getWorkItemManager().registerWorkItemHandler(
    "deployer", h3);
Map<String, Object> params = new HashMap<String, Object>();
params.put("project", "MyProject");
params.put("reqDescription", "My new Requirement");
ProcessInstance instance = ksession.startProcess(
    "sprintManagement-V1", params);
```

In the preceding code, we first created our session (using the APIs we saw in
Chapter 2, BPM Systems' Structure), named `ksession`, and we registered work item
handlers for it. The main process activity starts when we call the `startProcess`
method, which receives the process ID we defined and a map of parameters
(whose keys, you might notice, were described in the `Variable Definitions`
property of our process). This is the most basic API we will need on the runtime
to start a process instance.

Process modeling summary

Up to this point, we have learned to create and manage process definitions in the
KIE Workbench. We have also covered the steps required to design a process from
scratch using the elements available in the Web Process Designer's palette. We have
covered the most frequently used elements that jBPM6 supports, but we still might
need to get a better understanding of the rest of the nodes. I strongly recommend
reading the jBPM6 user guide, especially the chapter on the Web Process Designer.
It can be found at `http://docs.jboss.org/jbpm/v6.0.1/userguide/`.

Also, for a full reference of all the designer features, you should refer to its
documentation at `http://docs.jboss.org/jbpm/v6.0.1/userguide/chap-
designer.html`.

The Web Process Designer advanced topics

Even if the functionalities already covered in this chapter are enough to create a process, the Web Process Designer has some other features that will make life easier. These features include things like importing existing process definitions into the designer, validating our processes, creating custom task nodes, and so on.

Let's cover these features now to improve our productivity in the designer.

Importing process definitions

Sometimes, we already have a process definition outside of the KIE Workbench that we want to modify. One example is all of the `.bpmn2` files that come with the source code of this book; another example would be if someone e-mails us a process definition that they are working on. The Web Process Designer has a feature to allow importing these files and creating a visual representation. In the toolbar, there's the **Import Definition** menu that we can use if we want to import an existing process definition. The supported languages are BPMN 2.0 and JSON. The latter is the internal representation used by the Web Process Designer to maintain the definition of the process while we edit. There is a third option, **Migrate jPDL 3.2 to BPMN2**, that is used to migrate jBPM Process Definition Language (the proprietary language jBPM used until version 4 of the product) to BPMN2 files.

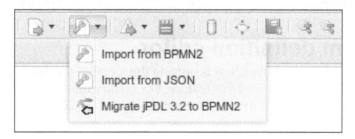

When we select one of the options in this menu, a pop-up window will open that lets us browse for the file containing the definition we want to import. We can also paste the definition of the process directly into the text area of the window. The editor will prompt you on whether you want to overwrite your existing process. If you choose to do so, the diagram will be overwritten. If you choose not to do so, the imported process will be pasted on top of your already-existing process definition.

Regardless of how we choose to import a definition, the process definition will be displayed in the editing canvas. If an error occurs in the importing process, a generic error message will be displayed in the designer.

Service tasks

As we now know, the BPMN 2.0 specification defines eight different task types that we can use in our processes. We also know that jBPM6 uses Abstract tasks as a way of extending the process definition functionality to fulfill our business needs (even if we are not aware of the specifics yet). But there is one thing that makes this extension mechanism possible; we need to define a specific task type. These predefined task types will then be made available through the **Shape Repository** panel in the **Service Tasks** tab.

For this purpose, jBPM6 allows us to create a definition of a task and then reuse it in our processes without having to redefine it every time we want to use it. The definition of this task is created in the KIE Workbench, outside of the Web Process Designer.

Let's take the example of the "Notify Developer of Requirement Changes" task that we are using in the sprint management process. This task can be changed from a Script task to a Service task. To do so, all we have to do is go to the action toolbar in the **Project Authoring** perspective of the KIE Workbench and select **Create New | Work Item Definition**. Work Item is the technical name for what are called Service tasks in the Web Process Designer. They are also referred to as **domain-specific tasks**.

Work Item definition editor

A complete description of this editor is outside the scope of this book. We are only going to give a brief overview of this feature. For further information, you can refer to the jBPM6 documentation: `http://docs.jboss.org/jbpm/v6.0/userguide/jBPMDomainSpecificProcesses.html`

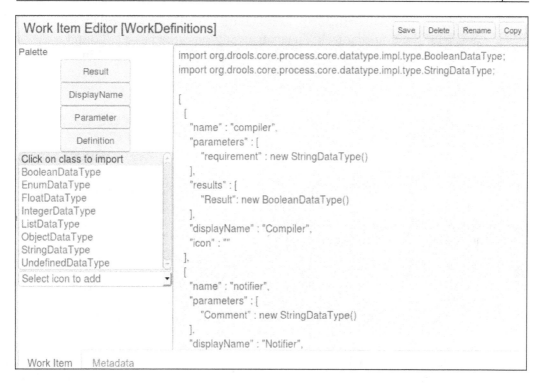

The editor is basically a text area where we can write the structure of a Work Item definition. The format of this structure is similar to JSON syntax, but in reality is MVEL syntax.

A Work Item definition is composed of the following five sections:

- **Name**: This section will define the key for registering work item handlers in jBPM6 runtime.

- **Parameters**: These are the input variables of the resulting task. Each of the elements in this array is going to be a variable definition in the `DataInputSet` property of the task.

- **Results**: This section is the same as parameters but for output variables. Each of the elements in this array is going to be a variable declaration in the `DataOutputSet` property of the resulting task.

- **Display name**: This section is the name that the resulting task is going to have in the Web Process Designer's Service task palette.

- **Icon**: This property defines the icon that the Web Process Designer is going to use for the resulting task. The icon must be specified as a URL and is going to be used both in the Web Process Designer's palette and in the task representation inside the editing canvas.

Using Work Item definitions in the process designer

For each Work Item definition, the Web Process Designer is going to add a new element to the **Shape Repository** panel, under the **Service Tasks** option. Only the Work Item definitions belonging to the same project (where the project is being edited) are going to be used by the process designer. All of the Work Item definitions are placed inside the **Full** perspective, under the **Service Tasks** tab.

 As this book is being written, a better editor for Work Item definitions than the one shown in the previous screenshot is being created. The current editor has a problem that causes any problem in the structure of the MVEL description of Work Item definitions to break the Service task importing, leaving only messages in the server log about any problems parsing the Work Item definitions file. The future editor will have a friendlier UI, which will be less error prone and will avoid this problem.

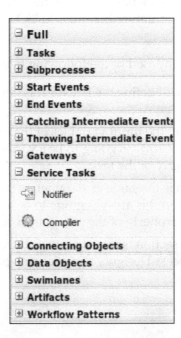

In the preceding screenshot, we can see two domain-specific tasks—**Notifier** and **Compiler**.

 In order to see the domain-specific tasks we have created, we need to close the process we are designing and reopen it. If we still can't see our saved Work Item definitions (or the **Service Tasks** tab), review the last logs of the server to check whether there were any errors parsing the Work Item definitions.

In the properties of these new tasks, we can check that the `DataInputSet` and `DataOutputSet` variables are prepopulated with the values we have defined in the Work Item definition.

Providing a runtime for our process

Process definitions are not considered standalone components in the KIE Workbench, but part of a project instead. These projects contain all the configurations to provide a runtime environment for our processes, and in order to get the most out of the KIE Workbench, we need to know how to configure a runtime for them. To do so, we need to edit certain properties of the project, deploy it, and decide in what manner we are going to run our processes.

The project editor

From the **Tools** option in the action toolbar of the **Project Authoring** perspective, we have one of the tools we can use to configure our runtime in the KIE Workbench—the **Project Editor** tool. In it, we can define through user-friendly tools all the KIE Module and Maven project-related components, such as project dependencies and knowledge base and session configuration.

From a process runtime point of view, this is where we should start working to check that our processes will have all the extra components they will need to work inside the KIE Workbench directly, such as Work Item handler configurations, dependencies where rules or other processes might be defined that our process definition needs to run properly, whether it should run with persistence or not, and so on.

The full extent of this configuration exceeds the scope of this book. To get a full explanation of this editor, visit the jBPM6 documentation.

Build and deploy

Once all the components in our project are ready to be compiled, all the required dependencies are defined, and all knowledge configurations have been settled, we need to create a compiled unit with the project assets. In our project, where we only have a process definition with a very basic data model (which doesn't define extra classes), we have reached said state, so we're ready to compile the project. For that, the project editor comes with its own toolbar with a **Build & Deploy** button:

Upon clicking on this button, the project editor will try to compile all the project assets into a JAR file and deploy it to the local Maven repository. From then onwards, we are just one configuration away from having a running environment for our process definition.

Configuring the deployment unit

Once the KIE Module project is compiled and installed in the Maven repository, we can define an environment for it to run in a standardized way. This environment will be available from the **Deploy | Deployments** perspective in the KIE Workbench, and it is called **Deployment Unit**.

A **deployment unit** is a specific configuration based on a KIE Module that will define one KIE base, one KIE session, and one runtime manager type to define a way to run process instances. A project might define multiple KIE bases or KIE sessions. Even if it defines just one of each, you still might want to create different configurations whether you share statuses between different process instances or not. Deployment units allow you to configure these components to define the exact configuration in which specific instances will run later on.

To configure a deployment unit, you need four things: a KIE Module, identified by a Maven release ID, composed of group, artifact, and version, that can be defined in the project editor seen in the previous chapter, a specific KIE base name (can be default), a specific KIE session name (can also be default), and a runtime manager type (can be singleton, by process or by request). We'll look at runtime managers in more detail in *Chapter 7, Defining Your Environment with the Runtime Manager*.

Summary

In this chapter, we covered the main characteristics and features of the Web Process Designer. We learned how to create and manipulate process definitions and other related assets in the KIE Workbench and how to design our processes.

Using one of the processes introduced in *Chapter 3, Using BPMN 2.0 to Model Business Scenarios,* as a guideline, we have reviewed the different BPMN 2.0 elements and properties that we might use if we want to create an executable version of that process in jBPM6. While designing the process, we learned about some of the most frequently used BPMN 2.0 elements as well as the properties required by the jBPM6 engine for execution.

This chapter introduced some executable examples that we can use to test not only the processes introduced by this chapter, but also any other process we might create using these tools.

Now, we should be familiar not only with the Web Process Designer's UI, but also with the underlying BPMN 2.0 code it generates.

Let's move on to some of the most advanced topics of jBPM6, such as runtime managers, Human tasks, and persistence management.

6
Human Interactions

Business processes express the way an organization works toward a well-defined business goal. Both humans and systems play important roles in reaching this goal. We need an understanding of interactions between people and an organization's business processes and how responsibilities are assigned and managed for different human interactions involved in those processes.

This chapter will focus on understanding the framework provided by the BPM discipline—and the jBPM6 framework—to handle human interactions. We will also introduce the **Web Service Human Task (WS-HT)** standard specification that has been created to standardize the information, life cycle, and interaction with software components specialized in managing human interactions.

In this chapter, you will learn the following topics:

- The role that human tasks play in the BPM discipline
- How jBPM6 handles human interactions at the code level
- User interfaces of KIE Workbench specialized in human interactions

Understanding human interactions

Many studies have been made to improve human-to-system interactions in the software industry. We will see how the BPM discipline approaches these interactions in a way that distils decades of experience. Some changes will be introduced to how we think and design user interfaces, from thinking about standalone applications to integration components. First, we need to take a look at the context in which Human tasks take place inside business processes.

Human interactions inside our processes

Modeling business processes using the BPMN 2.0 standard notation allows you to define many different types of activities. Two of the most frequently used activities are User tasks to handle human interactions and Service tasks to handle external system interactions. Our processes will be in charge of coordinating system-to-system and human-to-system interactions to guide an organization's day-to-day activities.

From a BPM discipline perspective, the distinction exists to guarantee a higher level of descriptive content in our process diagrams. At an interaction level, both human and system interactions are the same: something that happens outside the process scope.

When a User task is reached in one of our processes, a new User task will be created and handed to the correspondent business actors. At that point, we will create a new task in another system—the Human task component. This system is the main focus of this chapter and will have the responsibility of notifying the users and handling interactions with the newly created task along with its status changes.

User tasks contain information that is relevant in the context of a specific process' execution, which will allow the user to execute the task. Also, an actor will need to handle more than one task at a time, and the contextual information, including the type and/or name of the task, will differentiate each task from the rest.

Depending on the number of business processes in which the actor is involved, there will be different types of tasks that the user must be ready to execute. The ability of a user to perform a certain job will be determined easily through his/her user role. However, the processes themselves might be a component that the end user will not be interested in. In the same way as that of the process engine that sees the Human task as merely an external interaction, the Human task only sees the process engine as its origin and as a listener for the changes in its status.

At this point, we need to have a list of user interaction components to manage notifications, displaying, interaction, and completion of Human tasks. Both humans and the process engine itself will interact with those components at runtime.

Many different vendors have implemented these mechanisms in many different ways. Eventually, a standard specification appeared that formalized these mechanisms as well as the task's life cycle for all human interactions. The following section introduces this standard called the WS-HT standard specification. For further details, you can review the WS-HT specification definition in a PDF format at `http://docs.oasis-open.org/bpel4people/ws-humantask-1.1.pdf`.

WS-HT standard specification

OASIS Group is an international consortium that drives open source adoption of standards. It has defined the WS-HT specification to standardize human interactions, their structure and information, and make them interoperable between different vendors. The WS-HT specification serves as a guideline of the features that every human component should have; it is based on industrial best practices and on the most implemented end user features. Being compliant with this kind of specification will help you to replace components provided by one vendor with the components of another vendor without affecting other components, as long as both vendors apply the same standards.

Most BPM systems architectures provide a built-in component that is in charge of handling human interactions. This becomes a problem when trying to expose human interactions to other systems, besides the BPM system. It is because of this reason that even if jBPM6 provides a built-in Human task component, it can be created as a standalone component, accessible through external services. The overall structure for a jBPM6 BPM system core, considering only the main components relevant to our current scenario, looks like the following figure:

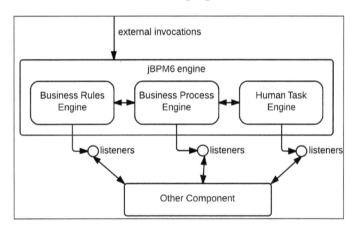

In the preceding figure, we can see that external components can interact with any of the components related to jBPM6, regardless of whether we're talking about processes, rules, or human interactions. The sort of information exposed through the listeners in the Human task engine is, however, closely related to the task's internal life cycle. We'll now provide an overview of it.

Human tasks' life cycle

The WS-HT specification defines a detailed and complete set of states that every task can be in as well as operations allowed to change a task from one status to the next. These states are designed to cover almost every possible scenario related to Human tasks.

These statuses also cover what we call Group tasks, which are assigned to a group instead of a particular person. Business processes can create these tasks, and anyone who belongs to the defined groups can complete them. When tasks are created, every person in the group who wishes to complete them will have to claim each task in order to work on it. Claimed tasks are assigned to the claimer only, and no one else can *claim* that task. If the claimer of the task cannot work on it, he or she has the option to **release** it.

The following graph represents the possible states and transitions of a task according to the specification:

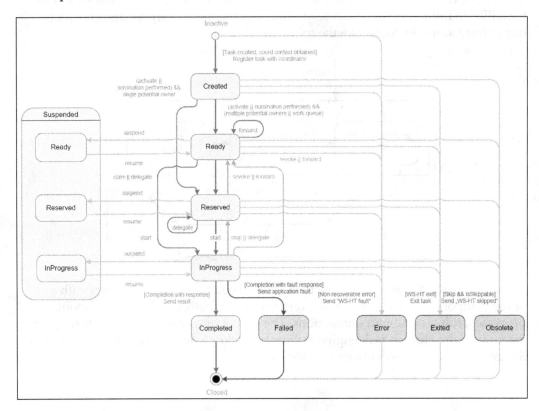

When you invoke a specific task operation on a particular task instance, you can change the internal status on said task. If you call an invalid operation for the current state of the task, the Human task component will throw an exception.

Usually, when our business process creates a User task, it will be set up at the **Created** state. If the task has no direct assignment (that is, the process or the task definition doesn't contain information about who is in charge of it), the task will be placed at the **Ready** state until someone can claim it.

A task in the **Ready** state still needs a potential owner of the task to claim it. Potential owners can both claim it into the **Reserved** state and release it back into the **Ready** state. At this point, the task will be ready and waiting for a user assignment.

A task in the **Reserved** state is only available for one user, so it is ready to be started by the claimer. The claimer, once ready to begin working on the task, can start it by moving it to the **InProgress** state. The task will usually remain in that state until the user in charge of that task completes it, moving it to the **Completed** state. Alternatively, we can suspend or stop the task, which means that we need to resume it or start it again.

In situations where a task cannot be successfully completed, we can use four other close strategies for the tasks. If it cannot be successfully completed, the Fault task operation moves the task to the **Failed** state. This is usually done when the user in charge of the task doesn't have all the information or the means that is required to finish the task. **Error**, **Exit**, and **Obsolete** are used when there is an error inside the task or the task is no longer needed.

Determining who is the right person to complete a specific task is the responsibility of the Human task service, and it will do it based on the input information received from the task creation process. Now that we understand the states that a task can be in, we can get into the API side to understand how these operations translate to code invocations and how this extra information is shared between processes and tasks. The following section introduces the Human task component provided in jBPM6 by showing us an example of how to create Human tasks.

jBPM6 Human task component's overview

Based on the WS-HT specification, the current version of the Human task component is composed of multiple projects that can be found inside the master Git repository, where you can download the full code of the jBPM project. The following link will allow you to see the source code directly from the browser:

```
https://github.com/droolsjbpm/jbpm/tree/master/jbpm-human-task
```

From the architectural perspective, this component can be configured to run in different ways, depending on your application needs. Because the Human task component is a very simple and lightweight component, the simplest way to start using it is to embed it in the same runtime with the process engine.

The following figure describes the different interactions with the Human task component:

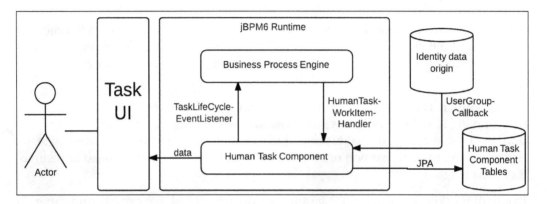

This option instantiates the Human task component inside your application. The Human task component is a service that is implemented using **Java Persistence API (JPA)** to persist information in a database. This implies adding special configurations to our application to make it work: a persistence provider must be specified (which by default is `hibernate` in jBPM6) and a persistence unit must be defined in order for JPA to understand specific objects as database table mappings.

An application that holds the Human task component as a library inside it will have a way to access information on our Human tasks from a database. As a con, we will need to add the database access configurations inside our application; if we have multiple applications embedding the Human task component features, we will have to maintain all the configurations for every application, which increases complexity.

The second option is to use this component as an external component. Our application will have to configure how to connect to the Human task component — located in a different server — through some specific communication protocol. In *Chapter 10, Integrating KIE Workbench with External Systems*, we will see ways in which KIE Workbench provides such an external Human task component and process engine.

The following figure shows how communication would happen with an external Human task component:

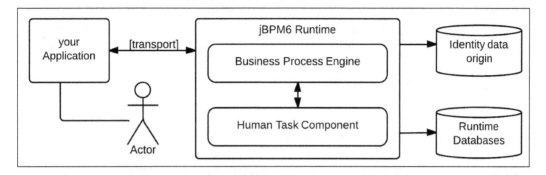

Before we get into any more details regarding how to externalize the Human task component, we should probably get into more detail about how it is implemented, its internal elements, and its exposed APIs.

Human task component APIs

For this particular case, we've extended the process definition with which we started working in the previous chapters. We added two new User tasks to test and bug fix the requirement, and we added a model class to it called **requirement** to handle all process variables, data inputs, and outputs.

The following screenshot shows the process definition we will be using in this chapter:

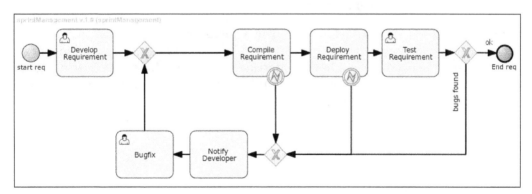

With these modifications, we now have two different groups in charge of Human tasks, namely, developers, and testers. This will enrich the process enough to give us a playroom for the next configuration steps.

The task service

The Human task component in jBPM6 follows the guidance of the WS-HT standard specification to construct a service that is accessible by both people and the process engine. This specification defines specific calls that must be made to switch the state of Human tasks. The main API for the Human task service is defined in the `org.kie.api.task.TaskService` interface, as shown in the following code:

```
public interface TaskService {
    ...
    void claim(long taskId, String userId);
    void start(long taskId, String userId);
    void delegate(long taskId, String usrId, String tgtUsrId);
    void fail(long taskId, String usrId, Map faultData);
    void skip(long taskId, String usrId);
    void forward(long taskId, String usrId, String tgtEntityId);
    void complete(long taskId, String usrId, Map outputData);
    List<TaskSummary> getTasksAssignedAsPotentialOwner(
            String userId, String language);
    List<TaskSummary> getTasksOwned(
            String userId, String language);
    ...
}
```

This is just a simplification with the most used methods of the `TaskService` interface. The behavior they provide is guided by the graph of the Human tasks' life cycle that we saw in the *Human tasks' life cycle* section. In order to use it, we must initialize an implementation of it.

In order to have our Human task component available inside our classpath, we need to add the dependencies necessary to get the task service classes working. In a Maven-based project, we can add those dependencies by adding the following three dependencies to your own Maven-based project's `pom.xml` file, just like the project in the code section of this book, which is in the `chapter-06/human-task-components-api` folder:

```
<dependency>
  <groupId>org.jbpm</groupId>
  <artifactId>jbpm-kie-services</artifactId>
  <version>6.1.0.Beta3</version>
</dependency>
<dependency>
  <groupId>org.jbpm</groupId>
  <artifactId>jbpm-human-task-core</artifactId>
  <version>6.1.0.Beta3</version>
```

```
  </dependency>
  <dependency>
    <groupId>org.jbpm</groupId>
    <artifactId>jbpm-human-task-audit</artifactId>
    <version>6.1.0.Beta3</version>
  </dependency>
```

Once we have these dependencies in our project, we can configure the persistence unit that will be used by our Human task component's implementation.

As previously mentioned, the Human task component is basically a JPA-backed application that will handle the stateful nature of Human tasks with a database. For it to work, it needs a persistence unit configured in the META-INF/persistence. xml file in our classpath, pointing to all the database entity class mappings and data source configurations. In the human-task-components-api project inside this chapter's code, you will find the persistence.xml file in the src/main/resources folder. The content of this file is as follows:

```
<?xml version="1.0" encoding="UTF-8"?>
<persistence version="2.0"
        xmlns="http://java.sun.com/xml/ns/persistence"
        xmlns:orm="http://java.sun.com/xml/ns/persistence/orm"
        xmlns:xsi="http://www.w3.org/2001/XMLSchema-instance"
        ...>
  <persistence-unit name="org.jbpm.services.task"
        transaction-type="JTA">
  <provider>org.hibernate.ejb.HibernatePersistence</provider>
  <jta-data-source>jdbc/testDS</jta-data-source>
  <mapping-file>META-INF/Taskorm.xml</mapping-file>
  <class>org.jbpm.services.task.impl.model.AttachmentImpl</class>
  <class>org.jbpm.services.task.impl.model.ContentImpl</class>
  <class>org.jbpm.services.task.impl.model.BooleanExpressionImpl
  </class>
  <class>org.jbpm.services.task.impl.model.CommentImpl</class>
  <class>org.jbpm.services.task.impl.model.DeadlineImpl</class>
  <class>org.jbpm.services.task.impl.model.DelegationImpl</class>
  <class>org.jbpm.services.task.impl.model.EscalationImpl</class>
  <class>org.jbpm.services.task.impl.model.GroupImpl</class>
  <class>org.jbpm.services.task.impl.model.I18NTextImpl</class>
  <class>org.jbpm.services.task.impl.model.NotificationImpl
  </class>
  <class>org.jbpm.services.task.impl.model.EmailNotificationImpl
  </class>
  <class>
```

```
        org.jbpm.services.task.impl.model.EmailNotificationHeaderImpl
    </class>
    <class>org.jbpm.services.task.impl.model.PeopleAssignmentsImpl
    </class>
    <class>org.jbpm.services.task.impl.model.ReassignmentImpl
    </class>
    <class>org.jbpm.services.task.impl.model.TaskImpl</class>
    <class>org.jbpm.services.task.impl.model.TaskDataImpl</class>
    <class>org.jbpm.services.task.impl.model.UserImpl</class>
    <class>org.jbpm.services.task.audit.impl.model.BAMTaskSummaryImpl
    </class>
      <properties>
        <property name="hibernate.dialect"
                value="org.hibernate.dialect.H2Dialect" />
        ...
      </properties>
    </persistence-unit>
  </persistence>
```

Also, the said persistence unit will need a transactional data source to work against the database. In our test file called `HumanTaskSampleTest.java`, you will find its configuration in the method marked by the `@Before` annotation called `setUp`. This is a JUnit (`http://junit.org/`) markup to let the test runtime know that this method will initialize components for every test run:

```
@Before
public void setUp() {
    this.ds = new PoolingDataSource();
    this.ds.setUniqueName("jdbc/testDS");
    this.ds.setClassName("org.h2.jdbcx.JdbcDataSource");
    this.ds.setMaxPoolSize(3);
    this.ds.setAllowLocalTransactions(true);
    this.ds.getDriverProperties().setProperty("URL",
            "jdbc:h2:mem:db");
    this.ds.getDriverProperties().setProperty("user", "sa");
    this.ds.getDriverProperties().setProperty("password", "sasa");
    this.ds.init();
}
```

The test will start a **Bitronix** (`http://www.bitronix.be`) transactional data source to be used by the persistence unit. Bitronix is the framework that defines the `PoolingDataSource` class, which is used to wrap a data source with a transaction manager.

In order for all these components to compile, we will need to add a few extra dependencies to our pom.xml file. We do this so that our classpath can have the JPA APIs, an implementation of those APIs (we will use hibernate for our case), and the Bitronix transaction manager dependency as well, as shown in the following code:

```
<dependency>
    <groupId>org.hibernate.javax.persistence</groupId>
    <artifactId>hibernate-jpa-2.0-api</artifactId>
    <version>1.0.1.Final</version>
</dependency>
<dependency>
    <groupId>org.hibernate</groupId>
    <artifactId>hibernate-entitymanager</artifactId>
    <version>4.2.0.Final</version>
</dependency>
<dependency>
    <groupId>org.hibernate</groupId>
    <artifactId>hibernate-core</artifactId>
    <version>4.2.0.Final</version>
</dependency>
<dependency>
    <groupId>org.codehaus.btm</groupId>
    <artifactId>btm</artifactId>
    <version>2.1.3</version>
</dependency>
```

Finally, because we will be working with an H2 database as the persistence accessed through JPA, we will also need to add the H2 dependency:

```
<dependency>
    <groupId>com.h2database</groupId>
    <artifactId>h2</artifactId>
    <version>1.2.128</version>
</dependency>
```

Once we have started our data source and configured our persistence unit, we can start the JPA persistence by just creating an EntityManagerFactory object with the persistence unit name, as follows:

```
EntityMananagerFactory entityManagerFactory = Persistence.
        createEntityManagerFactory("org.jbpm.services.task");
```

Adding a users and groups data source origin

Another thing we need to configure before we create and use our task service is a way for it to understand who the valid users are and the groups they belong to. Depending on the way your software or organization defines these structures, you might need to connect to one of the many different identity software components. These range from something as simple as a file with users and roles to a database or to an LDAP or **Active Directory (AD)** server.

As this configuration can be so varied, the Human task component provides a specific interface (with multiple available implementations) to connect itself to any of these data sources called `UserGroupCallback`:

```
public interface UserGroupCallback {
    boolean existsUser(String userId);
    boolean existsGroup(String groupId);
    List<String> getGroupsForUser(String userId,
        List<String> groupIds,
        List<String> allExistingGroupIds);
}
```

For our test case, we will use a properties file, and an implementation called `JBossUserGroupCallbackImpl`, which will allow us to define our users and groups at runtime through a `Properties` object:

```
Properties userGroups = new Properties();
userGroups.setProperty("john", "developers");
userGroups.setProperty("mary", "testers");
JBossUserGroupCallbackImpl userGroupCallback =
        new JBossUserGroupCallbackImpl(userGroups);
```

There are other implementations of this interface that are already available for use, such as `DBUserGroupCallbackImpl` that allows you to configure a couple of queries to validate users and groups, or `LDAPGroupCallbackImpl` that can be used to connect to an LDAP/AD server to validate users and groups. You can even implement your own to connect to any legacy system you might have to validate users within your organization.

Starting your task service

Finally, once we have our JPA persistence started and our identity data source configured, we can start our task service. Doing so is very simple, and the Human task component provides a factory class called `HumanTaskServiceFactory` to quickly create a task service instance, as follows:

```
TaskService taskService = HumanTaskServiceFactory.
        newTaskServiceConfigurator().
        entityManagerFactory(entityManagerFactory).
        userGroupCallback(userGroupCallback).getTaskService();
```

At this point, we can start using our task service that is backed up by JPA-based persistence, which is connected to our users and groups' data source. This task service will give us the possibility to create new tasks; interact with them, one user at a time; complete them; and so on. The next step in our configuration will be to connect it to the actual process runtime.

Connecting to the KIE session

By now, we have a task service instance running against a database and a user data source. We now need to connect it to the process runtime so that each process instance can create tasks in the Human task component and the Human task component can notify the process runtime when a Human task has been completed.

The connector, as we saw in *Chapter 2, BPM Systems' Structure,* is based on the `WorkItemHandler` interface, and for our particular case, it is going to be the `NonManagedLocalHTWorkItemHandler` implementation, as shown in the following code:

```
WorkItemHandler htHandler = new NonManagedLocalHTWorkItemHandler(
        ksession, taskService);
ksession.getWorkItemManager().registerWorkItemHandler(
        "Human Task", htHandler);
```

Using the `Human Task` reserved key, we can register a work item handler specific to handling User tasks. In this opportunity, the instance we selected is prepared to create a new task every time a process instance enters a new task. At the same time, this handler will register a listener on the task service to receive notification when the created task is completed, skipped, or failed, in order to call the `completeWorkItem` method on the work item manager.

The most interesting thing about the interaction between the process runtime and the task service is that it minimizes the interaction with the process runtime. The more the systems take care of notifying the process instance that it should continue, the less you have to do it. You'll find out that the only interaction with the KIE session for the test available in `human-task-components-api` is to start the process; all the subsequent activities are handled directly through the task service. We request specific tasks available for a developer or a tester and complete them using the available methods:

```
List<TaskSummary> tasks = taskService.
        getTasksAssignedAsPotentialOwner("john", "en-UK");
TaskSummary firstTask = tasks.iterator().next();
taskService.claim(firstTask.getId(), "john");
taskService.start(firstTask.getId(), "john");
Map<String, Object> results1 = new HashMap<String, Object>();
results1.put("reqResult", req);
taskService.complete(firstTask.getId(), "john", results1);
```

The calls that we see in the preceding code snippet are made after a process is started to get the tasks available for the user, john (one of the developers defined in the user data source). Once we have the task available, we claim it, start it, and complete it. After this is done, the process will be notified about the task completion and it will move to the next wait state. This will be a User task owned by testers, so mary will be able to get a task now to work on, as follows:

```
List<TaskSummary> marysTasks = taskService.
        getTasksAssignedAsPotentialOwner("mary", "en-UK");
TaskSummary marysTask = marysTasks.iterator().next();
taskService.claim(marysTask.getId(), "mary");
taskService.start(marysTask.getId(), "mary");
Map<String, Object> results2 = new HashMap<String, Object>();
req.addBug("bug 1");
results2.put("reqResult", req);
taskService.complete(marysTask.getId(), "mary", results2);
```

As you can see, these interactions are done exclusively through the Human task component. This translates to an actual application where you have people who only need to worry about working directly with Human tasks and let the application run the process in the background, creating new tasks according to what the process dictates. The interfaces needed for such a user perspective of the process runtime is defined in the following section.

Task-oriented user interfaces

A good way to finish the understanding of APIs provided by the Human task component is to understand what kind of generic UIs will relate to it. These task-oriented user interfaces should be generic enough to work for any kind of User task, but descriptive enough to show sufficient information to the users to determine the task they should be working with.

These screens will contain and handle Human tasks in two different ways usually:

- Through the task lists
- Through the task forms

Task lists

When a user needs to check pending tasks, they need a screen that displays these tasks and have an initial interaction with them. The list should contain enough information to understand the pending task, but the information should be generic enough to be available for most of the tasks.

The **Tasks List** view provided by tools such as KIE Workbench allows the user to choose which tasks in the list to start working on first. A **Tasks List** view is an entry point for users to understand what needs to be done. Users should have enough information from the list to understand the nature of the tasks at hand and be able to prioritize them in order to know which one to do first.

Some of the common pieces of information displayed in the **Tasks List** view are as follows:

- **Task Name**: This is a short and descriptive name of the task.
- **Priority**: This can help us sort tasks depending on their urgency.
- **Status**: A task could be in many different statuses and available to a user. It could be reserved to that user, ready for one of its groups, or in progress when it is already started.
- **Created On**: This is the date when the task was created.
- **Due On**: This is the date and time for when the task is due.
- **Description**: This is some textual description of the task that can contain contextual information to clarify its purpose.
- **Last Update**: This is the last date when it was modified.

The Human task component clients should build a UI to represent this information for many tasks at a time; they should do this to let the users decide which task to work on.

This view, whether you use KIE Workbench or a custom UI, should be generic enough to show information of any kind of tasks. However, when we have to work on a specific task, standardization becomes complicated, and specialization is what we will need for each specific task. To provide said specialization for each task type at a time, we will use task forms.

A **Tasks List** screen looks like the following screenshot in KIE Workbench, where we can see some of the properties we previously mentioned:

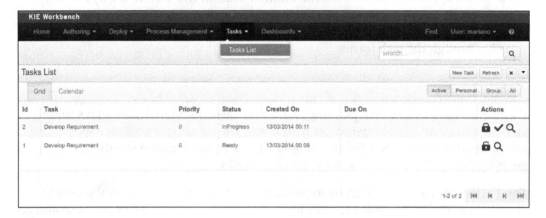

Task forms

Once we are able to view, discriminate, and prioritize the pending tasks, we need a way to work with the full representation of each task, one task at a time.

Each type of task needs to have a different task form that enables user interaction. These forms can be created from the process designer's contextual menu in KIE Workbench. This menu will allow us to create and edit both the forms used by User tasks as well as the form that can be used to create a new process instance, as we can see in the following screenshot:

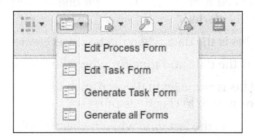

Each specific User task should have a specialized task form to show the exact information the user needs to perform their job. The task forms usually have the following requirements:

- Reviewing and approving information
- Gathering information required by the task
- Doing manual work and reporting the outcome

Each task form needs to be created to handle the information managed on each task. An example of a task form is shown in the following screenshot:

The **Hiring a Developer** task form provides the user with all the components to determine the name of the developer to be hired. Like almost all the task forms, this one contains information that is only relevant to the specific domain of this task. When the user needs to do the real work, they need specific tools to make the decisions involved in said job. However, when it comes to listing tasks, we want to be able to assess multiple cases simultaneously. The formula to get both the things working in the same environment is to provide abstract task lists and specific domain task forms. The other cool thing about task forms is that multiple processes that require this functionality can reuse them.

Keeping an external reference inside the process can be enough for most cases. There is no need to keep all the content of a document as a process variable, especially if there are external services to access, query, or even modify the said documents from outside the process scope. You will find it a common practice to keep documents in a content repository and have a process variable that points to the actual document. If for some reason the business process requires some bits of information from inside the document to make some decisions, you can usually store the metadata about the document inside the repository and use that information inside the process' context.

Web Process Designer also provides us with an option in the aforementioned menu to automatically generate all the task forms. This will create a generic implementation of the task forms. The main responsibility of generic implementations of task forms is to get the task's input and output information. Based on this mapping, provided by the BPMN file, we can construct a dynamic form that will display all of the input and provide simple form fields to fill all of the task output. The kinds of output a mechanism like this could handle are as follows:

- Text input fields
- Password/hidden text fields
- Calendar components to handle dates
- Select lists (list of values)
- Multiselection lists
- Checkboxes/radio buttons

The previously mentioned visual components are available in most of the UI-related frameworks. They can be enough to start working on a generic initial form display, but eventually, we will want to provide as much real-world information to the end user as they need to do their job more efficiently. This is one of the most important steps toward improving the performance of business processes. Depending on the nature of the task, we need to create custom components to deal with the interactions of domain-specific users.

External components can be used to render our forms, so we need to search and decide which component is best for each one of our forms' needs. Also, each of these task forms can be handled as a knowledge asset, which will be used as a bridge between the process and the users. The eventual task form that the user sees is the combination of a form definition used as a template and input data from the task to populate the said template.

We need to understand that this is just one possible solution to enable the user interaction. We need to be open minded about how we can expose the task lists and task forms so that users can easily access the information required to complete their tasks.

The following are some of the things that we can do to improve how the end users access the information related to Human tasks:

- Provide mobile implementations for task lists and task forms
- E-mail-based services
- SMS-based services
- Social networking client interfaces (such as Twitter and Facebook implementations)
- Excel-based task forms

The more options the users have to work on their tasks, the easier it is for them to adapt to the new services provided by the process engine.

The following section discusses how we can extend the functionality of the Human task component.

Building your own extensions to Human tasks

Now that we've understood the APIs provided by the Human task component, we can start discussing the possible extension points that the API provides to allow users to extend its functionality and connect the component to other tools. This proves most useful when you think of the Human task component as a piece of a big puzzle, for example, the overall enterprise architecture of an organization. In such contexts, the possibility of handling human tasks is not the only thing that is important, but how information from those tasks can also impact other components.

The main responsibility of the Human task component is to handle the life cycle of tasks, and leave many connection points for other pieces of software to be notified about the changes in said life cycle or affect it in a simple way. In the following subsections, we will see some details on how to configure different pieces of software that can provide a lot of added value to you. We will concentrate on three main extension points:

- Task life cycle event listeners
- Task service interceptors
- Task model providers

Task life cycle event listeners

In jBPM6, the task service provides a configuration facility to expose the behavior of tasks to external components. This configuration allows you to construct all sorts of publishing for task operations. In a way, every time a task is changed from one state to another, the current status of said task could be exposed. This is achieved through a specific listener class called `TaskLifeCycleEventListener` that can be implemented in virtually any way you see fit, as shown in the following code:

```
public interface TaskLifeCycleEventListener extends EventListener {
    public void beforeTaskActivatedEvent(TaskEvent event);
    public void beforeTaskAddedEvent(TaskEvent event);
    //omitted methods
    public void afterTaskActivatedEvent(TaskEvent event);
    public void afterTaskAddedEvent(TaskEvent event);
    //omitted methods
}
```

In the current status of the API, the methods provided by this listener interface allow you to implement your own code before and after any changes made to a task. The `TaskEvent` class used to describe the occurrence of each event gives you a reference to the task instance and a `TaskContext` object that will hold a few useful references, as shown in the following code:

```
public interface TaskContext extends Context {
    TaskPersistenceContext getPersistenceContext();
    void setPersistenceContext(TaskPersistenceContext context);
    UserGroupCallback getUserGroupCallback();

}
```

A `TaskPersistenceContext` object gives you data access methods to query and/or change the task persistence, especially tasks, groups, users, and task data. It also has methods to control the status of the database connection and the transaction, so they do provide a lot of power when deciding to alter the persistence of our model.

In the project `human-task-extension-points`, you will find a test file called `HumanTaskListenersTest.java`. In this file, you will find an example of using a listener to keep an in-memory list of all the activities done in the tasks. We create a special listener implementation called `LogTaskChangeListener` and add a very simple `TaskLog` object for each `after` method of the listener, as follows:

```
public void afterTaskClaimedEvent(TaskEvent event) {
    logs.add(new TaskLog(event.getTask().getId(), "TaskClaimed"));
}
```

After this, we provide a `get` method for the logs we create and validate it from the test.

The process of configuring listeners for the Task Service can be done through the `HumanTaskServiceFactory` class, as shown in the following code snippet:

```
TaskService taskService = HumanTaskServiceFactory.
        newTaskServiceConfigurator().
        entityManagerFactory(emf).
        userGroupCallback(ugCallback).
        listener(new LogTaskChangeListener()).
        getTaskService();
```

You can also add a new listener to an existing task service instance by executing the following code:

```
( (EventService<TaskLife cycleEventListener>) taskService)
    .registerTaskEventListener(listener)
```

The preceding code section first casts the `taskService` instance to an `EventService` interface and then registers the listener. The `HumanTaskServiceFactory` helper class will do this for us if we use it to build the task service.

However, sometimes configuring information about the tasks themselves is not enough. We might be interested in not just the task change, but any sort of invocation for the Human task component. For those cases, the Human task component provides another set of interactions called **interceptors**, which will be discussed in the following section.

Task service interceptors

One more extension point provided by the Human task component is what is called the interceptors. In order to explain the nature of interceptors, we must first understand the way that the task service is internally implemented, and to do so, we will need to explain the command pattern.

The **command pattern** is based on having every method in a particular service represented by the exact same call to a command object. An adapter class between the interface and the invocation of those command objects need to be created. The resulting class structure for the task service implemented through a command pattern looks like the following screenshot:

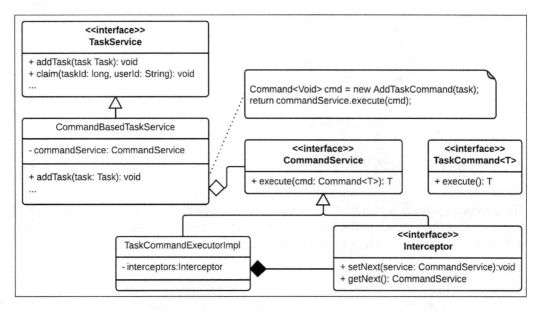

In the preceding class diagram, we can see that the addTask method is translated to a command invocation as follows:

```
public void addTask(Task task) {
    Command<Void> cmd = new AddTaskCommand(task);
    return commandService.execute(cmd);
}
```

A similar structure is followed for every single method invocation in the task service API. As you can see, the commandService.execute() method invocation will be the one done for every method.

The next step to understand the interceptors is to understand the CommandService class. This class will have the responsibility of invoking the actual execute method in the Command object. The idea behind the interceptors is that you can decorate the class by creating wrappers for it. Each one of the wrappers can invoke special pieces of code before and/or after the method invocation. The result is the creation of different components that can do anything you want before or after every method that is called on top of the task service.

The following sequence diagram shows how the interceptor pattern allows you to add steps before and after the execution of commands:

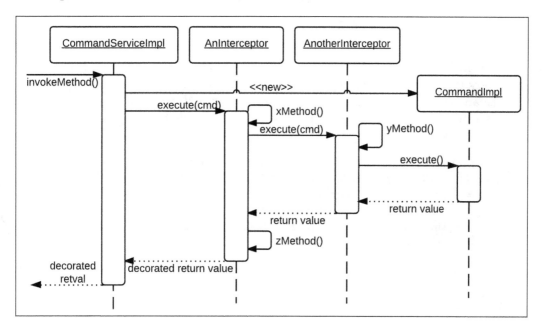

Now that we have understood a bit more about what the interceptors do and how they influence the behavior of a command pattern's application, we can get into the details of specific interceptors you can build for the task service, how to configure them, and what classes constitute our model to create these interceptors.

Interceptors for the task service can extend an abstract class with some helper methods called `AbstractInterceptor`. It provides basic implementations for all the methods, except for the `execute` method, and provides an `executeNext` method to invoke the next interceptor in line. With it, it becomes very simple to create a new interceptor.

In the project, `human-task-extension-points`, you will find that we created an interceptor called `UserLogInterceptor`. It is just for demonstration purposes. The main activity it provides around every method is the process of finding out whether it is a user-related operation according to the type of the invoked command. If it is, it stores a log of the operation that is called, inferred from the command name as well. The `execute` method for `UserLogInterceptor` looks like the following code:

```
public <T> T execute(Command<T> command) {
    String userId = getUserId(command);
    String operation = getOperationName(command);
```

```
    if (userId != null) {
        logs.add(new OperationLog(userId, operation));
    }
    return executeNext(command);
}
```

Later on, in the `HumanTaskInterceptorTest` class, we can see that we register it and check its logs after every user action to see that they are correctly populated. The `HumanTaskServiceFactory` class provides a method to configure interceptor objects inside your task service's implementation. The code to configure them looks like the following code snippet:

```
TaskService taskService = HumanTaskServiceFactory.
        newTaskServiceConfigurator().
        entityManagerFactory(emf).
        userGroupCallback(ugCallback).
        interceptor(priority, new UserLogInterceptor()).
        getTaskService();
```

In the preceding code, the `priority` variable is an integer that defines in what place this interceptor will be in the chain of interceptors that a task service instance could have.

 It is not recommended to add a new interceptor to an already existing task service, due to it being an internal component of the implementation of the `TaskService` interface.

When to use task event listeners or interceptors

Whether to use interceptors or task life cycle event listeners is a tough discussion, but the best rule of thumb to make a decision in that aspect is to consider transaction management.

Task life cycle event listeners provide a simple connection point. However, this extension point is usually detached from the invocation stack. It will be solely invoked from inside the task service when the task service finds a change in a task. It is great to connect external systems to the internal information of the task, but not a great place to make once-per-method-invocation operation inside the task service.

Interceptors, on the other hand, will be invoked for each method's invocation and will be able to wrap a lot more of execution than each method of the listener; for one invocation in a task service method, many different task life cycle event listeners might be fired, all detached from one another. However, the interceptor will be able to handle what happens before and after that whole invocation and even take care of exception handling if some of the actions taken in the proprietary code need to roll back the task service operation if there is an error.

For some cases, using both on a single class could be an alternative. For example, let's consider a cache for tasks. Whenever a task is changed, we want to mark it to update the cache. However, we don't want the cache to be updated until we finish the method's invocation. A good way to manage such a case would be to implement an interceptor to handle the cache update and a life cycle event listener to control which tasks are being changed by a particular method's invocation in the task service.

Many more possible cases might trigger the necessity of one over the other. The important thing to understand is that they are not mutually exclusive, and each deal with a different aspect of the task management, something we can take advantage of.

Task model provider

One final extension point that we will discuss in this chapter is the possibility of changing the JPA entity model used by the application. This will be an advanced feature that users can use that will allow people to add extra attributes (and therefore, extra columns) to the domain model to make it easier for you to create your own queries on the persistence.

You could have the possibility of adding, for example, an external entity ID passed to the task as a data input to your task objects. Later on, you could use this ID to create queries with your particular model, provided that they are both working in the same persistence unit.

This is possible because no components of the core of the Human task component construct any of the model objects directly. Instead, they use a factory called `TaskModelFactory`. This factory provides a concrete implementation of the interfaces that compose the core model of the task service, as follows:

```
public void TaskModelFactory {
    public Task newTask();
    public TaskData newTaskData();
    public Content newContent();
    //omitted methods
}
```

The `TaskModelFactory` class has an implementation called `JPATaskModelFactory` that defines JPA-based implementations for the interfaces defined in the model. What the task model provider does is that it discovers the `JPATaskModelFactory` implementation through Java's `ServiceLoader` and uses it to create its own components.

Therefore, you can configure the actual `TaskModelFactory` class that your project will use by adding a file called `META-INF/services/org.kie.internal.task.api.TaskModelFactory`, with the actual name of the implementation in it. You can see an example of this configuration in the `human-task-extension-points` project in the code section of this book, which just defines the default implementation class for the interface. If any of its methods is constructed to return a different type of object, it will replace the actual JPA implementation by the one you need. The only thing you will have to be careful is to make sure you replace the classes that will be persisted in the `META-INF/persistence.xml` file as well as in the newly registered implementation of the `TaskModelFactory` interface.

Summary

In this chapter, we discussed the main points of providing human interactions. They are not necessarily tied to a business process execution and can be independently created by any other application. We have learned how we can configure the Human task component to interact with the process runtime, how users interact with it through task lists and task forms, and how we can extend it to provide the functionality we need.

The next chapter will show how the Human task component can be provided in a common frame of execution with the process runtime called the runtime engine, how it is configured, and how we can construct our own runtime engine for any special cases we might have in our organization.

7
Defining Your Environment with the Runtime Manager

By now, we have seen the two main components of a jBPM6 runtime, the KIE session and the Human task service. These components are provided as the basic components needed to run process interactions between humans and systems. As the responsibilities of the process runtime grows, connectors to external systems should be added to transform the process engine into a highly configurable enterprise integration platform, where coordination between different systems can be easily managed in a business-friendly way.

The entire configuration involved in creating a runtime for the process engine, the Human task component, and all the external systems connectors could become cumbersome if not managed in a single place. In this chapter, we will learn about the **runtime manager** component, which is designed to create a bridge between all the components and configurations involved in a process execution. This component can be used to create a full runtime for the process engine. For this chapter, our goals will be as follows:

- Understand the role of the runtime manager in the jBPM6 architecture
- Get familiar with the available runtime managers and interfaces
- Start extending the API to create our own custom runtime managers

Understanding the role of the runtime manager

The runtime manager's main role in an application is to provide an application-wide point to access process runtimes (all the necessary interconnected services to execute a process execution within a specific domain). The nature of those runtimes and how many different runtimes can exist in a particular domain is a decision that each of the runtime manager implementations available has to make. By default, a runtime will be composed of two main components: the KIE session where the process is executed and the Human task component where human tasks will be handled. Both are grouped and returned from the runtime manager through the `RuntimeEngine` interface:

```
public interface RuntimeManager {
    RuntimeEngine getRuntimeEngine(Context<?> context);
    void disposeRuntimeEngine(RuntimeEngine engine);
    String getIdentifier();
    void close();
}

public interface RuntimeEngine {
    KieSession getKieSession();
    TaskService getTaskService();
}
```

Runtime managers will return a specific number of runtime engines, depending on their specific nature. There is a singleton implementation that will return a single session for all required runtimes in an application, no matter how many you ask. On the other hand, there is a runtime manager for each process instance that will provide a separate session for each process instance started in the runtime. The following diagram shows how the classes involved in the runtime manager component interact with each other:

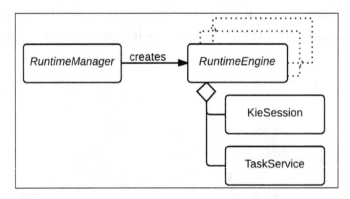

Determining what type of runtime manager we should use for our environment is a complex decision that involves an equilibrium between synchronization of operations and the number of concurrent calls that can be performed by a BPM environment at the same time. We will try to explain the advantages and disadvantages of each type of runtime manager as we explain them. Regarding the architectural decisions on which runtime manager to use, we will see a few considerations to help us in *Chapter 10, Integrating KIE Workbench with External Systems*.

The nature of the KIE sessions will impact the amount of information shared between process instances and how recoverable that information will be by other threads later on. The KIE sessions have a memory group called working memory, which groups a set of objects that will be evaluated by business rules. If you feed information to this working memory from the process instance or decide to fire rules during the process execution, depending on the level of isolation of the KIE session, the working memory might contain objects from a single process instance or many.

Rules evaluate this working memory to find patterns between different objects. Depending on what a business rule states, you might want to match different objects that come from different process instances, or isolate them on the instance level/request level of each process. For these cases, the runtime manager provides different alternatives to access a process instance in different session environments.

Understanding the runtime environment

Runtime managers provide you with a strategy to access different levels of isolation for your runtime, but it depends on another component to define all the configurations that allow the runtime to run in a specific way. The component that allows you to define these configurations is called the **runtime environment**, which is a grouping of all the different elements required for the process runtime. In the runtime environment, you can configure several things:

- Whether your engine will use persistence (we will see persistence configurations in detail in *Chapter 8, Implementing Persistence and Transactions*) or if it will run in memory only
- The knowledge definitions you will use in the runtime
- The specific user group callback object to connect the Human task component to a user and groups data source

The following code section defines the `RuntimeEnvironment` interface:

```
public interface RuntimeEnvironment {
    KieBase getKieBase();
    Environment getEnvironment();
    KieSessionConfiguration getConfiguration();
```

```
        boolean usePersistence();
        RegisterableItemsFactory getRegisterableItemsFactory();
        UserGroupCallback getUserGroupCallback();
        ClassLoader getClassLoader();
        void close();
    }
```

As you can see, there are methods to provide all the different components involved in providing the necessary information to the runtime to run correctly, including the KIE session configuration properties, class loaders, and runtime connectors, which are defined inside the **registerable items factory**. This is explained in the next section.

Registerable items factory

The runtime environment has a particular subcomponent that takes care of registering all the different connectors to external systems. This subcomponent is called `RegisterableItemsFactory`, and it provides a contract for the process engine to populate its work item handlers and different listener types for process and rule executions:

```
    public interface RegisterableItemsFactory {
        Map<String, WorkItemHandler> getWorkItemHandlers(
                RuntimeEngine runtime);
        List<ProcessEventListener> getProcessEventListeners(
                RuntimeEngine runtime);
        List<AgendaEventListener> getAgendaEventListeners(
                RuntimeEngine runtime);
        List<WorkingMemoryEventListener> getWorkingMemoryEventListeners(
                RuntimeEngine runtime);
    }
```

As you might have noticed already, external connectors can be implemented in a bidirectional way — both to expose the internal functionality of the engine to the rest of the application components and to configure signaling methods from external components back into the engine. It is because of this reason that listeners and work item handlers are provided with a reference to the runtime engine, so you can pass it on to your own connectors whenever they might need them.

Defining our runtime environment

Another thing to notice is that all these interfaces (except for RuntimeManager) define just getters for different components that the runtime will need at specific instances of rules and processes execution paths. You can implement your own to return the different implementations you wish as you see fit. However, the jbpm-runtime-manager project provides two implementations: SimpleRuntimeEnvironment and DefaultRuntimeEnvironment.

The SimpleRuntimeEnvironment implementation provides setters as well as getters for all the configuration components, or enough setters to create the configuration components based on simpler parameters. The DefaultRuntimeEnvironment instance extends the first implementation to add the most usual configurations as a default template. This default configuration will provide a persistent environment for sessions to be created, with history logs and the Human task component preconfigured.

Since persistence will be covered in detail in *Chapter 8, Implementing Persistence and Transactions*, we will save it for later use and just focus on working with SimpleRuntimeEnvironment for now. However, in order to simplify the code a little, we will not use it directly, but through a builder class called RuntimeEnvironmentBuilder. In the following code snippet, we can see how this builder class will let us initialize a RuntimeEnvironment instance really fast:

```
SimpleRegisterableItemsFactory factory =
        new SimpleRegisterableItemsFactory();
factory.addWorkItemHandler("Human Task", MyWIHandler.class);
RuntimeEnvironment environment = RuntimeEnvironmentBuilder
        .Factory.get().newEmptyBuilder()
        .userGroupCallback(userGroupCallback)
        .knowledgeBase(kbase)
        .registerableItemsFactory(factory)
        .get();
```

As you can see in the previous code, we can provide our own implementations of different components to a RuntimeEnvironment instance really fast without creating multiple lines of code to invoke each of the setters provided by a specific implementation.

You might have also noticed the `SimpleRegisterableItemsFactory` implementation that we used to register a work item handler type (by a class name) to its correspondent key. While the API provides two different implementations of the `RuntimeEnvironment` interface, it also provides several different implementations or the `RegisterableItemsFactory` implementation that we can use in different situations. The different implementations available are:

- `SimpleRegisterableItemsFactory`: This implementation defines type setters for work item handlers and listeners. When a runtime engine asks for the implementations, it will try to build the different handlers. It will create each of the specified types looking for a constructor with a `KieSession` parameter, a `TaskService` parameter, a `RuntimeEngine` parameter, or no parameter at all.

- `DefaultRegisterableItemsFactory`: This implementation extends the previous one to provide default listeners and work item handlers. Particularly, it will create a Human task component work item handler and listeners to trigger rules from processes and keep history logs in a persistent environment.

- `KModuleRegisterableItemsFactory`: This implementation extends the previous one to add any configuration defined in the `kmodule.xml` file of a specific `KieModule` object. It is constructed with a `KieContainer` reference and a session name from which to obtain the correspondent mappings.

- `InjectableRegisterableItemsFactory`: This implementation extends the default implementation to discover the different configuration components from CDI injection.

Now that we understand how the environment for a runtime manager is configured, and before we start working with the actual `RuntimeEngine` implementations, we need to understand how the lifecycle of the runtime is expected to be executed.

Runtime lifecycle management

We have already reviewed the idea behind the runtime manager and the runtime engine to understand their purpose. The runtime engine is a grouping of all the running configurations connected together that are provided by the runtime manager. We now need to understand how these components reside in the server and at what times they must be created or discarded. First of all, let's discuss the runtime manager's lifecycle.

The runtime manager usually behaves like a singleton in an application; we just need one instance of it. From that one instance, we will construct one or many runtime engines. So, it is important that even if we create many different runtime managers, they all behave in the same manner; otherwise, we might have different behaviors depending on how many runtime managers we have.

In the next section, we will see how different implementations of the runtime manager interface provide solutions for this problem. Whichever implementation we choose, the behavior against the obtained `RuntimeEngine` instance is the same as explained in the following sequence diagram:

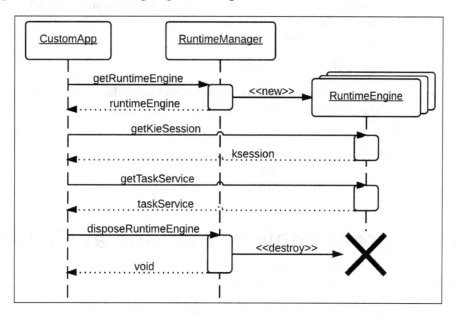

The `RuntimeManager` implementation will return a specific runtime engine, depending on the `RuntimeManager` type and the `Context` parameter we pass to it:

```
RuntimeManager manager = ...;
RuntimeEngine engine = manager.getRuntimeEngine(
        EmtpyContext.get());
```

Once we receive a `RuntimeEngine` instance, we will be able to interact with its subcomponents using the following options:

- We can use the KIE session to start processes, fire rules, and send signals. The code is as follows:

```
engine.getKieSession().startProcess("procId");
engine.getKieSession().fireAllRules();
engine.getKieSession().signalEvent("signalX", null);
```

- We can use the task service to interact with human tasks. The code is as follows:

```
List<TaskSummary> tasks = engine.getTaskService().
        getTasksOwned("john", "en-UK");
Long taskId = tasks.iterator().next().getId()
engine.getTaskService().start(taskId, "john");
```

The `RuntimeEngine` interface could also be extended to add other interactions if necessary for a particular domain.

When we're done using `RuntimeEngine` in the current transaction or thread, we let `RuntimeManager` know whether it can try to free resources by calling the `disposeRuntimeEngine` method:

```
manager.disposeRuntimeEngine(engine);
```

Once we do that, the `engine` instance will be rendered unusable. If we want to interact with the processes or tasks, we will need to get another instance of `RuntimeEngine`.

Now that we understand the lifecycle of both the `RuntimeManager` and `RuntimeEngine` instances, we can discuss the different types of runtime managers available for use in the jBPM6 code base.

The different implementations available

The `RuntimeManager` and `RuntimeEngine` are interfaces that can be implemented in any way a specific domain requires. There is no correct way of using the runtime managers, because the specifics of what your organization is trying to accomplish will determine whether a KIE session should be shared between different processes or not. Nevertheless, the jBPM6 project provides a number of implementations for the most common situations.

Depending on which implementation of the runtime manager we use, we will need to request a `RuntimeEngine` instance with different parameters. The runtime manager provides the `getRuntimeEngine` method to obtain a `RuntimeEngine` instance using a `Context` object as a parameter. This `Context` object will have the responsibility of identifying the actual instance of the KIE session and other configuration components for our runtime that we need for each different context.

The following implementations of the `RuntimeManager` interface are already provided in jBPM6:

- Singleton Runtime Manager
- Per Process Instance Runtime Manager
- Per Request Runtime Manager

We will discuss each one in detail, learn how they can be used, and see the different types of `Context` objects that should be used to obtain the `RuntimeEngine` instances from each one of them.

Singleton Runtime Manager

The **Singleton Runtime Manager** makes sure a single KIE Session is used for all interactions with the runtime engine, as shown in the following diagram:

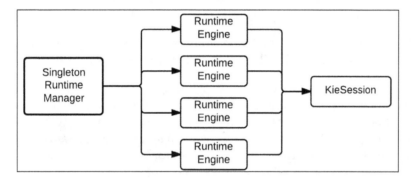

The jBPM6 code base provides a factory method to create a Singleton Runtime Manager. A code section from the `singleton-runtime-manager` project for this chapter where this factory method is being used is shown here:

```
RuntimeManager manager = RuntimeManagerFactory.
        Factory.get().
    newSingletonRuntimeManager(
            runtimeEnvironment, "node-identifier");
```

As you can see, it receives two parameters. The second one is optional, and it identifies a runtime manager uniquely. Given that runtime managers should behave as singletons, the factory keeps a register of all runtime managers until they're closed to make sure that you cannot instantiate the same runtime manager twice.

The `get` factory method mentioned before will instantiate a `SingletonRuntimeManager` object. This object stores a file with the KIE session ID that should be used. Every time a new instance of `SingletonRuntimeManager` is created, it checks if that file is already created. This session ID is later on retrieved from the database, or if persistence is not being used, from an in-memory `HashMap`.

Each time a runtime engine is created, a reference to a `TaskService` instance is also created. Since the `TaskService` instance acts as a stateless service with only the persistence keeping state information, no distinction is made between the different built-in runtime managers when it comes to creating the Human task component.

The Singleton Runtime Manager will require a context parameter to retrieve the `RuntimeEngine` instance. Since there is no distinction required between different environments (because they all share the same KIE session), we can use an `EmptyContext` instance or null parameters to retrieve the runtime engine:

```
RuntimeEngine engine = manager.getRuntimeEngine(
        EmptyContext.get());
```

With `SingletonRuntimeManager`, every `RuntimeEngine` instance returned will have the same KIE session object. This has its own advantages and disadvantages.

On the one hand, all processes that will be running on the same session can interact with each other through the rule engine memory, and feed combined rule executions with data. This allows you to have many processes interacting with each other as well as with rules, letting the processes remain simple enough, and complex decisions being handled by rules. Also, it allows for performance monitoring rules to be written and executed on the same environment as the processes are running.

On the other hand, having rules sharing information between different process instances can also lead to complications, particularly if we want to write rules that take into account only the objects of a specific process instance in a Business Rule task. Also, when persistence and concurrent invocations of process instances are being used, all of them will be derived form the same session that will have to execute them one at a time. This could lead to performance degradation.

The CDI injection

The jBPM6 project provides CDI annotations to directly inject a
`SingletonRuntimeManager` instance in your managed beans. To distinguish it
from other types of runtime managers, you should mark it with both the `@javax.`
`inject.Inject` annotation and the `@org.kie.internal.runtime.manager.cdi.`
`qualifier.Singleton` annotation. That way, the CDI initialization will know to
inject a singleton runtime manager instance without having to declare its specific
type. It can mark a `RuntimeEnvironment` instance as well:

```
@Inject @Singleton
RuntimeManager manager;
@Inject @Singleton
RuntimeEnvironment environment;
```

Remember that CDI is called upon initialization, so always inject the manager but
not the `RuntimeEngine` instance.

Per Request Runtime Manager

The **Per Request Runtime Manager** does the opposite of the singleton instance;
it creates a new KIE session the first time a request is made in a particular thread.
Each runtime engine returned from the manager will have a new KIE session for the
duration of the thread, as the following diagram depicts:

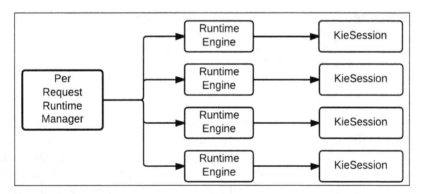

The jBPM6 code base provides a factory method to create a Per Request Runtime
Manager. A code section from the `per-request-runtime-manager` project for this
chapter where that factory method is being used is shown here:

```
RuntimeManager manager = RuntimeManagerFactory.
        Factory.get().
        newPerRequestRuntimeManager(
                runtimeEnvironment, "node-identifier");
```

As you can see, it receives two parameters. The second one is optional, and it identifies a runtime manager uniquely, in the same way as we explained for the Singleton Runtime Manager.

The `get` factory method instantiates a `PerRequestRuntimeManager` object. This object will keep a `ThreadLocal` reference pointing to the KIE session in one particular thread. If it is a nonpersistent environment, the reference will be lost the moment the runtime engine is disposed of. This doesn't make much sense unless you run fully-synchronous, automatic processes that will be completed the moment they return from the `startProcess` method invocation, or in a single code block.

However, if you are in a persistent environment, all references to long-lived process instances will be kept in the database, as well as any process instance reference that is waiting for a specific signal. In these cases, the Per Request Runtime Manager provides the most isolation regarding execution of processes and rules. All rules will be fired with only the data that is present in the process instance or explicitly added to the working memory before calling a process related invocation in the KIE session.

The Per Request Runtime Manager will require a context parameter to retrieve the `RuntimeEngine` instance associated to a specific process instance ID. However, in the same way as the Singleton Runtime Manager, it will not condition the KIE Session to be used (in this case, it will always be a new one), so we can use the `EmptyContext` instance:

```
RuntimeEngine engine = manager.getRuntimeEngine(
        EmptyContext.get());
ProcessInstance pInst = engine.getKieSession().
        startProcess("procId");
Long procInstId = pInst.getId();
manager.disposeRuntimeEngine(engine);
```

The `PerRequestRuntimeManager` injection provides enough isolation of processes to guarantee the highest scalability possible, but the rules associated with the process execution cannot take advantage of gathering cross-process instance information. Information that could be used in cross referencing complex events fired by different process instances will not be available, because every time a new KIE session is created, the working memory is initialized from scratch.

The CDI injection

The jBPM6 project provides CDI annotations for the `PerRequestRuntimeManager` injection in managed beans. To distinguish it from other types of runtime managers, you should mark it with both the `@javax.inject.Inject` annotation and the `@org.kie.internal.runtime.manager.cdi.qualifier.PerRequest` annotation. CDI initialization will inject a runtime manager instance per request without having to declare its specific type. It can mark a `RuntimeEnvironment` instance as well:

```
@Inject @PerRequest
RuntimeManager manager;
@Inject @PerRequest
RuntimeEnvironment environment;
```

Remember that CDI is called upon initialization, so always inject the manager but not the `RuntimeEngine` instance.

 If you use a Per Process Instance or Per Request Runtime Manager, never inject KIE sessions or Human task service objects as CDI beans. They will be managed by the runtime manager and different KIE session instances and services could be created. Instead, you should only inject the manager and request sessions and services from a specific runtime engine.

Per Process Instance Runtime Manager

The **Per Process Instance Runtime Manager** takes care of registering the specific KIE session where a process was created. Each runtime engine returned from the manager will later on use the same session that created a specific process instance, as shown in the following diagram:

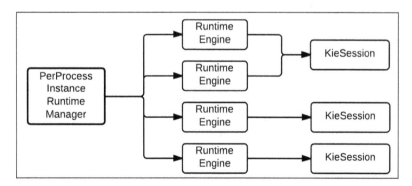

The jBPM6 code base provides a factory method to create a Per Process Instance Runtime Manager. A code section from the `per-process-instance-runtime-manager` project for this chapter where this factory method is being used is shown here:

```
RuntimeManager manager = RuntimeManagerFactory.
        Factory.get().
        newPerProcessInstanceRuntimeManager(
                runtimeEnvironment, "node-identifier");
```

As you can see, it receives two parameters. The second one is optional, and identifies a runtime manager uniquely, in the same way as we explained for the Singleton Runtime Manager.

The `get` factory method instantiates a `PerProcessInstanceRuntimeManager` object. This object will keep a reference of which session started which process instance. If it is a nonpersistent environment, the reference will be kept in an internal `HashMap`. If it is uses persistence, the reference is kept on a JPA-managed table called `ContextMappingInfo` as well, but is cached internally to minimize database use.

The `PerProcessInstanceRuntimeManager` will require a context parameter to retrieve the `RuntimeEngine` instance associated to a specific process instance ID. If we want to start using a new KIE session, we can request a runtime engine with a fresh session by using the `EmptyContext` instance. This is usually the practice to start a new process:

```
RuntimeEngine engine = manager.getRuntimeEngine(
        EmptyContext.get());
ProcessInstance pInst = engine.getKieSession().
        startProcess("procId");
Long procInstId = pInst.getId();
manager.disposeRuntimeEngine(engine);
```

However, if we want to retrieve the same session that started a previous process instance, we can retrieve it with the process instance ID and the help of a context class called `ProcessInstanceIdContext`:

```
Long procInstId = ... // process instance ID provided by code
RuntimeEngine engine2 = manager.getRuntimeEngine(
        ProcessInstanceIdContext.get(procInstId));
engine2.getKieSession().getProcessInstance(procInstId);
```

Even if the `PerProcessInstanceRuntimeManager` object can return a new session for each process instance we manually start, this is not mandatory. There is no limitation to the number of process instances a KIE session could use. Also, process instances started by internal process signaling and subprocesses will end up sharing the same KIE session. Nevertheless, each new process instance will register a new mapping between the KIE session and the new process instance, which means that you can use the `ProcessInstanceIdContext` to retrieve the specific KIE session.

Also, if you wanted to explicitly create a process instance in the same session where another one resides, you could just get the `RuntimeEngine` instance using the process instance ID of the previous process instance and start the new process in its session:

```
RuntimeEngine engine = manager.getRuntimeEngine(
        EmtpyContext.get());
ProcessInstance inst1 = engine.getKieSession().
        startProcess("procId");
Long oldProcInstId = inst1.getId();
manager.disposeRuntimeEngine(engine);
RuntimeEngine reuseEngine = manager.getRuntimeEngine(
        ProcessInstanceIdContext.get(oldProcInstId));
ProcessInstance inst2 = reuseEngine.getKieSession().
        startProcess("procId");
```

This allows for a greater control over which process instances are executed in each session. We can have several groups of process instances running in parallel in multiple KIE sessions that can run in multiple threads, which allows for better performance and scalability. Process instances inside the same session can share events and rule data between each other.

However, we must understand that process instances residing in a different KIE session will not have this data available unless we explicitly share it through our own code. We must explicitly search for KIE sessions using process instance IDs, which means that we must store other details associated to the mapping we want to keep elsewhere. The Per Process Instance Runtime Manager is a component that sacrifices a little of this ease of use in exchange for better performance (by providing the possibility of having multiple sessions).

The CDI injection

CDI annotations are provided as well for `PerProcessInstanceRuntimeManager`. To distinguish it from other types of runtime managers, you should mark it with both the `@javax.inject.Inject` annotation and the `@org.kie.internal.runtime.manager.cdi.qualifier.PerProcessInstance` annotation. CDI initialization will inject a `PerProcessInstanceRuntimeManager` instance without having to declare its specific type. It can mark a `RuntimeEnvironment` instance as well:

```
@Inject @PerProcessInstance
RuntimeManager manager;
@Inject @PerProcessInstance
RuntimeEnvironment environment;
```

Remember that CDI is called upon initialization, so always inject the manager but not the `RuntimeEngine` instance.

> For the `RuntimeEnvironment` injected instance in CDI, you could use multiple annotations for the different runtime manager types. The following code is completely valid and often used in test cases:
>
> ```
> @Produces
> @Singleton @PerProcessInstance @PerRequest
> public RuntimeEnviornment createEnv() {
>     return RuntimeEnvironmentBuilder.Factory.get().
>         newDefaultBuilder().get();
> }
> ```

The UI configuration of runtime managers

The KIE Workbench (which we explained in *Chapter 4, Understanding the KIE Workbench*), among its functionalities, provides a runtime environment for process executions. It uses the provided runtime manager implementations to allow the user to configure how each module they create is going to be executed. In order to do so, you must follow specific steps to provide the workbench with all the necessary information. You will have to perform the following operations:

- Configure a KIE session for a specific project and deploy it
- Configure a runtime manager type for the specific deployment

We'll provide a step-by-step guide to be able to do so.

Configuring a KIE session for a KIE module

Every provided instance of the runtime manager depends on a KIE session being defined and the Human task component being available. The KIE Workbench provides a running instance of the task service, but the KIE session requires a KIE module to be configured inside a project before being available for use. In this section, we will go into detail about defining our knowledge bases and sessions in a project inside the KIE Workbench.

First of all, we need to go to the **Project Editor**. You can find it in the **Project Authoring** perspective under **Authoring**, and then navigating to **Tools | Project Editor**. There, you will have a drop-down list from where you will be able to select the option **Knowledge bases and sessions** as shown in the following sessions:

When you select the **Knowledge bases and sessions** option, the project editor contents will change to show a series of user friendly form components to define a `kmodule.xml` file inside the project. We will use it to define a KIE base with the name `kbase1` and a stateful KIE session called `ksession1`. Any name we want to use will do, as we will only use them as a reference later on.

Make sure you mark the KIE base as default by selecting it and clicking on the **Make Default** button; for the moment, let's leave the rest of the configuration as is. The KIE session menu is to the bottom-right corner of the project editor.

After you finish editing the `ksession1` components (you can edit its preconfigured work item handlers and listeners as well), you can click on the **Build & Deploy** button to make the deployment available for the runtime configuration components:

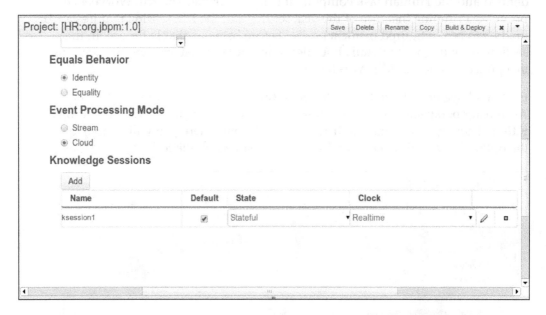

Once the **Build & Deploy** stage is finished and the compilation is successful, we can go to **Deploy | Deployments**, because by default the KIE Workbench will initialize a Singleton Runtime Manager for the default KIE session of the default KIE base of every deployed project. This is shown in the following screenshot:

Configuring a runtime manager type

We can delete the existing deployment units by clicking on the **Delete** action button to the right of each row, or create new ones by clicking on the **New Deployment Unit** button on the header of the table. When we click on the **New Deployment Unit** button, a pop up will guide us to select a specific release of a project, a KIE base, and a KIE session from that project, and also to select the type of provided runtime manager that we will use to operate with the KIE session:

Once we complete all the fields and click on the **Deploy Unit** button, we will see the unit details available as a new row in the deployment units table as shown in the following screenshot:

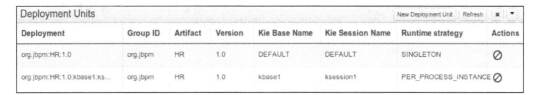

By default, the KIE Workbench will allow you to have one runtime manager per KIE session definition. If you define multiple different sessions, you should be aware that the place where they will be used (from the KIE Workbench perspective) is the Process Definitions and Process Instances perspectives. In these perspectives, you will have access to the process definitions from which you can start process instances.

Having a specific runtime manager configured for a specific KIE session configuration will allow us to not only run a process in the KIE Workbench, but also to customize it with the specific configuration we chose. We can configure our KIE session name to run on a specific KIE base with many rules and processes together and to run them all in a single KIE session or in multiple ones.

You have to make sure that for the same KIE Workbench installation, if you have multiple deployment units, you can only access a process definition from one of them, which is a limitation of the tooling. The API has access to anything you want, though. If you wish to have any kind of runtime manager in different parts of your application for the same KIE session configuration, you just have to provide the proper CDI annotations to use the one you prefer.

You could also extend the available runtime managers to provide different strategies for KIE session and Human task component initialization. We will discuss that topic in the next section.

Creating your own runtime manager

The provided runtime manager implementations are enough to start working with jBPM6 without going into the details of how components are created. However, several organizations reach a point where they need to define specific sharing between processes in a simple way to allow special process instance collaborations through rules. One example of this would be writing monitoring rules that count how many process instances of a specific domain are being created within the last hour that are not yet finished, and take actions when that number reaches high values. This is something that can be easily written in the internal **Drools Rule Language** (**DRL**), as shown in the following DRL code:

```
rule "too many processes"
when
    $n: Number(intValue > 1000) from accumulate(
        $p: WorkflowProcessInstance() over window:time(1h)
        eval($p.getVariable("domainXProcess") != null)
    )
then
    externalService.sendWarning("Too many processes created in the
last hour: " + $n);
end
```

In order for this rule to work, all process instances that have the `domainXProcess` variable assigned should reside in the same working memory, and therefore, in the same KIE session.

Also, they might need specific levels of isolation determined by external policies. For example, a company working on legal processes might want to make sure that all rules and processes that make legal decisions for a specific client remain isolated with respect to the client. Since the runtime manager is the one that creates the KIE session and the Human task service, it is the perfect place to decide whether to share an existing session or create a new one, based on context information.

The main components that we will need to provide to create our own runtime manager are as follows:

- A `RuntimeManager` interface implementation
- A `Context` interface implementation to pass the domain key we will use

We'll discuss how to provide said components for a Per Process Definition Runtime Manager implementation.

Per Process Definition Runtime Manager

In the `custom-per-process-runtime-manager` project, we've provided an implementation of a runtime manager that will store a KIE session for each process definition. By default, when you use this runtime manager, it will use the same KIE session for all instances of a specific process definition. The implementation is composed of three custom classes:

- `ProcessDefContext`: This class defines the context key to be the `String` representation of the process definition ID
- `PerProcessDefinitionRuntimeManager`: This class implements `RuntimeManager` to register the KIE session of each process definition
- `CustomRMFactory`: This class provides a factory method to create the specific runtime manager for us

Other classes are also used, but they are part of the already available implementation. Most of them are explained through comments in the provided runtime manager implementation code, and we will learn about them as we get into detail about how this runtime manager works.

We've based this custom implementation on `PerProcessInstanceRuntimeManager`, with some modifications on top of it. They work by getting a local or database mapping from the specific context ID to a KIE session ID. If the mapping is found, the same session is reloaded. Otherwise, a new session is created. The mapping is retrieved from an interface called `Mapper`, which acts as a Data Access Object for the relation between KIE session IDs and context IDs.

The mapping, however, is not stored immediately after the creation of the KIE session; it is stored when a process instance is created, if not present. To connect that functionality with the internal functions of the KIE session, we provide an implementation of the ProcessEventListener interface called MaintainMappingListener, which stores the relation before the process instance is created. The overall class structure looks like the one shown in the following diagram:

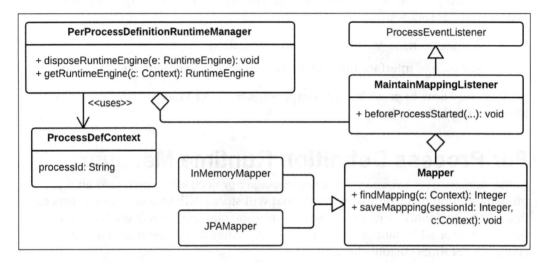

The Mapper interface, as you can see, has two different implementations depending on whether you use database persistence or not. The MaintainMappingListener implementation will use the reference to said Mapper object to store the reference:

```
public void beforeProcessStarted(ProcessStartedEvent event) {
    String processId = event.getProcessInstance().getProcessId();
    if (mapper.findContextId(ksessionId) == null) {
        mapper.saveMapping(
                ProcessDefContext.get(processId), ksessionId);
    }
}
```

After the KIE session, the getRuntimeEngine method in the RuntimeManager interface, which is either created or loaded, creates a new TaskService instance using the same methods we saw in *Chapter 6, Human Interactions*. The context domain (a process definition ID) has no relevance for the Human task component, so no special treatment is done to keep different instances for each task service. However, this could be easily done and kept under a mapping as well through a custom mechanism to have a full separation of runtime functionality.

The resulting functionality is a KIE session that is registered on a by-process-definition basis, making a runtime structure similar to the one shown in following figure:

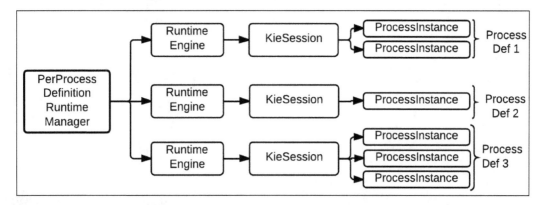

Later on, we can construct a new Per Process Definition Runtime Manager by calling the factory method in the CustomRMFactory class, as shown in the following code:

```
RuntimeManager manager = CustomRMFactory.getInstance().
        newPerProcessDefinitionRuntimeManager(
                environment, "node-ID");
```

Summary

In this chapter, we saw how to use and create runtime managers, runtime engines, and how they affect the way processes can interact with each other. We learned the consequences of both KIE session sharing and isolation from a process execution perspective. Also, we learned how to define the environment configurations to start our runtime.

The following chapter will show us how to configure persistence mechanisms for our KIE sessions in order to keep database copies of our processes' current execution paths for reuse and concurrency.

8

Implementing Persistence and Transactions

In real-life scenarios, we need to have process instances running for many hours, days, or even years. If we want to be able to run processes for such a long time, we cannot rely on something as volatile as the memory of a server to keep track of all our process instances statuses. We need a way to provide persistence for them.

This chapter focuses on providing a persistence and transaction mechanism to our process engine environment, which will allow us to store enough information about our executions to be able to recreate them afterwards. This feature brings the possibility of having more than one thread or server trying to access the same persisted runtime environment at the same time. So, we will also learn how to generate a transaction around said persistence to make sure no concurrency issues occur.

Persistence and transactions are topics that are hard to handle for newcomers, mostly because they entail a lot of different configuration points that need to be carefully orchestrated to get the expected behavior from our application. Once you have finished this chapter, you will learn about the following:

- How the jBPM6 persistence works
- How to configure all the different components of the persistence and transaction
- Why we need transactions in our systems

Why do we need persistence and transactions?

So far, we've dealt with very short-lived processes. Running inside a JUnit test, process instances last very few milliseconds, and having them in memory is sufficient for those environments. However, in real-life situations, we don't usually create interactions between systems and humans without having long wait states in between. This is especially relevant for the case of processes with human tasks, where users backed up with too much work might have a pending task assigned to them for hours, days, or even more. For each of the processes in your environment, you should be able to determine whether it should be a persistent or a nonpersistent process depending on how long-lived each of its process instances will be. From this perspective, you will find these two top-level categories:

- In-memory processes
- Long running processes (also known as persistent processes)

In-memory processes are usually short-lived processes that perform entirely automatic synchronous interactions. Depending on the complexity of each automatic interaction, some processes might take longer to complete than others, but with this type of process, in general, a range that might go from a few seconds to a few minutes is more likely.

Long-running processes, on the other hand, might take several minutes to complete the fastest process instance—with more *real* values ranging from hours to even years, depending on the nature of the process. Keeping an in-memory reference for such processes becomes impractical and even impossible to guarantee in some cases. For such processes, we need a persistence mechanism to keep a recoverable reference to the process whenever it is needed.

Several questions will help you determine whether your process will need to be persisted or not:

- Does your process interact with other components? How slow are they? How prone to failure are they? If external interactions are really slow and asynchronous by nature, or prone to errors and retries, then a persistent process will be able to handle it better than an in-memory process.

- Should the process be able to recover from a failure state? If we should manually recover from an error state, we will need to keep a reference of the process to recover it later on.

- Does the process interact with humans? Human interactions are intrinsically slow from a computer perspective. Persistent processes should be used whenever human interactions are involved.

- Does the process have a high demand? This might imply that we need to handle the process in a distributed environment. A persistent process will allow you to retrieve an existing process from any other system with connection to the database.

Persistence of the process' internal state needs a set of characteristics that we need to understand in order to take full advantage of the mechanism. We'll proceed to explain each component of the persistence to make it as clear as possible to configure it in the way that best suits your needs.

Persisting long running processes

The main reason we need to persist processes is because they are yet to be finished. From a process' perspective, we say that the process is still active, which means its business goal hasn't been accomplished yet. This means that the process is still running from its internal perspective; however, from a more technical view (and if we are using asynchronous work item handlers), the process is going to be waiting for some external interaction, either a human interaction or a system interaction. To understand these wait states, consider the following process flow:

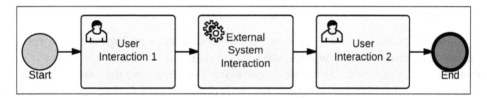

As you can see in the preceding process definition flow, the first thing a process instance will do is execute the **Start** event, and then the User task **User Interaction 1** will be started. However, since it is an actual human interaction, it will be waiting for the user to complete said task before continuing with the execution. As we saw in *Chapter 6, Human Interactions*, this will leave the process instance in an active state, and wait for the user interaction to be finished to continue with the process execution. The following process flow shows how this interaction will look from a technical perspective:

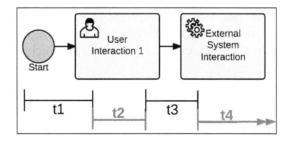

As you can see, there are four time lapses to which we should pay attention in the previous process definition section. The first one, **t1**, starts when we call the `startProcess` method on a KIE session object. Once it reaches the start of a User task, it will return control to the invoking thread, and wait for the User task to be finished. This could take a really long time, and we don't want to have to depend entirely on memory until a user decides to finish the task. This is one of the reasons persistence is needed for jBPM6.

Persistence is also needed for external system interactions, because of two main characteristics:

- An external system interaction might take a lot of processing time. This could be because it's using a slow, overused system. The problem is we might have many different process invocations waiting for the next state in a single BPM system, and if we leave all waiting states on external interactions in memory, we might exceed the BPM system capacity.

- The external system could fail and need a retry at some other time. This is mostly a consideration for asynchronous external interactions rather than for persistence. However, while the process instance is waiting to do a retry at a given time, we can release resources from the server if we store those process instances now and reload them later on.

Now that we have understood that we might need to store and reload our process instances at different time intervals, we have to deal with another particular problem: making sure two different threads don't try to access the same process instance at the same time, causing an internal conflict. The solution for said problem is also the solution to some other much more important issues, which we will discuss in the next subsection.

The server failover and distribution mechanism

Whenever we have generic systems that might cover very diverse cases of our organization, it becomes more and more important that we have a way to scale up such applications. In order to do so for a BPM system, process persistence is the key. This is because it will not only release precious memory resources when not needed, but also allow the creation of different nodes in a High Availability grid managing said processes if they have more idle time, all synchronized through the database.

However, this carries another issue that we should discuss: the possibility that two different servers (or even two different threads in the same server) may try to access and change the same process instance simultaneously. This can be solved in the same server with very simple in-memory synchronization mechanisms. However, when you have different servers competing for the same process instance, we need something more powerful, that is, transaction management.

Transaction management allows us to make sure that different servers will not work on the same process instance at the exact same time, and persisted process instances will not be persisted if a runtime error occurs (a possibility provided by the rollback capacity of transactions).

Now that we understood the necessity of persistence and transactions in a BPM system, it's time to analyze how these components are provided in jBPM6.

Persistence in jBPM6

The persistence and transaction mechanisms in jBPM6 are not considered to be an externally consultable source of information; they provide a quick store and recovery mechanism, mainly to have a high-performance distributed platform. This means that the simplest way to configure the persistence in jBPM6 will have two characteristics:

- Only enough information to recreate the runtime is persisted. This means that we will have limited information about our process instances; only currently running processes will be stored, and only the information of the currently active nodes and used variables will be available. The rest of the information can be persisted as well, but through other mechanisms (see the *History logs – extending the basic functionality* section further in this chapter).

- The runtime information is persisted in the fastest way possible: serialized information in a byte array structure. This makes information for the basic persistence mechanism hard to read from external tools.

The persistence and transaction mechanisms for jBPM6 are directly applied from the KIE session. This means that not only the process runtime has a persistence mechanism for jBPM6, but also the rule runtime. This is because the same mechanism that is used by Drools to store content in a database is extended by jBPM6 to also store process instance information.

This is the best way to guarantee that the exact same environment that started running a process in one server or thread will be the one that will continue running it in another place. This is especially important if you're using rules that are invoking references to different process instances. We will see some examples of such types of rules in *Chapter 9, Integration with Other Knowledge Definitions*.

The configuration needed to create and load a JPA persistent KIE session with persistent process instances converges in code similar to the following:

```
KieServices ks = KieServices.Factory.get();
Environment env = ks.newEnvironment();
EntityManagerFactory emf = ...;
TransactionManager tm = ...;
env.set(EnvironmentName.ENTITY_MANAGER_FACTORY, emf);
env.set(EnvironmentName.TRANSACTION_MANAGER, tm);
KieBase kbase = ks.getKieClasspathContainer().getKieBase();
```

The preceding code section performs a series of steps needed to configure a persistent environment and load a KIE knowledge base. These components will be used while creating (and further down the line, loading) a KIE session that is persisted in a JPA persistence unit.

For brevity reasons, we skipped the creation of some of the components, such as the JPA `EntityManagerFactory` object, and the initialization of `TransactionManager`, leaving only the code relevant for the configuration of the `Environment` variable. If you want to see a full example of this code, it's available in the `JPAPersistentProcessTest.java` file in the `persistent-process-examples` project.

You can see that we have set special entries in the environment variable for the entity manager factory and transaction manager. These are the most basic properties a persistent environment defined with JPA will need. Later on, the KIE components will use the specified environment to determine how the persistence is configured in your environment.

Also, we are defining the KIE knowledge base. This is because, as we mentioned earlier, the persistence is only going to store minimal information for the runtime to be reloaded in another context. For this reason, the persistence mechanisms don't have the trouble of serializing the full knowledge base, and it must be provided each time we create or reload a persistent KIE session.

KieStoreServices – creating and loading KIE sessions

Once all environment components are created, we will not directly create the persistent KIE session implementation. Instead, we will use a special service to handle that creation for us. As a matter of fact, we will not even load the special service class directly; we will use the `KieServices` helper class to load it for us, as shown in the following line of code:

```
KieStoreServices kstore = KieServices.Factory.get().
        getStoreServices();
```

The `KieStoreServices` interface will define two methods—one to create a new persistent KIE session and another to load an existing one, as shown in the following code:

```
KieSession ksession = kstore.newKieSession(kbase, null, env);
Integer sessionId = ksession.getId();
...
//on a different part of your code
KieSession reloadedKsession = kstore.loadKieSession(sessionId,
  kbase, null, env);
```

The KIE session ID is the only data that the application will need to remember to retrieve the same KIE session later on. Depending on how much we wish to reuse the KIE session, we might consider temporarily storing the ID, or maybe even registering it in a database reference or file to be reused all the time.

The actual implementation behind the `KieStoreServices` interface knows we have to use JPA to persist our runtime and create all the necessary components to make a persistent KIE session. In order to have the specific implementation of the service in the classpath, we will need to add a dependency to our projects that holds that implementation:

```
<dependency>
    <groupId>org.jbpm</groupId>
    <artifactId>jbpm-persistence-jpa</artifactId>
    <version>6.1.0.Beta3</version>
</dependency>
```

Different forms of persistence can be provided behind the `KieStoreServices` interface. Since the `KieServices` helper class will try to load the actual valid class from the service loader, we could implement our own persistence strategy and hide it behind the same interfaces, minimizing the changes needed in existing code to start using a different persistence mode. The runtime manager (explained in the previous chapter) uses the `KieStoreServices` class behind the scene so that users don't have to use it directly, and it will work for any part of the jBPM6 code that uses persistent processes.

How does persistence work?

So far, we've seen how to start a persistent KIE session using helper classes from the jBPM6 API. We are now going to take some time to understand the components that are generated by those helper classes. Understanding the internal composition of a persistent KIE session will help you understand how and when the persistence is being used, and it will help you to easily detect problems in your persistence configuration.

Persistence is provided to a KIE session is through a specific set of adapters that use a **command pattern** implementation. Command pattern shows that every operation is encapsulated by a single contract (specifically, a `Command` interface with an `execute` method). Using this contract, you can implement different `Command` objects for all the different methods of a class (in our case, the KIE session). Then, you can decorate every method invocation by just deriving each command execution through another class, called a `CommandService`, which will have the responsibility of knowing what you have to do before and/or after each command execution.

An example of how this is done to provide a persistent KIE session can be seen in the following class diagram:

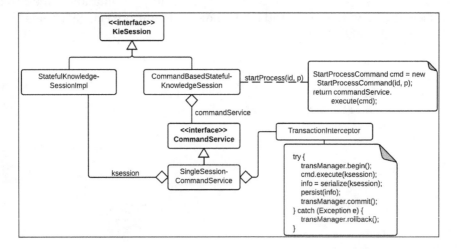

Here, we can see that we have two implementations of a `KieSession` interface: `StatefulKnowledgeSessionImpl`, which is the real implementation of a KIE session, and `CommandBasedStatefulKnoweldgeSession`, which is the command pattern adaptation of the KIE session interface. The latter will implement each method by creating a specific `Command` object and assigning its execution to a `CommandService` object.

The actual implementation used by the JPA persistent KIE session is called `SingleSessionCommandService`, and it provides a wrapper around the KIE session command execution that creates a database transaction before the command execution, serializes the actual KIE session object to a persistent object, and commits the transaction.

The `SingleSessionCommandService` session doesn't directly implement the transaction management, but it has an `Interceptor` list that defines all the different method decorations needed, similar to the way the Human task component explained in *Chapter 6, Human Interactions* uses.

Eventually, the interaction between persistence and the KIE session activity happens on a per-method invocation basis, as shown in the following diagram:

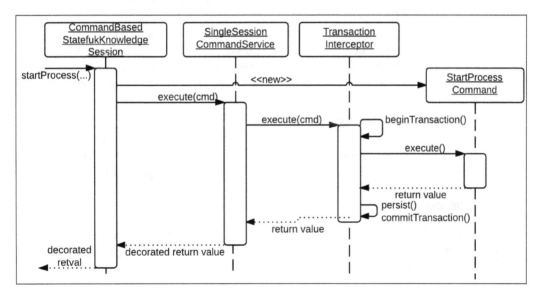

We can infer the following points from the preceding diagram:

- The runtime won't be stored at every single change, but after a specific method invocation is completed. This means our runtime will only be storing itself when its internal execution reaches a static return point. Think of it as a very complex, configurable state machine, which will only be persisted after it reaches a defined state.

- Every process in the runtime will be persisted only when it reaches a safe state. That means, if we have multiple automatic steps and a few asynchronous steps in a process, the process runtime will only be persisted at the asynchronous step's wait states.

Internally, the JPA persistence strategy will store the process runtime separated in three different entities:

- `SessionInfo`: This class is a serialization of the KIE session, and it is persisted exclusively from the command pattern whenever a method on the persistent KIE session is invoked. It basically stores a byte array with the deserialized information of the KIE session at a particular state and an integer ID.

- `ProcessInstanceInfo`: This class is a serialization of a specific process instance's runtime information. It stores a byte array with the deserialized information of the process instance runtime, its ID, state, and pending event information. There is a special manager class used by the persistent KIE session, called `JPAProcessInstanceManager`, which takes care of notifying the persistence of any changes the KIE session does to each process instance's internal status.

- `WorkItemInfo`: This class stores information about a specific state in a process instance. It specifically stores a byte array with the input and output information of a step, its ID, a process instance it references, and the particular step's internal state flag. There is a special manager class used by the persistent KIE session, called `JPAWorkItemManager`, which takes care of notifying the persistence of any changes in each step done by the KIE session.

In order for the JPA to be able to perform all the required steps to actually store the content of the KIE session and its components in a database, it requires certain configurations:

- JPA implementations and jBPM6-related dependencies
- A data source with access to an existing database
- A persistence unit with all the entity mappings
- A transaction manager configuration

We'll see all these configurations in detail during the next section of this chapter.

Persistence and transaction configuration for jBPM6

In order to configure the JPA persistence in our environment so that jBPM6 can create and load persistent KIE sessions and process instances, we need to configure a set of components and tie them together.

The first components we will need are the JAR files in our classpath to be able to use JPA directly from our code, and also directly from jBPM6. The dependencies we will use will be implementing JPA 2.0, and the Maven references to the relevant JAR files can be found in the `persistent-process-examples` project's `pom.xml` file:

```xml
<!-- JPA 2.0 standard library -->
<dependency>
    <groupId>org.hibernate.javax.persistence</groupId>
    <artifactId>hibernate-jpa-2.0-api</artifactId>
    <version>1.0.1.Final</version>
</dependency>
<!-- Hibernate implementation of the JPA 2.0 standard library -->
<dependency>
    <groupId>org.hibernate</groupId>
    <artifactId>hibernate-core</artifactId>
    <version>4.2.3.Final</version>
</dependency>
<!-- JPA management in jBPM6 -->
<dependency>
    <groupId>org.jbpm</groupId>
    <artifactId>jbpm-persistence-jpa</artifactId>
    <version>6.1.0.Beta3</version>
</dependency>
<!-- in-memory database -->
<dependency>
    <groupId>com.h2database</groupId>
    <artifactId>h2</artifactId>
    <version>1.2.128</version>
</dependency>
<!-- simple transaction manager -->
<dependency>
    <groupId>org.codehaus.btm</groupId>
    <artifactId>btm</artifactId>
    <version>2.1.4</version>
</dependency>
```

As you can see, each dependency has a different purpose. The `hibernate-jpa-2.0-api` defines the interfaces (the internal contract) of the JPA 2.0 specification. The actual implementation of said specification is provided by the `hibernate-core` dependency. We also need to provide a dependency for our data source and transaction manager (in our case, a simple test case, we can use h2 as an in-memory database and `btm` for the transaction manager). The jBPM6 management of the JPA persistence is done thanks to the classes we previously mentioned implemented in the `jbpm-persistence-jpa` dependency.

Once we have the dependencies, we need to define the required component configuration for each one of them. Let's start with JPA/hibernate, where the configuration we will need to add is the specific persistence unit that defines entities that should be mapped to our database. The most basic content that needs to be added to the `META-INF/persistence.xml` file in our classpath, as shown in the following code:

```xml
<?xml version="1.0" encoding="UTF-8"?>
<persistence version="2.0" ...>
  <persistence-unit name="org.jbpm.persistence.jpa"
                    transaction-type="JTA">
    <provider>org.hibernate.ejb.HibernatePersistence</provider>
    <jta-data-source>jdbc/testDS</jta-data-source>
    <mapping-file>META-INF/JBPMorm.xml</mapping-file>
    <class>org.drools.persistence.info.SessionInfo</class>
    <class>org.drools.persistence.info.WorkItemInfo</class>
    <class>
      org.jbpm.persistence.processinstance.ProcessInstanceInfo
    </class>
    <class>
      org.jbpm.persistence.correlation.CorrelationPropertyInfo
    </class>
    <class>
      org.jbpm.persistence.correlation.CorrelationKeyInfo
    </class>
    <properties>
      ...
    </properties>
  </persistence-unit>
</persistence>
```

Let's take some time to understand this file. It follows the JPA 2.0 standard XML notation to define five entities (`SessionInfo`, `WorkItemInfo`, `ProcessInstanceInfo`, `CorrelationPropertyInfo`, and `CorrelationKeyInfo`), a provider (which is defined in the `hibernate-core` dependency, called `HibernatePersistence`), and a JTA data source (which we will implement using `btm`).

Since we are using JTA to define a transaction manager for our data sources, we need to define a JNDI registry where the transactions are discovered. We can define that easily by having a `jndi.properties` file within our classpath that defines, in our case, the `btm` naming registry, with the following content:

```
java.naming.factory.initial=bitronix.tm.jndi.BitronixInitial
    ContextFactory
```

From then onward, all other components are defined in our case through code. Specifically, we will start a data source, use `btm` to start a transaction manager around that data source, and start an entity manager factory (a class used by JPA to interact with our database in runtime).

From inside our test cases, we define a method marked with the `@Before` JUnit annotation in our `JPAPersistentProcessTest` class by using the following content:

```
private PoolingDataSource ds = null;
...
@Before
public void startUp() throws Exception {
    ds = new PoolingDataSource();
    ds.setUniqueName("jdbc/testDS");
    ds.setClassName(
            "bitronix.tm.resource.jdbc.lrc.LrcXADataSource");
    ds.setAllowLocalTransactions(true);
    ds.setMaxPoolSize(3);
    ds.getDriverProperties().put("driverClassName",
            "org.h2.Driver");
    ds.getDriverProperties().put("Url", "jdbc:h2:mem:mydb");
    ds.getDriverProperties().put("password", "sasa");
    ds.getDriverProperties().put("user", "sa");
    ds.init();
}
```

The preceding code section will do two different things. First, which is easy to infer, is the creation of the `PoolingDataSource` class (a data source class provided by `btm`). What is hard to understand first-hand is that this is not our real data source, but just a wrapper that we will use to provide transaction management around the `LrcXADataSource` class (the actual in-memory database data source). Secondly, the preceding code section will also publish the created data source in the JNDI context. That way, the persistence unit that we previously configured in the `persistence.xml` file is going to be able to take the connection from the `jta-data-source` parameter configuration:

```
<jta-data-source>jdbc/testDS</jta-data-source>
```

This way, the persistence unit will be using the specific data source information that we define in our unit test. We just need to make sure that we create the data source wrapper before instantiating the persistence unit's entity manager factory. This is something that the code you create to start the persistence unit needs to do beforehand, and it is the main reason we create the persistence unit's `EntityManagerFactory` object in the test method, and start the data source wrapper in the `@Before` section:

```
@Test
public void testPersistentKieSessionInstantiation() throws Exception {
    KieServices ks = KieServices.Factory.get();
    KieStoreServices kstore = ks.getStoreServices();
    Environment environment = ks.newEnvironment();
    EntityManagerFactory emf = Persistence.
        createEntityManagerFactory("org.jbpm.persistence.jpa");
    TransactionManager tm = TransactionManagerServices.
        getTransactionManager();
    environment.set(EnvironmentName.ENTITY_MANAGER_FACTORY, emf);
    environment.set(EnvironmentName.TRANSACTION_MANAGER, tm);
    KieBase kbase = ks.getKieClasspathContainer().getKieBase();
    KieSessionConfiguration ksconf = ks.
        newKieSessionConfiguration();
    KieSession ksession = kstore.newKieSession(
        kbase, ksconf, environment);

...
}
```

We will go into detail about each of the steps we saw in the previous code section, in the order they appear:

- We created the data source wrapper to handle the connection transactions for us. This initialization code is usually provided by the JEE container or by a context initialization framework such as CDI or Spring. We will need to obtain a `TransactionManager` object once we have initialized this. In our case, we do it with the following code:

```
TransactionManager tm = TransactionManagerServices.
    getTransactionManager();
```

- We first created the `EntityManagerFactory` object by calling the following code:

```
EntityManagerFactory emf = Persistence.
    createEntityManagerFactory(
    "org.jbpm.persistence.jpa");
```

- We provided both the transaction manager and the entity manager factory to an `Environment` variable, as shown in the following code:

```
Environment env = KieServices.Factory.get().
    newEnvironment();
env.set(EnvironmentName.TRANSACTION_MANAGER, tm);
env.set(EnvironmentName.ENTITY_MANAGER_FACTORY, emf);
```

Once we have this information, we simply use the previously explained `KieStoreServices` interface to access a persistent KIE session.

While all these components will provide enough information to make a KIE session recoverable from another thread or server node, it is just the most basic information we can store inside a database. If we want to store and/or retrieve extra information, such as specific tables related to our domain model or statistical information, we can extend our configuration in multiple ways. We will concentrate on two of the most popular components for extending the persisted information:

- **History logs**: This component is used to store extra historical information about our process executions
- **Object marshalling strategies**: This component is used to store extra entities in specific ways in our model

History logs – extending the basic functionality

We previously mentioned that jBPM6 stores the minimal information to be able to recover a KIE session and its process executions in another place. Most of the time in productive environments, we want to keep information that is not directly required by the runtime, but is instead used by KPIs. These KPIs can be used to know about which tasks took longer, how many process instances are completed or pending, and many other inquiries.

In order to provide that information to the database and also to publish any piece of process information to external tools, we will use a specific implementation of the `ProcessEventListener` interface.

Process event listeners will expose all the process execution information through different methods that expose process starts, completions, and node and variable changes. We explored them previously in *Chapter 7, Defining Your Environment with the Runtime Manager*. In this case, we use the interface as a connection point to expose all that information in a different set of entities: the `NodeInstanceLog`, `ProcessInstanceLog`, and `VariableInstanceLog` classes. All the information can be checked later through a series of services. Summarizing all things needed to work with the history logs, we need the following four components:

- The `jbpm-audit` dependency added to the classpath:

```
<dependency>
    <groupId>org.jbpm</groupId>
    <artifactId>jbpm-audit</artifactId>
    <version>6.1.0.Beta3</version>
</dependency>
```

- The history log entities added to the persistence unit (the three classes enumerated previously, `ProcessInstanceLog`, `NodeInstanceLog`, and `VariableInstanceLog`)

- Adding the specific `ProcessEventListener` implementation to our KIE session:

```
ksession.addEventListener(
    AuditLoggerFactory.newJPAInstance(environment));
```

- Instantiating and using the audit log service to query the generated history logs:

```
AuditLogService service = new JPAAuditLogService(emf);
```

Once we have a version of the `AuditLogService` class (and some process executions to feed the history logs), we can start checking some of its information directly from the already provided methods:

```
List<ProcessInstanceLog> findProcessInstances();
List<ProcessInstanceLog> findProcessInstances(String procId);
List<ProcessInstanceLog> findActiveProcessInstances(
    String procId);
List<NodeInstanceLog> findNodeInstances(long processInstanceId);
List<VariableInstanceLog> findVariableInstances(
    long processInstanceId, String variableId);
...
```

You can also extend these methods quite easily, since they're only JPA queries executed against the existing entities. You can see an example of using the audit service in the `testHistoryLogs()` method of the `JPAPersistentProcessTest` class.

Object marshalling strategies

Object marshalling strategies are used to configure our persistent KIE session to understand that specific objects are going to be persisted or loaded into the KIE session in a very specific way. By default, the persistent KIE session will try to serialize every object in the working memory, process variables, and task inputs and outputs to a series of byte arrays. However, if you have a specific way of storing certain objects in a data storage, you can use a persistence strategy to let the KIE session know how to persist such objects. This is a very common way of simplifying interaction- and domain-based monitoring of the process engine. To be able to provide such functionality, the Drools and jBPM6 API define an interface called `ObjectMarshallingStrategy` to specify different strategies of storing your model:

```
public interface ObjectMarshallingStrategy {
    boolean accept(Object object);
    void write(ObjectOutputStream os, Object object);
    Object read(ObjectInputStream os);
    byte[] marshal( Context context, ObjectOutputStream os,
                    Object object);
    Object unmarshal( Context context, ObjectInputStream is,
                      byte[] object, ClassLoader classloader );
    Context createContext();
}
```

The implementations are rather simple. The `accept` method will determine whether a specific object is suitable for the specific persistence strategy. If accepted, writing and reading the objects will involve two things:

- Storing or reading an ID or any other way of referencing the object in the provided byte array
- Reading and/or writing the object in a specific persistence strategy

There are a few implementations provided and they are ready to be utilized. The `SerializablePlaceholderResolverStrategy` implementation is the one used by default, and it simply attempts to write the full object to the byte array. The `JPAPlaceholderResolverStrategy` implementation is used to read objects from a JPA database. It only stores the ID in the byte array, and it doesn't store the objects if something changes. We extend it in the `testProcessModelStorage` method of the `JPAPersistentProcessTest` class by creating the `JPAReadAndWriteStrategy` object and adding it to the corresponding environment variable:

```
Environment environment = kservices.newEnvironment();
...
environment.set(EnvironmentName.OBJECT_MARSHALLING_STRATEGIES,
```

```
            new ObjectMarshallingStrategy[] {
                new JPAReadAndWriteStrategy(emf),
                new SerializablePlaceholderResolverStrategy(
                    ClassObjectarshallingStrategyAcceptor.DEFAULT)
});
```

This configuration works by providing an array of the `ObjectMarshallingStrategy` objects, and the engine will try to find the first strategy in the provided array that accepts each specific object and uses it to persist or read the correspondent objects. This configuration needs to be the same when restoring a specific KIE session; otherwise, you might get marshalling problems.

Other persistence mechanisms

The `KieStoreServices` interface can be implemented in any way for any type of persistence you can imagine. The JPA persistence is currently the most robust implementation available, but there is also another implementation available on top of Infinispan (`http://infinispan.org`). Also, any other `KieStoreServices` implementation could be registered and used directly from the `KieServices` helper class by just registering the actual implementation through the following code:

```
ServiceRegistryImpl.getInstance().registerLocator(
    KieStoreServices.class, new Callable<KieStoreServices>() {
    @Override
    public KieStoreServices call() throws Exception {
        return (KieStoreServices) Class.forName(
                "path.to.my.Impl").newInstance();
    }
});
```

Let's take a moment to review the Infinispan persistence usage with a small code example.

Infinispan persistence

Similar to the JPA persistence provided for jBPM6, there is another experimental implementation provided by the code base that allows you to store and load the contents of persistent KIE sessions in an Infinispan cache. This implementation uses the exact same command pattern to wrap every KIE session method execution with a transaction; however, instead of using the data access objects provided for JPA, it uses new ones created to work directly with Infinispan.

There is a project provided to see the Infinispan persistence implementation in action in the `infinispan-persistence-examples` project. The following code examples are taken from the `InfinispanPersistentProcessTest` class.

There are three main differences between the JPA-based and the Infinispan-based `KieStoreServices` implementations:

- The dependency needed in the classpath is as follows:

```
<dependency>
    <groupId>org.kie</groupId>
    <artifactId>jbpm-infinispan-persistence</artifactId>
    <version>6.1.0.Beta3</version>
</dependency>
```

- The configuration of an Infinispan configuration (provided in our example in the `infinispan.xml` file) is as follows:

```
<infinispan ...>
  ...
  <namedCache name="jbpm-configured-cache">
    <eviction strategy="NONE" />
    <transaction ...
        transactionManagerLookupClass="
            org.infinispan.transaction.lookup.
            BitronixTransactionManagerLookup"/>
    ...
  </namedCache>
</infinispan>
```

- The configuration parameters needed in the environment variable are as follows:

```
KieServices ks = KieServices.Factory.get();
DefaultCacheManager cm =
    new DefaultCacheManager("infinispan.xml");
Environment env = ks.newEnvironment();
env.set(EnvironmentName.ENTITY_MANAGER_FACTORY, cm);
env.set(EnvironmentName.TRANSACTION_MANAGER,
    new JtaTransactionManager(
        TransactionManagerServices.getTransactionManager().
            getCurrentTransaction(),
        TransactionManagerServices.
            getTransactionSynchronizationRegistry(),
        TransactionManagerServices.
            getTransactionManager()));
env.set(EnvironmentName.PERSISTENCE_CONTEXT_MANAGER,
    new InfinispanProcessPersistenceContextManager(env));
```

As you can see, the environment uses many more components. This is because the Infinispan connection is still experimental and default configurations are not yet fully supported from the initializing code. It forces us to be much more verbose, but still in a manageable way. The main new components added to the environment that we need to discuss are as follows:

- `JtaTransactionManager`: The `TRANSACTION_MANAGER` key had a simple `TransactionManager` implementation in the JPA examples. This is because the actual JPA implementation would create this instance of `JtaTransactionManager` as a wrapper to be used directly by the command pattern in order to manage transactions that could have been started by external components. This component has to be manually created for the Infinispan implementation.

- `PERSISTENCE_CONTEXT_MANAGER`: This is a special object that, in the JPA examples, is automatically created as a `JPAPersistenceContextManager` object. If we manually create an object in that key, it is not overridden by the underlying implementation. Therefore, we override it with a specific Infinispan implementation in our case.

After these changes are made, we can use the create and load methods of the persistent KIE session directly from the relevant `KieStoreServices` instance. Persistence in Infinispan is still just a serialization strategy, and it is not yet recommended for production environments. However, it can be easily extended to provide extra functionality for NoSQL adopters.

Summary

Persistence is an excellent way to maintain and resolve long running processes, as well as to release resources from an environment when they're not needed. We've seen that persistence is not a way to provide searchable information, but a way to provide a recovery point that is not directly readable by people. However, we've also seen that we can provide such functionality either by enabling object marshalling strategies and history logs, or by implementing our own strategies or persistence mechanism.

During the next chapter, we will understand how jBPM6 integrates with other types of entities, such as **rules**, **events**, and **complex event processing**, a concept we started discussing in *Chapter 2, BPM Systems' Structure*.

9

Integration with Other Knowledge Definitions

In this chapter, we will cover the different aspects of collaboration between processes and other forms of knowledge, particularly rules and events. We will also discuss the importance of rules in the business domain and define what business rules are. To understand how business rules work in jBPM6, we will need to understand how a rule engine works and how it interacts with the jBPM6 process engine, while comparing the way this interaction occurs for jBPM6 and other BPM frameworks. We will discuss all these aspects with a group of examples that will be easy enough to integrate into multiple business scenarios, as well as flexible enough to be extended to cover very complex situations.

After we gain some practice in the rules realm, we will introduce more complex concepts, such as adding temporal information into our rules to define events, time correlation between them, and inferences to detect more complex, indirect events. This will allow us to understand the full power of the rule engine and, in particular, how jBPM6 uses its runtime internally to run both rules and processes from the same set of APIs.

The topics you will learn in this chapter are as follows:

- How the Drools rule engine is related to jBPM6
- How to apply business rules to business processes and vice versa
- How to define events and temporal rules
- How to configure our environment to be able to detect complex event situations

What is a rule?

The first thing we need to define in a clear manner before proceeding is what rules are. A **rule**, from the rule engine's perspective, is a constraint within a particular domain that will evaluate to true or false. When specific components within the domain evaluate the constraint of a specific rule to be true, we say that the particular rule is activated. When activated rules are fired (an operation that is usually separated from the activation of a rule), a particular action—specified within the rule—will be taken. Depending on the syntax, a rule structure can vary from implementation to implementation. However, the general structure of a rule will always be similar to the following code:

```
rule "rule name"
/* optional rule attributes */
when
     /* a specific set of constraints in our domain */
then
    /* a specific set of actions to be taken when
       the constraints evaluate to true */
end
```

A single rule by itself doesn't provide much value to describe a complex decision. Nevertheless, a group of (many) rules will be far more descriptive. The rule engine responsibility is to evaluate all rules together for a group of objects in the most efficient way possible.

A business process can invoke groups of rules to make complex decisions in specific parts of its execution. At the same time, a rule can have specific actions that start, signal, or interact in some way with an existing process instance. This integration between rules and processes is managed in a special way with jBPM6, which we will discuss in the next section.

Old-fashioned integration

A rule engine can become extremely useful when evaluating situations that would become very difficult to determine through a business process, either because the situation is too complex to make a clear diagram out of the sequence of steps required to evaluate the decision, or because the sequence itself is not relevant to the evaluation itself. In the past, adopting the process engine and the rule engine technologies was complicated due to the integration work required to make both engines share the necessary information to operate as expected. As the rule engine and the process engine were completely different applications, communication protocols had to be established between each other. This usually caused a few problems:

- Communication protocols between both engines could fail, creating a whole new group of issues that needed to be tested for a specific implementation of our business domain—even if both engines were running in the same environment.

- Interaction between rules and processes implied specific mappings of both the location of the other system, as well as the required inputs and expected outputs of process and rule executions. This is because every piece of relevant data needs to be sent back and forth between each engine.

- Transaction management could become a difficult issue to handle, because all transactions should be considered from a business perspective and have to be cross-engine execution.

- If you need both processes invoking rules as well as rules invoking processes, handling the communication could become troublesome and hard to maintain, and can increase the possibility of error due to increased complexity in the communication.

The overall intercommunication architecture needed to have both the rule engine and the process engine collaborating with each other, as shown in the following figure:

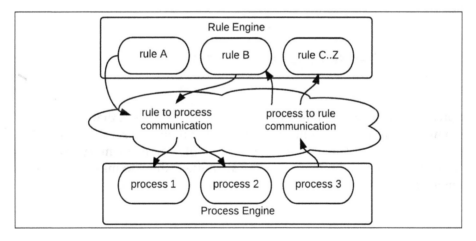

In the preceding figure, every arrow you see is a potential communication problem. This is not an issue with jBPM6 and Drools, because the rule and process engine are the same thing. You can seamlessly invoke rule executions from a process instance, and a rule can trigger a specific signal or interact with a particular process instance—all without creating any intercommunication mechanism between both components, unless a clear separation of both engines is desired. This simplifies the initial adoption of rules and processes interactions.

The Drools rule engine

Drools is a rule engine framework that provides the possibility of creating rules in a script language called **Drools Rule Language** (**DRL**) and running the rules inside an in-memory inference engine that provides great performance. Rule languages have a declarative nature, which means that the next action to be taken is determined by the input data that triggers specific conditions in the rules, unlike the imperative nature of languages such as Java, where the next action to be taken is determined by the sequence of actions written in the code.

Rules written in DRL follow a very specific syntax for constraints and a configurable syntax for the actions of the rule (which we will keep as plain Java for simplicity). The constraint part of the rule shouldn't be interpreted as regular imperative code such as a Java code, where we specifically tell the system what to do at a particular point in time. Instead, it should be considered as a declarative statement, similar to a SQL query, where we will search anything that matches a specific criterion. For every match, we will execute the consequence of the rule (the "then" part of the rule). The structure of a DRL rule is similar to the following code:

```
rule "prioritize requirements with lots of bugs"
lock-on-active
when
    r: Requirement(bugs.size() > 3)
then
    r.setPriority(20 / r.getBugs().size());
    update(r);
end
```

In the preceding rule, we searched for all `Requirement` objects that have a bugs list with more than three elements. For each one of them, we set the priority to a calculated value and update the reference in the rule engine memory to evaluate other possible rules. The `lock-on-active` attribute is there to make sure we don't re-evaluate the same rule for the same object after we update it.

The power of rules grows as we add more rules. The internal algorithm of the rule engine (called PHREAK on the current version) will optimize the structure of all rules and make sure that all added objects evaluate rules in the shortest execution path possible. Afterwards, using rules is very simple, and it uses the same runtime component we already learned in order to use processes, that is, the KIE session:

```
KieServices ks = KieServices.Factory.get();
KieSession ksession = ks.getKieClasspathContainer().newKieSession();
ksession.insert(new Requirement("req1", "description"));
...
ksession.fireAllRules();
```

The preceding code uses two new methods: `insert` (that adds objects to the rule engine memory for evaluation) and `fireAllRules` (that executes all the rules that are ready to be triggered by the engine). The full code can be seen in the `drools-simple-example` project in the chapter's code bundle.

The preceding code uses the same API that is used to invoke process executions through the `startProcess` method. However, some configuration considerations need to be taken to have both processes and rules interacting together. The next sections explain those considerations in detail.

What Drools needs to work

To start with, all that Drools needs to work is a KIE session. In order for it to work with rules, we need to include the DRL files in the KIE base that will be used, either through the `kmodule.xml` configuration or through the programmatic API.

The following four methods are the most important calls that we need to know in the KIE session to interact with the rules:

* `FactHandle insert(Object fact)`
* `FactHandle update(FactHandle handle, Object fact)`
* `void delete(FactHandle handle)`
* `int fireAllRules()`

The first three methods allow you to insert, update, and remove objects from the rule execution memory. The FactHandle class is a reference to the internal status of an object in said memory. Finally, the fireAllRules method allows you to fire any rules that matched any rule constraints for the inserted objects.

Every time we add, change, or remove objects from the internal memory of the KIE session, evaluations of these objects are created that determine what rules should execute. The fireAllRules method later invokes the following flow of execution:

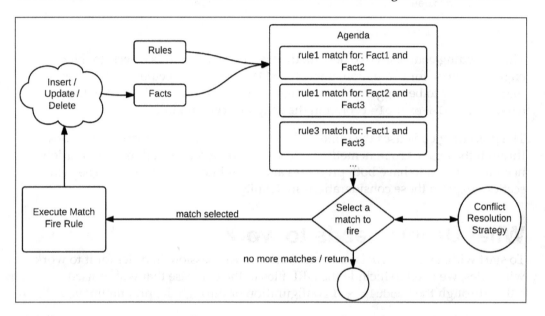

The previously mentioned methods are enough to interact with the rules. However, to simplify process and rule interaction, we will see a few other components of the DRL language and the KIE session.

The DRL language allows us to define attributes to our rules. Three of these attributes allow us to define groupings for our rules in order to activate small groups of rules at a time instead of activating all of them at the same time. These attributes are as follows:

- agenda-group: This attribute has a string parameter. It defines a group of rules that can be manually set through code using the following method:

  ```
  ksession.getAgenda().getAgendaGroup("group-x").setFocus();
  ```

  When this group is activated, only the rules inside of it will be matched or fired.

- `activation-group`: This attribute is similar to the agenda group, except it marks a group of rules where only one should be executed. The decision of which rule is executed is determined by the conflict resolution strategy of the rule engine.

- `ruleflow-group`: This attribute is the one we will see the most. It determines a group of rules that will not be activated manually, but instead will be activated by a specific process instance execution. It is one of the most used points for process/rule interaction.

Another component that we previously mentioned in *Chapter 8, Implementing Persistence and Transactions,* is called event listeners. There are three types of event listeners we can add to a KIE session through the `addEventListener` method:

- `ProcessEventListener`: This event listener, as previously mentioned, exposes methods to add specific hooks to all changes in a process instance internal state

- `AgendaEventListener`: This event listener exposes methods to notify when a match to a rule constraint is detected or negated, changes in the activated groups of rules, and when each rule is fired within the KIE session

- `RuleRuntimeEventListener`: This event listener allows us to follow all changes done to the objects in the rule execution memory (insertions, updates, and deletions)

Now that we have mentioned these components, we can see them in action in the `process-rules-examples` project in the next section.

Applying rules to our processes

Invoking business rules from inside a business process and vice versa can provide a lot of power to our knowledge representation. Both components deal with decisions in two very different ways; rules provide simple ways of representing complex solutions, where the order to find said solution is not always relevant. Processes, on the other hand, focus on the order of the steps that need to be taken to reach a goal.

Inside jBPM6, you can invoke rules and processes or even perform nested invocations, where rules invoke processes that can then invoke other rules with very little configuration.

We will start by learning the different ways to execute rules in our business processes. In the `process-rules-examples` project, you will find a test that will be used in the rest of this section called `RulesAndProcessesTest`, where processes are invoked from rules and rules from processes as well.

Gateway conditions

The simplest way to define conditions in our processes is inside an exclusive or inclusive gateway's outgoing sequence flows. Inside sequence flows, you can determine a condition expression to decide whether that flow should be followed or not. This condition is defined as Java code by default in the web process designer used in *Chapter 3, Using BPMN 2.0 to Model Business Scenarios*. However, if you select Drools in the expression language attribute of the sequence flow, you can define a condition expression that will be evaluating the rule memory with a DRL-based condition. This is quite useful to evaluate complex conditions, but it depends on that all the relevant objects being "inserted" in the KIE session's rule memory.

Business Rule tasks

The most common way of invoking rules from a process is through Business Rule tasks, which was explained briefly in *Chapter 3, Using BPMN 2.0 to Model Business Scenarios*. In a Business Rule task, you will have to define two important things: input mappings for the task that will determine what process variables should be made available in the KIE session's rule memory, and a `RuleFlow Group` attribute that will define what group of rules are to be invoked. In the `RulesAndProcessesTest` class, we invoke a process with a Business Rule task, such as the one shown in the following diagram:

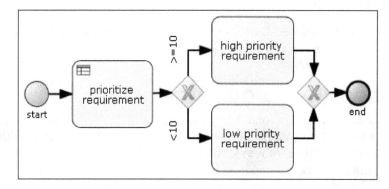

The preceding process diagram has a Business Rule task called **prioritize requirement**. The task has an input mapping of a Requirement object, such as the one we saw in the model of *Chapter 6, Human Interactions,* and *Chapter 7, Defining Your Environment with the Runtime Manager.* It also defines establish-reqs-priority as the RuleFlow Group attribute value. This attribute will define that when the process instance reaches the **prioritize requirement** task, only rules that define the same RuleFlow group variable will be activated. You can see examples of such rules in the reqRules.drl file. The following code snippet is a small skeleton of a rule that defines such group:

```
rule "prioritize requirements"
    lock-on-active
    ruleflow-group "establish-reqs-priority"
    when
        r: Requirement(priority == -1)
    then
        r.setPriority(5);
end
```

As you can see in the examples, you can have multiple rules that evaluate the model and change values to different objects in it. The output of the rules in a Business Rule task is usually a modification or addition in the model that will be easily checked by a gateway later on. In our case, the elements we check in each of the gateways' outgoing connections is the requirement's priority value, and determine two paths based on the values of the priority.

Ad hoc process instance evaluations

Ad hoc processes are processes whose sequence of actions cannot be predefined. When we define an ad hoc process, we do know what tasks will be needed to be performed, but the order and sequence of said tasks is either too complex to be defined in a flow or too variable to be considered fixed. As a diagram, they just seem as a bag of tasks with no connection between them. The following diagram shows a representation of the adhocProcess.bpmn2 file:

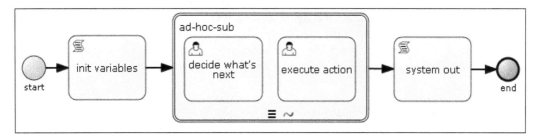

In jBPM6, ad hoc processes are supported in a way that makes it similar to a Business Rule task: the name of the ad hoc process will be a ruleflow group that will be activated when you reach the start the process. Using rules, you can determine which task needs to be created and you can start one of those tasks manually using a class called `DynamicUtils`. You can also determine the conditions to exit the ad hoc process using rules. In the `process-rules-examples` project, you can find a test called `AdHocProcessTest`, which uses this functionality to run an ad hoc subprocess called `adHocProcess` and uses the rules defined in the `ad-hoc-sub` ruleflow group to determine the next task. The rules are defined in a file called `adhocRules.drl`, and on finding specific conditions, fires a new work item to execute a specific task within the ad hoc process as the following rule shows:

```
rule "init rule"
salience 100
ruleflow-group "ad-hoc-sub"
when
    wf: WorkflowProcessInstance($nodes: nodeInstances)
    dn: DynamicNodeInstance() from $nodes
    eval(wf.getVariable("processVar1") == null)
then
    System.out.println(drools.getRule().getName());
    KieRuntime kr = kcontext.getKnowledgeRuntime();
    Map params = new HashMap();
    params.put("inVar1", wf.getVariable("processVar1"));
    params.put("TaskName", "decide what's next");
    DynamicUtils.addDynamicWorkItem(dn, kr, "Human Task", params);
end
```

In the preceding rule, we are looking for a process instance, which has an active dynamic node (which is jBPM6's internal representation for an ad hoc process) and has no process variable assigned with the name `processVar1`. This is done by checking for the `WorkflowProcessInstance` objects we might have in the rule engine memory, and checking whether its `nodeInstances` attribute (which we will assign to a `$nodes` variable) contains a `DynamicNodeInstance` object. Finally, we evaluate whether a process variable is not yet present in the process instance. When those conditions are met, we start a dynamic Human task (with a `WorkItemHandler` registered in the KIE session with the **Human Task** key). It is a responsibility of the "then" part of this rule to provide all the information to the work item generated, including all parameters and references to the KIE session and the node.

One more important step to know is which is the best way to start a process or invoke a process signal inside a rule consequence. To do so, we need to understand a specific predefined variable in the rules consequence called `kcontext`. This variable will have a reference to the KIE session so that we can use it to invoke our process executions. Using this variable, we can also call all the process related methods in the KIE session, such as `signalEvent`, `getProcessInstance`, `abortProcessInstance`, and so on.

Runtime configurations to activate rules

Even though rules and processes share the same runtime, they have very different memory scopes. The process instance memory (called process variables) and the rule memory (called working memory) do not share information unless it is specified that they should do so. In order to communicate information back and forth from the process memory to the rule memory, we need to configure event listeners to populate relevant information changes from one component to the other. Luckily for us, if we want to automatically add a process instance to the working memory (and communicate its internal changes to it for reevaluation when necessary), you can add a particular event listener called `RuleAwareProcessEventLister`:

```
ksession.addEventListener(new RuleAwareProcessEventLister());
```

This listener will make sure that when a process instance is added, changed, or removed, it gets inserted, updated, or deleted from the rule memory. Note that it finishes with the word `Lister` and not `Listener`. This is not a typo in the book, but in the code itself, and it has been maintained like this for backward compatibility issues.

Another important configuration that we need to be aware of is related to the use of ruleflow groups. Whenever we enter a Business Rule task or an ad hoc process, the KIE session will not fire all the rules associated with those ruleflow groups automatically. All it will do is notify the internal structure of the KIE session that the ruleflow group is activated, and the user needs to decide whether and when they should fire all the rules. In the majority of cases, we want to fire all rules activated in a ruleflow group when we reach a Business Rule task or an ad hoc subprocess. In order to do so, we have a method in the `AgendaEventListener` interface to take specific actions after a ruleflow group is activated, and we can invoke a `fireAllRules` method inside it:

```
ksession.addEventListener(new DefaultAgendaEventListener() {
    public void afterRuleFlowGroupActivated
      (RuleFlowGroupActivatedEvent event) {
        KieSession kses = (KieSession) event.getKieRuntime();
        kses.fireAllRules();
      }
});
```

With these event listeners, rules from a ruleflow group can be invoked and fired from a process instance.

On a side node, the previous event listener implementation is built in the jBPM6 code, in a class called `org.jbpm.process.instance.event.listeners.TriggerRulesEventListener`. However, the previous anonymous class was left intentionally to show that you can create your own event listeners as you see fit, and don't need to stick to built-in event listeners.

This covers the main interactions between rules and processes. The next section deals with some advanced rule concepts that allow for tracking different operations along a specific timeline.

Temporal reasoning and processes

Business rules allow us to define smarter processes depending on the contextual information we feed the rule execution engine. The combination of rules and processes is a very powerful mix that provides a way of merging specific sequence of actions with reactive behavior in a very performant way. It is now time to start learning about involving temporal information inside our rules definitions.

Adding temporal information such as fact time correlation, streams of data, or any live data will add a lot of power to your rule executions and their capacity to infer information from the real world. These procedures are encompassed in **complex event processing** (CEP), a methodology to infer complex situations out of simple ones, and **Event-driven Architecture** (EDA), which allows for a natural growth of applications that use CEP. We will see each of these concepts in detail.

Events and complex events

Before understanding CEP, we need to understand a series of other concepts tightly related to it. The first and most important concept we need to define is an event. From a temporal Business Rule perspective, we will define an event as any fact (an object in the rule memory) that has temporal constraints of some sort: a moment in which it occurred, an optional duration, and a life cycle.

Events can be anything that holds a relation to a specific point in time. A temperature measuring could be used as a fact, but it can be treated as an event if we consider at what time that measuring was taken. A phone call can have a price, a receiver, or a caller, but if we add data of the exact moment it happened or how long the call lasted, it can be treated as an event. Events usually represent things that already happened, so from a logical perspective, they should be immutable. The Drools framework doesn't enforce this to facilitate all kinds of use cases to be represented, including the possibility of mutable events.

Now that we clearly understand what an event is, and know how to define it in a DRL, we can work our way into defining a **complex event**. We will define a complex event as an aggregation, composition, or abstraction of other events, which can be simple events or complex events themselves, called component events. The concept implies that from some basic information about the world represented in events, we can define specific inferences that will be treated themselves as events.

Let's review an example of a complex event to understand how complex events can be composed of simple events. Imagine if we had a lot of seismic meters all over a city. Each measurement will tell us whether we have an earthquake, with intensity and location. But more importantly, it will have a timestamp to let us know at what moment in time the earthquake happened. Each seismic measure is our simple event.

Let's imagine that we detect a lot of very small earthquakes, not enough to disturb any buildings, but we detect that they all happen in a straight line through the city — one after the other, with maybe 2 or 3 seconds time difference. With temporal reasoning, we might make an inference and say that probably a very large object is moving through the city. This inferred event is our complex event, as explained in the following diagram:

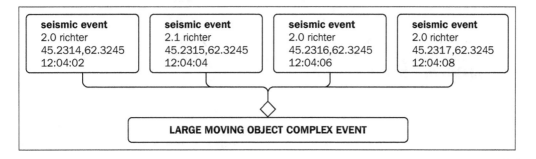

However, we won't stop there. Let's assume that we also have other meters around the city and we can detect fires and loud noises — thanks to the power of social media, we might even be measuring twitter messages to determine the general sense of alarm of a particular area. If we translate all that information into a fire spreading through the same general zone, at the same speed as our first complex event, we might consider the possibility (as bizarre as it might seem at the beginning) that Godzilla is going through the city. This Godzilla event would be a complex event as well, inferred from other complex events.

Once we detect our complex events, we will not want to stop at just the detection. 99 percent of the time, we will want to take a reactive action towards those events. For that particular case, we fall into the realm of CEP.

CEP

Now that we understand the concept of complex events, we need a way to actually correlate events, infer those events, and take specific actions from all the different correlations between events. Event processing is based on providing analysis and tracking tools of different events from different sources.

CEP extends that definition to add the possibility of combining said events into complex events by utilizing analysis tools, and later on using these events to feed more complex situations. Drools provides such a mechanism through business rules writing and execution. Rules provide a very quick and performing way to infer events and act accordingly, which is why it has been widely used by many real-time applications that need to have the fastest reaction possible.

CEP is all about analyzing events and reacting as soon as a situation of interest is found. Events might be coming from different sources, with different structures, and at different moments in time. It is the responsibility of the CEP agent to both define a structure of processing behind the specific data (in case of Drools, that structure is defined using rules) as well as a way to introduce information to the runtime (in case of Drools, through event insertion in the rule memory).

CEP agents are one piece of a system that will need to produce events, and usually the outputs of the rules will be fed to some other component that is prepared to consume said outputs. These components have been abstracted and defined within an **Event-driven architecture (EDA)**.

EDA

When working with events, we usually end up splitting the components involved in the event management into three main categories:

- Components that are creating specific, simple events
- Components that are processing simple events into complex ones
- Components that are waiting for specific events

EDA defines a decoupled way to build an infrastructure based on these three components, along with a way to communicate events between them. The following diagram depicts all the components in an EDA working together:

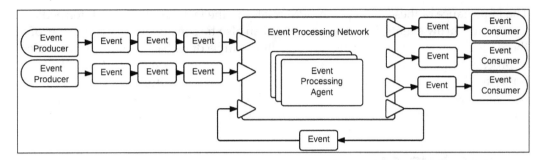

The main components the architecture proposes are event producers, event consumers, event processing agents, and event channels.

The sole responsibility of event producers is to generate streams of events. It is anything that emits any sort of information, regardless of how complex or basic the information might be. It can go from simple sensors to user interfaces to complex applications that can send very specific notifications. If it can send an event to an external scope, it is an event producer.

Event producers will need means to propagate their events to other components of the EDA. Event channels are the component through which event producers will be able to do so. Anything from a protocol definition to the logical representation of a wire between a sensor and a computer could be considered an event channel, as long as events are transmitted through that mean.

Usually, event producers send events to a series of event processing agents, which are software components in charge of consuming one group or many groups of events as inputs and produce complex events as outputs. These event processing agents will connect with each other depending on the type of events they consume or produce to form an **event processing network**.

The final outcome of this network is usually a final set of events, which are not needed to infer any other events, but are to be directly used by other components. These components that are waiting for specific events are called **event consumers**. They can be any component interested in receiving a notification of a state—from an application to a dashboard to a machine-state-based piece of hardware waiting for instructions.

One big advantage to these types of architecture is that event producers, consumers, and processing agents don't need to know each other. This allows EDA-influenced applications to grow in a nonintrusive way, even along with other architectures (such as **service-oriented architecture**) without breaking its structure, but rather enriching its functionality.

The importance of these concepts in BPM relates to the fact that thanks to Intermediate Catch and Throw events, business processes can also be consumers and producers of these sorts of events. Considering that signaling can be done back and forth from rules to processes, these concepts add a lot of value for inferring the state of the world and notifying this to our processes. At the same time, process instances themselves could be treated as events. All these possibilities will be explored in the next section when we will discuss how CEP can be implemented with jBPM6 and Drools.

Drools Fusion functionalities

The Drools framework has a lot of different operators, functions, and special syntax that could cover another book by itself. They deal with comparing different objects within the rule runtime memory. In this section, we'll concentrate to discuss the module more related to temporal reasoning, which is called **Drools Fusion**.

Drools Fusion is not a separate dependency of Drools, but just a logical separation to keep CEP-related documentation separate from the general body of knowledge of Drools Expert, the main rule engine project. It comprises a way to declare facts as events, temporal operators to compare them, splitting of the rule runtime memory by stream origin, and the possibility of using sliding windows to see the last events that match a specific condition. Let's discuss each of these concepts in detail.

Event declarations

In the DRL language, you need to declare our events from a specific imported object type, or you can even construct them directly. In the `process-cep-examples` project, you will find a `cepRules.drl` file that defines one of these event types with the following syntax:

```
declare ProcessEvent
    @role(event)
    processId: String
    state: Integer
    reqVariable: Object
end
```

Defining the @role annotation, we can tell the engine that a particular object type should be treated as a fact (the default scenario) or an event (with time association). A Drools event can have other attributes that will add special metadata to an object type. We'll enumerate them as follows:

- @timestamp: This attribute receives one parameter, which should be the name of an attribute in the object type. This attribute should contain a Date object, which specifies the time at which the event happened. This is an optional annotation; because if it is not present, the moment the event is added to the rule memory will be taken as the moment the event actually happened.

- @duration: This attribute receives one parameter, which should be the name of a long value determining the number of milliseconds the event lasted. This is an optional attribute, as events are considered punctual by default (that is, they only existed in a specific moment). For example, if we consider a phone call to be an event, the moment between answering the phone and hanging up are very important components to treat the phone call as a temporally defined object.

- @expires: The "expires" annotation receives a time-based string to determine that after a specific amount of time, events added to the rule memory should be automatically evicted.

An example of the preceding annotations could be similar to the following code section:

```
declare PhoneCall
    @role(event)
    @timestamp(callStartDate)
    @duration(callDuration)
    @expires(4h30m)
end
```

The preceding code section defines that a PhoneCall object (that could be an imported class) should be treated as an event, its callStartDate attribute should mark when it started, its callDuration attribute should mark its duration, and it should be automatically evicted after 4 hours and 30 minutes from the rule memory.

Once we define the events we are going to use, we will be able to compare them based on the time of their occurrence. We can do so using the temporal operators provided by Drools Fusion.

Temporal operators

Temporal operators are extensions to the DRL language that allow us to directly compare the timestamp of objects that we have declared as events. James F. Allen defines 13 temporal operators, some of which only make sense with interval events. These operators are `after`, `before`, `coincides`, `during`, `finishes`, `finishedby`, `includes`, `meets`, `metby`, `overlaps`, `overlappedby`, `starts`, and `startedby`.

As an example, `after` is used to define, obviously, that the timestamp of one event is after the other event's timestamp. Temporal operators can receive parameters within brackets; in case of the `after` operator, they indicate that the first event happened at least a certain time after the second event, and if it has a second parameter, this indicates that the second event happened within a range after the first event. The following code is an example of a rule condition using the `after` operator:

```
when
    p1: ProcessEvent($processId1 : processId)
    p2: ProcessEvent(this after[3m] p1, processId == $processId1)
...
```

In the preceding example, we are first detecting an event of type `ProcessEvent` and then trying to find another one that has the same `processId` attribute and happened at least 3 minutes after the first one. In `ProcessCEPTest`, you can see an example of a code running this structure in the `testAfterRule` test method.

Sliding windows

Another important concept behind Drools Fusion CEP functionalities are sliding windows. They define an interval of interest in which we want to start filtering or grouping our events. It comes in two flavors, windows of length and windows of time. The best way to explain them both is with a simple example:

```
HeartBeatEvent() over window:time(15s)
```

The preceding code should be read as follows: get all `HeartBeatEvents` that have happened in the last 15 seconds. Another example could be:

```
TemperatureEvent() over window:length(5)
```

The preceding code should be read as follows: get the last five `TemperatureEvents` that have been added to the rule runtime memory.

Drools Fusion in action

Now that we have seen all the components needed to define temporal reasoning in our business rules, we need to start considering the different configurations required to make our CEP business rules run smoothly, as well as how to integrate them with our business processes. All considerations needed to run simple business rules together with business processes apply to Drools Fusion (that is, having the `RuleAwareProcessEventLister` listener and the custom listener `AgendaEventListener` to fire rules added to the KIE session configuration). We will now concentrate on the extra features needed to configure temporal-based rules for our runtime.

The first consideration that we need to take into account is a special configuration we need to add to the KIE base that we build our KIE session from, to be able to manage the concept of now (used for sliding windows) and get an understanding of events as such, instead of just facts. This special configuration is called the **STREAM** mode, and by default, the rule engine works in the **CLOUD** mode. The STREAM mode provides a way for the engine to understand the concept of time and events and keep a reference of when are events added to the rule engine memory. The CLOUD mode doesn't understand these concepts and treats all elements added to the rule engine memory as simply facts, with no temporal data associated to them. The STREAM mode can be configured to the KIE base programmatically as follows:

```
KieServices ks = KieServices.Factory.get();
KieBaseConfiguration kbconf = ks.newKieBaseConfiguration();
kbconf.setOption(EventProcessingOption.STREAM);
KieBase kbase = ks.getKieClasspathContainer().newKieBase(kbconf);
```

The KIE base can also be configured through the `kmodule.xml` file with the `eventProcessingMode` attribute of the `kbase` tag. Please refer to the `process-cep-examples` project to see a full example of such a configuration.

Another configuration item, related in this case to the KIE session object, is the clock type. By default, the KIE session will understand how much time goes by between events by the internal clock of the computer it is running in. This might be good for productive environments, but it is definitely problematic for rule testing purposes.

During a test, we might want to debug our code, and if we depend on the internal clock of the computer to determine time correlations, we might find ourselves breaking rule conditions by debugging the code. Also, if we want to test a rule that correlates two events with a big time difference between insertions, we would need a lot of time to test it.

In order to avoid this problem, the KIE session can be configured to run with a **pseudo clock**, that is, an implementation which will have to be advanced at will. In order to configure it, you can use the following code:

```
KieSessionConfiguration ksconf =
  ks.newKieSessionConfiguration();
ksconf.setOption(
  ClockTypeOption.get(ClockType.PSEUDO.getId()));
KieSession ksession = kbase.newKieSession(ksconf, null);
```

You can also configure the KIE session clock using the `kmodule.xml` file by writing `clockType="pseudo"` in the `ksession` tag. Later on, you can access the clock and advance its time with the following code:

```
SessionPseudoClock clock = ksession.getSessionClock();
clock.advanceTime(3, TimeUnit.MINUTES);
clock.advanceTime(5, TimeUnit.DAYS);
...
```

Finally, the last configuration we'll mention here is regarding when to fire the rules. So far, all examples we saw involve firing rules when a process changes state, which adds new events to the KIE session. What about the case where you need to trigger a rule when no new event is added? For example, if you're monitoring the heartbeats of a patient, not having any events for 15 seconds could mean a heart attack event. For these cases where rules should be constantly evaluated, there is a method called `fireUntilHalt` in the KIE session. This method will continuously evaluate rules that match, and change sliding windows as time advances. The method will hang the thread, and you can cancel it from another thread or from a specific rule by calling the `halt` method on the KIE session object.

Summary

In this chapter, we saw how to use business rules and CEP integrated with jBPM6 to produce smarter applications and processes. Business rules can be used in multiple ways to assist our business processes when event reaction analysis is required. They can also manage some of the business process executions.

The next chapter will focus on integrating all of the seen components into a solid architecture, and you will learn how to add processes, rules, and events to an enterprise infrastructure. We will see the sprint management application, which shows all three technologies (business processes, business rules, and CEP) in action.

10
Integrating KIE Workbench with External Systems

In the previous chapters, we learned the specifics of using jBPM6 as an API, both by itself and integrated with other components such as business rules. We also learned about the tooling available in jBPM6, and how it is used. In this chapter, we will focus on the previously mentioned tools, not from an end user perspective, but as an administrator with the job of deciding whether this is the right tooling for our project or company.

Understanding architectures implies getting answers to two main questions: "how is an application composed?" and "why is it composed in such way?" We will have to understand all the internal components proposed by the KIE Workbench in order to evaluate them accordingly, and to define whether their purpose will meet our needs. We will split the chapter into the following sections:

- Understanding the internal components of a jBPM6 project architecture
- How the KIE Workbench is applied to those architectural components
- Steps and examples on how to extend the KIE Workbench to meet our needs of BPMS middleware components

Defining your architecture

In order to define the architecture for a BPM system, we first need to understand the necessities such systems will have. There are many considerations to take into account when defining these requirements, and we will try to explain the main ones here.

First of all, the main purpose of the BPM systems is to provide an environment where process definitions can quickly change to adapt to a changing complex situation of the company domain, and how it will change to drive the company to its goals. This means we need a way to quickly define the change in our processes, in a manner that it can be notified and impacted quickly in the runtime. In order to provide a quick way to change the representation of our knowledge, we will use a repository strategy to quickly change content as well as to keep track of the changes introduced to the knowledge definitions used.

Secondly, we need to understand that even if initially just one or a few applications will use the BPM system, it will grow to be the centric point of access for all the company process definitions and runtimes. In order to cover such growth, the BPM system needs to provide a strategy to be distributed between multiple nodes. In order to provide such functionality, we need to handle our process instances through a persistence that should be synchronized with transactions. This can be done by using another repository strategy: in the KIE Workbench case, this is done with a JPA database.

One final concept we need to cover in a BPM system is the possibility of running as many tasks as possible in an asynchronous fashion. This will result in a more manageable environment, where threads are not just spawned on demand, but rather managed according to the environment capabilities. In the KIE Workbench (and any other jBPM6-based environment), there is a component called `ExecutorService`, which provides a `org.kie.internal.executor.api.Command` interface to give asynchronous executions seamlessly, in a way that it can handle failure retrial and thread pool management. Allocating how many threads can be used at the same time from processes will limit the chances of a BPM server from crashing due to excessive calls.

The overall structure of our BPM system architecture will look like the following diagram, considering the integration of all the mentioned components:

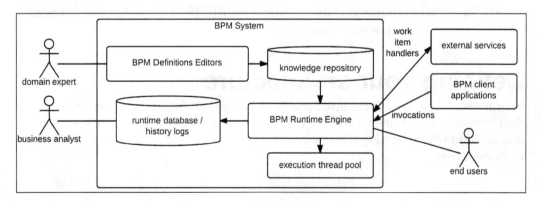

In order to make such an environment scalable, we need to be more specific about the particular strategy we pick to solve our nonfunctional requirements. These considerations will be covered in the following section.

Scalability considerations

Scalability is something to always consider when defining the internal components of a BPMS, mainly because it will be used or evolved into middleware that will later on be used by several other applications in our company, usually exceeding the initially defined requirement for the application. Even if you use it from your applications, the more you end up needing management in your BPM cycle, the more you need your processes to exist in an isolated, reusable environment where said life cycle is more controlled and configurable.

Once you reach this plateau where all your processes are managed through a common BPM system, you will feel the weight of many projects depending on the BPMS. Every application that needs to define a process execution and dynamic knowledge creation will at least consider the possibility of using the BPMS you will be defining now. You need to find a way to manage an ever growing demand for environment capacity.

Not only this, but also because of the dynamic nature of defining correlations between applications, the BPMS will have a responsibility to become an application coordinator. This would put a BPM system in two complex situations: at one side, it should be prepared to handle multiple requests, and at the same time, it should be able to quickly distribute them among many other applications without losing performance. This can be quite challenging if special considerations are not made in advance. The following correlation diagram, regardless of a good management, could transform a BPM system into a bottleneck in the overall enterprise architecture:

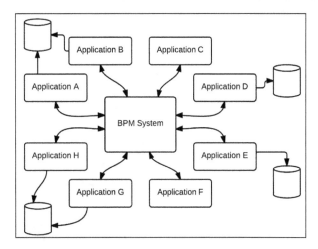

The KIE Workbench was created with such considerations in mind. The persistence for the process runtime is managed in a transactional fashion because it might need us to distribute the work across many servers. The **process definition repository** is defined as a virtual filesystem in order to manage the possibility of being shared between many nodes using the same APIs. Even the jBPM6 executor service is implemented using a database to manage queued tasks, considering the possibility of any other server in a grid being able to handle the tasks created by another node as soon as a thread is made available.

When defining architectures for our BPM systems, we need to take those considerations into account as a bare minimum, for they represent the natural progression of using the BPM discipline, even for projects that might start as modestly as having a few automated processes embedded in a single application.

Taking each of our nonfunctional requirements into account, we need to see whether the KIE Workbench (as it is distributed) or similar architectures are well-suited for our case. If not, do not despair as jBPM6 is — in its very core — just a process engine with configurable extensions to plug any sort of external system or functionality, and embeddable in any other kind of Java-based system.

We can use event listeners to publish auditing information to external systems and components, regarding the internal execution of our jBPM6 process engine. We can also configure **work item handlers** and **executor commands** to customize the way our tasks are executed. There are even pluggable systems for every internal component used in the `KieServices` class. If we change our classpath to have the Drools persistence JAR for Infinispan instead of the ones that implement JPA, we can change the way our system persists runtime information at its very core. Any different configurations can be thought of and created for any kind of environment specification. The following diagram shows a few different architectures based on distinct requirements:

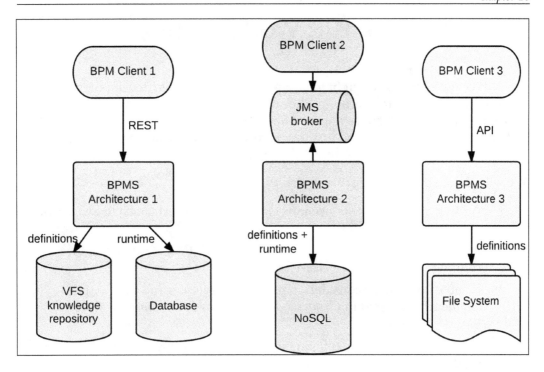

In the preceding diagram, we can see a few possible combinations. The first one to the left-hand side of the diagram shows the configuration as it is available in the KIE Workbench using a **Virtual File System** (**VFS**) for knowledge definitions, a database to persist runtime information, and a REST interface to expose information to clients. At the center, we see a possible alternative where we use a NoSQL persistence for both our runtime and definitions, and a JMS broker to communicate with clients.

Finally, we see the simplest configuration, where definitions are stored in a plain filesystem as files, access is provided through the jBPM6 API, and no persistence is configured. This is the least scalable scenario, but it is also a possibility that might be fit for the simplest cases.

In the next section, we will discuss how we can start changing the KIE Workbench to adapt its internal architecture to our specific needs.

Extending the KIE Workbench architecture

The KIE Workbench was thought to be a pluggable, extensible development environment and runtime for our jBPM6 applications. We will start discussing some of the most requested changes required for enterprise use, in order to serve as both utilities for your necessities and inspiration towards which changes can be applied to the application to make a customized version of it.

We will discuss the following integration topics:

- Adding a SOAP web service interface to the KIE Workbench to expose jBPM6 as web services

- Adding custom work item handlers that will be the default for all the runtimes managed in the KIE Workbench

- Remote invocations considering preexisting services and the runtime engine API (covered in *Chapter 7, Defining Your Environment with the Runtime Manager*)

- Considerations about deploying in the cloud, with specific demonstrations for deploying in OpenShift (http://www.openshift.com)

All integrations that follow are inside a KIE Workbench distribution project called `kie-wb-edition`, available in the chapter's code bundle. It is a Maven project prepared to use the assembly plugin to modify the original KIE Workbench, prepared to run on JBoss Application Server, in order to have our own extra modules and modifications to its internal configuration files. Checkout the `assembly-kie-wb-edition.xml` file under `src/main/assembly/` to see what changes are being introduced in the project. We will go through each one of them in detail as we explain the reason and structure of each configuration.

Web service addition

One very common request that most companies have due to internal policies is to provide a SOAP-based web service interface to interact with the BPM system. The KIE Workbench provides a RESTful interface by default, mainly because it can be accessed through web service clients as well as from other tools, such as JavaScript client APIs or mobile devices. Adding a SOAP-based web service, however, is far simpler than it would seem.

In the code bundle of this chapter, there is a project called `web-service-module`. Inside this project, you will find the definition for a simple web service. It uses a rather simple interface, which, for the simplicity of demonstration, only exposes two important methods: the `startProcess` and `signalEvent` methods of the KIE session. It defines a JAX-WS-based web service that will interact directly with a runtime engine (specified by the release ID passed as a parameter to the web service invocations).

Its configuration is rather simple. To have it added to our KIE Workbench, we need to do the following two things:

1. Add the compiled JAR file from the `web-service-module` project to the `lib` folder under `WEB-INF` of the KIE Workbench.

2. Add the corresponding servlet mapping to the `WEB-INF/web.xml` file of the KIE Workbench:

```
<servlet>
    <display-name>rmWebService</display-name>
    <servlet-name>rmWebService</servlet-name>
    <servlet-class>com.wordpress.marianbuenosayres.
        service.RuntimeManagerWebService</servlet-class>
</servlet>
<servlet-mapping>
    <servlet-name>rmWebService</servlet-name>
    <url-pattern>
        /RuntimeManagerWebServiceImpl
    </url-pattern>
</servlet-mapping>
```

Once that configuration is added to the application, we will have the web service exposing our internal services. As the web service is going to look for any runtime manager configured in the same environment from the specified release ID in the invocation, we will need no extra configuration to run its code. The `signalEvent` method of the `RuntimeManagerWebServiceImpl` class can be simplified into the following code snippet:

```
public void signalEventAll(String releaseId, String signalRef) {
    RuntimeEngine engine = RuntimeManagerRegistry.
        getManager(releaseId).getRuntimeEngine(
            EmptyContext.get());
    if (engine != null) {
        engine.getKieSession().signalEvent(signalRef, null);
    }
}
```

As shown in the preceding code snippet, when we have a preexisting runtime manager, we get a runtime engine from it and fire the `signalEvent` method to its KIE session object. These configurations, as we mentioned previously, are automatically added to a WAR file when compiling the `kie-wb-edition` project.

Work item handler default configurations

This is a powerful trick for reconfiguring our KIE Workbench environment to have our own default work item handlers, and it works for both the KIE Workbench as well as for any other jBPM6- or Drools-based application that uses a KIE session. There is a configuration file, called `drools.session.conf`, which defines the internal configurations of some of the components in a KIE session. By default, this `drools.session.conf` file has the following content inside the classpath:

```
drools.workItemHandlers = CustomWorkItemHandlers.conf
```

What this configuration has is a set of default values for our KIE session configuration objects. The `drools.workItemHandlers` property will allow us to define an MVEL file path, relative to the `drools.session.conf` file, which will contain a map of our `WorkItemHandler` instances indexed by their registry key. This MVEL map will be used by the KIE sessions constructed in its specific environment to prepopulate its work item handlers. We will use it, along with specific work item handlers added to our classpath, to do the following:

- Override existing configurations for task behavioral definitions
- Make our own configurations for new task types

We can make use of work item handlers to create interactions with pretty much any form of external system. Also, by adding the `jbpm-workitems` dependency to our project, we can create or extend from a wide range of previously existing work item handlers that allow us to access web services, RSS feeds, interact with filesystems, FTP servers, databases, Java beans, and many more components, as follows:

```
<dependency>
    <groupId>org.jbpm</groupId>
    <artifactId>jbpm-workitems</artifactId>
    <version>6.1.0.Beta3</version>
</dependency>
```

This dependency is available inside the KIE Workbench libraries, so you can use them to extend configurations without even writing a new `WorkItemHandler` definition.

We have defined a `CustomWorkItemHandlers.conf` file with extra features for our custom KIE Workbench edition. In it, you can find definitions that come from the project `custom-work-item-handlers`. There is one more component in the said project that implements the `org.kie.internal.executor.api.Command` interface, which we are going to discuss in detail in the next section.

Executor service commands

Configuring `WorkItemHandlers` is a great way of creating interactions with external systems. However, the more complex those interactions are, the more time the thread that interacts with the process will be waiting for the task to finish. This is a natural consequence of complex executions; they do take time. However, having a behavior that is detached from the actual process execution in our tasks will allow us to invoke more process executions with fewer resources. In order to provide this detached, asynchronous management of tasks, we will use the following three components:

- The `org.kie.internal.executor.api.Command` interface, which provides a new way of writing external interactions

- The `ExecutorService` class, which creates a managed thread pool for executing the said commands

- The `AsyncWorkItemHandler` class, which ends up connecting the process execution with the `ExecutorService` method in an asynchronous fashion

The `Command` interface is a very simple one. It provides an `execute` method that will receive a `Context` object and return an `ExecutionResults` object, as follows:

```
public interface Command {
    ExecutionResults execute(Context ctx) throws Exception;
}
```

The interface isn't just meant to work with `WorkItemHandlers`, but with anything that requires a pluggable and pooled asynchronous behavior. In order to use it as an interaction with process tasks, we will have a variable in the context marked by the key `workItem` to access the parameters of the task. The `custom-work-item-handlers` project in this chapter's code bundle defines a very simple command for handling a specific domain task:

```
public ExecutionResults execute(CommandContext c)throws Exception{
    WorkItem wi = (WorkItem) context.getData("workItem");
    Object domainXParameter = wi.getParameter("domainXParameter");
    //Your specific domain operations should go here
    ExecutionResults results = new ExecutionResults();
    results.setData("domainXResult", domainXParameter);
    return results;
}
```

As you can see, the `ExecutionResults` object has a `setData` method where we can add specific output for our commands. The specific work item handler prepared to pass tasks to the executor service, called `AsyncWorkItemHandler`, will take these parameters to match each result with a task output.

Overall, the `ExecutorService` object, the specific handlers, and the command it will use can all be specified through a single line of code. This is clearly visible in the `CustomWorkItemHandlers.conf` file that can be found in the `kie-wb-edition` project:

```
[
...
   "DomainX" : new com.wordpress.marianbuenosayres.handlers.
      DomainXWorkItemHandler(),
   "DomainXAsync" : new org.jbpm.executor.impl.wih.
      AsyncWorkItemHandler(
         org.jbpm.executor.ExecutorServiceFactory.
            newExecutorService(
               javax.persistence.Persistence.
                  createEntityManagerFactory(
                     "org.jbpm.domain")
            ),
         "com.wordpress.marianbuenosayres.handlers." +
            "DomainXExecCommand"
      )
]
```

The line for using the `AsyncWorkItemHandler` component looks a bit complicated, but it does a lot in a single line. First, it creates a JPA persistence manager, then it creates the executor service, and then it passes it to the `AsyncWorkItemHandler` component along with the name of the `Command` class to execute its tasks.

The main advantage of using the executor service is that it provides the possibility of handling many more concurrent calls that interact with process executions. Whenever we invoke an interaction with a process instance (without the executor service strategy), we will be hanging a thread until the automatic tasks involved in said process are finished or reach a wait state. So, if we have 10 users invoking processes with a task as the first step that takes 2 seconds to process, we will have 10 threads hung up for 2 seconds each.

With the executor service, this is far more manageable, because passing tasks to the executor service takes barely any time, and it will queue tasks for deferred execution until a thread inside its pool is made available. This translates to a far more scalable situation for our previous case, because we will have 10 threads hung up for very few milliseconds (the time it takes to queue a task), and then a limited number of threads solving elements from that queue. The following diagram shows how a server that uses the executor service (at the bottom of the diagram) scales better on high concurrency situations than the one that solves tasks using a synchronous work item handler (at the top of the diagram):

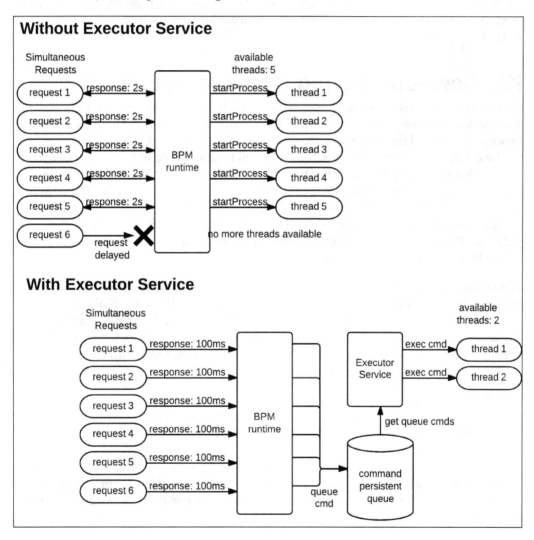

The preceding diagram shows how, even with fewer threads, the response time decreases because the actual tasks are not being finished by the BPM system invocation. Instead, they're just queued for another group of threads to actually perform them. This strategy with an executor service will even provide a retry mechanism if the tasks fail, because it can be configured to retry each command a number of times if they throw an exception, or even leave them in a pending state until a solution to the failure can be found.

This management issue becomes much more important when those 10 invocations a second become a hundred, or a thousand. The processes that use an asynchronous mechanism, such as the executor service, will scale far better when high concurrency is used.

KIE Session Sharing Considerations

Finally, another consideration to have when running on highly concurrent environments is one further consequence of sharing a KIE session between many process instances. Due to the way the persistence is configured (See *Chapter 8, Implementing Persistence and Transactions*), it will be able to recover and continue the KIE session execution from another thread, but only one thread at a time will be able to manage invocations to a KIE session. This is because they will edit the same tuple in the database (for the `SessionInfo` table) and internal locks on the database connection configuration will either throw an exception or lock the tuple in the database. Either way, only one thread will successfully access a KIE session at a time to avoid data change collisions.

When considering high concurrency environments, we will need to take this situation into account, as two process instances that share the same KIE Session won't be able to execute from two different threads at the same time. On a single standalone server, this could be managed with a synchronized block around a KIE session method invocation; however, with multiple nodes, this could become a problem that could occur a certain number of times.

In order to avoid this error, the implementation of the persistence for Drools provides an `OptimisticLockRetryInterceptor` component, that when a concurrent modification problem arises, hangs the latest thread and retries the execution milliseconds afterwards. This usually saves the few cases where this problem could happen if you don't share the session too much. However, in order to avoid having this situation too often, we will need to consider partitioning our KIE sessions in a specific way, and try to see whether a per-process instance runtime manager could fit our needs.

Remote engine invocations

Once we have a BPM system component to centralize our process engine, we will need a standard way to access that environment. It is important to expose such environments in order to not clutter other systems with complicated or dependency loaded APIs.

We've seen how to add a web service component to expose the KIE Workbench's internal components through a SOAP-based web service, but there are more standard ways of accessing our environment, which are preconfigured in the KIE Workbench. Those mechanisms also come with client components, based on the RuntimeEngine interface, for which implementations are provided to access the internal runtime engines of the KIE Workbench through the following two protocols:

- A RESTful HTTP interface
- JMS command invocations through Queues

The following diagram shows how these different ways of connecting external systems to the KIE Workbench are implemented:

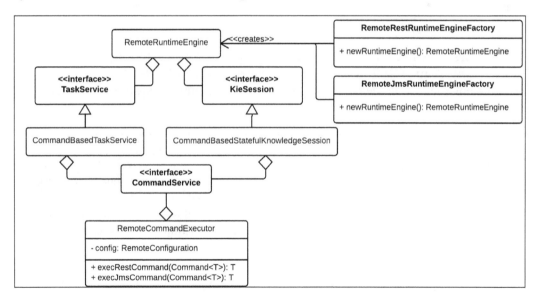

As the preceding diagram shows, the `RemoteRuntimeEngine` object takes advantage of the command pattern-based KIE session and task service to expose the exact same API by implementing a remote way to execute the commands. Using the `RemoteCommandExecutor` object, it can send XML serializations of each command through different protocols, and as long as a server is prepared to receive them, interaction between the client and server could be done through the same API you would use to run the process engine locally.

In order to use these remote APIs, you need to add the `kie-services-client` dependency to your projects, as follows:

```
<dependency>
    <groupId>org.kie.remote</groupId>
    <artifactId>kie-services-client</artifactId>
    <version>6.1.0.Beta3</version>
</dependency>
```

We will go into detail on how to use each one of these remote invocation strategies in the following sections.

REST interface

The simplest way to communicate with the KIE Workbench is through the REST interface. A group of REST service classes expose a series of URLs to access different runtime engines inside the KIE Workbench. The following table shows some of the URLs:

URL	Functionality
`/rest/runtime/{deployment-id}/ process/{process-id}/start`	This URL allows you to start a process instance. Here, the parameters are passed through the body.
`/rest/runtime/{deployment-id}/ process/instance/{process-instance-id}/abort`	This URL allows you to send the abort signal to a running process instance.
`/rest/runtime/{deployment-id}/ process/instance/{process-instance-id}/signal/{signal-ref}`	This URL allows you to send a specific signal to a running process instance.
`/rest/runtime/{deployment-id}/ signal/{signal-id}`	This URL sends a signal to the whole KIE session instead of just one process instance.
`/rest/runtime/{deployment-id}/ workitem/{workitem-id}/complete`	This URL allows the user to complete a work item remotely. Here, the parameters are sent through the body.

URL	Functionality
`/rest/runtime/{deployment-id}/workitem/{workitem-id}/abort`	This URL allows the user to abort a work item remotely.
`/rest/runtime/{deployment-id}/execute`	This URL allows the user to execute a command sent through the post body.
`/rest/runtime/{deployment-id}/process/instance/{process-instance-id}/variable/{var-name}`	This URL retrieves the value of a variable for a specific process instance.
`/rest/runtime/{deployment-id}/process/instance/{process-instance-id}`	This URL retrieves a specific process instance.
`/rest/task/{task-id}/{operation}`	This URL allows you to perform multiple different operations on top of the task service (claim, activate, complete, and so on). Here, the parameters are sent through the post body.
`/rest/task/query`	This URL allows you to perform queries on top of the task service database.
`/rest/task/{task-id}/content`	This URL retrieves the contents of a task (its task inputs, outputs, and errors).
`/rest/task/{task-id}/content/{content-id}`	This URL retrieves a specific content of one specific task.
`/rest/task/bam/history/clear`	This URL clears the audit information of the task database.
`/rest/runtime/{deployment-id}/process/history/clear`	This URL clears the audit information of the process database.
`/rest/runtime/{deployment-id}/process/history/instances`	This URL retrieves historical information of all completed and running process instances.
`/rest/runtime/{deployment-id}/history/instance/{process-instance-id}`	This URL retrieves all historical info about one specific process instance.
`/rest/runtime/{deployment-id}/history/instance/{process-instance-id}/node`	This URL retrieves all historical info about nodes of one specific process instance.
`/rest/runtime/{deployment-id}/history/instance/{process-instance-id}/variable`	This URL retrieves all historical info about variables of one specific process instance.
`/rest/deployment`	This URL show all the deployments that are available.
`/rest/deployment/{deployment-id}/deploy`	This URL updates a deployment.

URL	Functionality
`/rest/deployment/{deployment-id}/undeploy`	This URL removes a deployment.
`/rest/deployments`	This URL shows all the deployments that are available.

The most important URL exposed is probably the "execute" URL: `/rest/runtime/{deployment-id}/execute`. Through this URL, using the command pattern, every single function in the KIE session and the task service can be implemented using the same API. This is the one used by the implementation at the `kie-services-client` dependency to expose the `RemoteRuntimeEngine` class. The following code snippet shows how to build a REST remote runtime engine:

```
RuntimeEngine engine = RemoteRestRuntimeEngineFactoryBuilderImpl.
    newBuilder().addUrl(new URL("http://localhost:8080/kie-wb")).
    addDeploymentId("org.jbpm:HR:1.0").addUserName("mariano").
    addPassword("mypass").build().newRuntimeEngine();
```

You can see that we are passing four elements to the `RemoteRestRuntimeEngineFactoryBuidlerImpl` class: a URL for the KIE Workbench, a release ID for identifying a runtime manager, and a username and a password to log in to the application and pass credentials to what I will do on top of the created `RuntimeEngine`.

Once the `RuntimeEngine` object is created, we can use it as any other `RuntimeEngine` we built in our local environment. Internally, it will create commands for every method invoked in the KIE session and task service, serialize them into XML, and send them through the execute URL.

You can find an example in the `remote-invocations` project, in the `SignalEventAppREST` class. You can run it directly from the `remote-invocations` path by typing the following command:

```
mvn -Prest
```

JMS interface

Another way of accessing the KIE Workbench runtime engines is through the JMS implementations. It uses a set of queues to send serialized versions of the command objects for task service and KIE session method executions. These commands, whether they are sent to the task service or the KIE session, are sent through two different queues: `jms/queue/KIE.TASK` or `jms/queue/KIE.SESSION` queues, respectively. Responses are handled through the `jms/queue/KIE.RESPONSE` queue.

These are the default configurations in the KIE Workbench application, but they can be changed in the `bpms-jms.xml` file under the `WEB-INF/` folder of the KIE Workbench.

There is another queue we haven't mentioned because, for the moment, it is not managed by the `RemoteRuntimeEngine` interface. This queue is the audit queue. It manages requests for the `AuditLogService` interface, to access the history logs from outside applications.

In order to create code that could manage messages for the first three queues in a standard way, we must create the runtime engine through the provided API, as shown in the following code snippet:

```
InitialContext ctx = new InitialContext();
QueueConnectionFactory connFactory = (QueueConnectionFactory)
    ctx.lookup("jms/RemoteConnectionFactory");
Connection conn = connFactory.createConnection(
    "mariano", "mypass");
Session session = conn.createSession(true,
    Session.AUTO_ACKNOWLEDGE);
Queue ksQueue = (Queue) ctx.lookup("jms/queue/KIE.SESSION");
Queue taskQueue = (Queue) ctx.lookup("jms/queue/KIE.TASK");
Queue respQueue = (Queue) ctx.lookup("jms/queue/KIE.RESPONSE");
RuntimeEngine engine = RemoteJmsRuntimeEngineFactoryBuilderImpl.
    newBuilder().addDeploymentId("org.jbpm:HR:1.0").
    addConnectionFactory(connFactory).addKieSessionQueue(ksQueue).
    addTaskServiceQueue(taskQueue).addResponseQueue(respQueue).
    addUserName("mariano").addPassword("mypass").
    build().newRuntimeEngine();
```

The preceding code snippet does a lot more configuration, mainly to access all the JMS components needed. We first need to connect to an initial context to gain access to our JMS `ConnectionFactory` and `Queues`, and then we pass those to the factory along with a release ID, a username, and a password.

You will need to have the `jndi.properties` file in your classpath with all the configurations needed to access a remote JMS environment. You can find one with all such configurations to connect to a JBoss Application Server 7.1 remote JMS factory in the `remote-invocations` project.

There is an example provided in the `SignalEventAppJMS` class of the `remote-invocations` project. You can run it directly from the `remote-invocations` path by typing the following command:

```
mvn -Pjms
```

Due to default permission configurations in JBoss Application Server 7.1, you need to have the `guest` role added to the user with which you log in to the KIE Workbench. You can do so by editing the `application-roles.properties` file under `standalone/configuration`, changing `mariano=admin` to `mariano=admin,guest`.

Also, if you want to run the remote-invocations demo, you will also need to add the `mariano` user, with password `mypass`, to the application realm using the `add-user.sh` or `add-user.bat` script of the JBoss Application Server.

Deploying the KIE Workbench in the cloud

One trendy topic nowadays is the possibility of deploying different middleware solutions in the cloud, in order to relieve a company from the burden of managing hardware administration and allocation for their enterprise and development configurations. The KIE Workbench is a project that was developed with the cloud in mind, and evolved to be deployable within a cloud server.

The KIE Workbench is a web application and can run on any type of server. However, it is mainly tested on top of JBoss Application Server 7.1, the current production-ready Application Server from Red Hat. Because of that, the newest distributions are quickly available to run on JBoss-based cloud providers. This is the reason for having the cloud-based distribution of the KIE Workbench prepared to run on OpenShift (http://www.openshift.com), a multiplatform (of which one of them is JBoss) cloud service. We will see how to configure a running KIE Workbench on said cloud provider.

First, we will need to register on OpenShift by clicking on the **SIGN UP** button on the top-right corner of the OpenShift website. This button will take us to a registration screen, as shown in the following screenshot:

Once the registration is done and confirmed, we need to click on the Add Application button, which will take us to the cartridge selection screen. Cartridges are components installed into an environment to provide a specific functionality, such as a JBoss environment, a MySQL database, and so on. In our case, we're going to focus on two options that install KIE Workbench-like web applications on a server such as JBoss Application Server, described in the following list:

- The **JBoss Business Process Management Suite Cartridge**: This is the Red Hat maintained cartridge to access the product version of the KIE Workbench (called Red Hat BPMS). It requires a paid subscription to work properly, as it consumes a lot of resources.

- Use a custom cartridge: At the bottom of the page, you will see a text field that you can complete with a specific URL. We can select our manually created cartridges there. I've created a special cartridge to run the community version of this project, and if you type `https://raw.githubusercontent.com/marianbuenosayres/openshift-cartridge-kiewb/master/metadata/manifest.yml` into the text field and click on **Next**, you will see the page to configure the name of your application. We will select a name for it, a domain, and click on the **Create Application** button at the bottom of the page, as shown in the following screenshot:

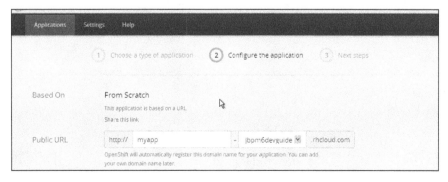

The application will take some time to be created. Once it is available, you should be able to access the application through the provided URL, and depending on the cartridge you used, a link will appear to access the BPMS, or an automatic redirection will take you to the KIE Workbench.

Summary

BPM adoption is a tough job, but its rewards are enormous. Not only has the speed of development dramatically increased, but the amount of intercommunication between technical groups and domain experts has increased significantly through a common language. No organization has ever regretted learning BPM, much less adopting it in their everyday activities.

In this chapter, we have learned about the architecture considerations of using jBPM6 as a BPM system, the different integration facilities the KIE Workbench provides, how to access it from outside tools, and even how to deploy it in the cloud. It is up to the end user to determine the best way to make use of these components to link jBPM6 to the existing enterprise infrastructure, but it is my honest hope that now you will have all the tools to make the right decision.

After all that we have covered in this book, I hope you have all the necessary tools to get started with jBPM6. It is such a big project that it is almost impossible to fit every single detail in just one book. For that reason, I strongly recommend going iteratively increasing the complexity of your projects, based on what you have seen in this book. I also recommend joining the community; it is by far the best way to learn about the project state and future directions. It is a very open group, and about half of the contributions made to the project are from people like you, who started learning about jBPM6.

This book will be used as a foundation to write more advanced articles describing extra topics, so keep an eye on my blog (http://marianbuenosayres.wordpress.com). Feel free to contact me through comments on my blog or using the community jBPM IRC channel. Don't be shy, and keep in touch!

The UberFire Framework

We have seen the different components of the KIE workbench throughout the book. This appendix will explain how all its components are bonded together through the UberFire framework, which allows us to have a configurable and extensible workbench environment. We will dedicate this appendix to discussing its structure and use, which will become useful if you wish to extend the tooling provided by jBPM6 for your own personal customization. This is an advanced topic, but will give you a full control over how to use the KIE workbench to fit it best to your company.

UberFire

UberFire is a JBoss-based framework developed and maintained by the Drools and jBPM team. UberFire creates a rich client platform built on top of GWT (`http://www.gwtproject.org`) and Errai (`http://erraiframework.org`). It is also the technology on top of which the KIE workbench project is built. It provides a series of components for a pluggable user administration, virtual file system management, and configurable perspectives and user interfaces. It is thought of as a work on top of an application server, and depends on JEE6 specifications (such as CDI, for dependency injection).

UberFire defines a few default implementations for a few of its services, but they are all highly configurable. For example, for user management, they use a user properties file as default, but the KIE workbench uses Java as a service implementation configured with a file in the classpath at `META-INF/services/org.uberfire.security.auth.AuthenticationSource` with the actual implementation to use for authentication.

We will discuss only a few of the components of UberFire here due to the need of perhaps a full book to cover every component. However, if you wish to go deeper into the framework utilities, visit `http://www.uberfireframework.org`.

Some of the most important functionalities that UberFire provides from our perspective are follows:

- Integration of components
- Existing components and services used by jBPM6
- How to extend and reuse components

 As I'm writing this book, UberFire is still in Alpha state, so some things might change in the near future. I'll try to cover the most important architecture components of UberFire you will more likely use, and that are less likely to change in the future.

Integrating components

As we mentioned before, UberFire is heavily dependent on GWT and Errai, integrated internally through a series of CDI injected events that each component either fires or captures to decide actions that need to be taken.

Context and Dependency Injection (CDI) is a standard defined by Java Enterprise Edition 6 to compose different components based on their types, names, and specific centralized configurations. The idea behind it is remove the need of writing legacy code to initialize and bind together different implementations of components, but allow them to be managed through specific annotations in classes and by configuration files.

Google Web Toolkit (GWT) is a framework created by Google that is used to define smart user interfaces using Java code, which are later (during project compilation) translated into JavaScript in order to run in a web browser without the need of having any plugins installed. Its goal is to enable productive development of high-performance web applications without the developer having to be an expert in browser quirks, Ajax requests, and JavaScript.

The main problem that a GWT translation of Java to JavaScript has is that it doesn't translate everything. There is a point where you have to split which classes run in the client as JavaScript and which classes run in the server as Java. Connectivity between the server and client don't take advantage of other frameworks such as CDI to inject communication stubs.

That's where Errai comes in. Errai provides several GWT extensions for UI templating, binding, and server communication through simple events. Errai allows users to define CDI annotations on GWT code and provides a way to translate those annotations and use them even if the actual component implementations are only server-side (that means, they weren't translated to JavaScript).

This allows components to directly communicate using events irrespective of whether they were server components or client components that will later on be translated to JavaScript. The level of unification in the design that this framework allowed made UberFire an incredibly powerful framework.

Thanks to all the already existing components in the workbench and the fact that all communication can be handled through events, extending components to listen to new events is very simple and new components that interact with other actions taken by the user or the server can be written with very loose coupled code.

The existing components and services

There are many existing components in the UberFire framework, and covering them all will take a book by itself. We will explore the most important components from the BPM perspective, and how they help in the generation of a BPM system for jBPM6.

Some of the backend features that UberFire has that are important for jBPM6 are as follows:

- **Security framework**: UberFire security is highly pluggable and assumes very little by default. Any class that implements the `org.uberfire. security.auth.AuthenticationSource` interface can tell the framework which credentials are valid and which are not. The framework comes with a starter set of `AuthenticationSource` implementations, but you can implement your own, add it to your workbench class path, and configure it using Java's standard `ServiceLoader` facility, by simply writing the full class name in the `META-INF/services/org.uberfire.security.auth. AuthenticationSource` file. If you want more than one authentication source at a time, list each fully qualified class name on its own line in the file; if your `AuthenticationSource` implementation also implements `RoleProvider`, then it can also provide role authorization.

- **Virtual File System API**: UberFire provides a configurable virtual file system and an implementation of said configurations using Git software configuration management (`http://git-scm.com`). This allows UberFire to store not only the knowledge assets created with the KIE workbench, but also perspective definitions and geometries for users' customized layouts. The interface provided for the virtual file system is created by backporting the NIO.2 API defined for Java 8 (`https://jcp.org/en/jsr/detail?id=203`) into the code base of UberFire. Just as the security framework, it can be configured using Java's standard `ServiceLoader` facility by writing content to the `META-INF/services/org.uberfire.java.nio.file.spi. FileSystemProvider` file. However, this isn't a recommended practice unless you know exactly what you're doing.

Thanks to these backend features, a lot of other features can be easily provided. Among the frontend features, we have the following:

- **Perspective generation**: Perspectives provide a powerful mechanism for task-oriented interaction with resources, multi-tasking, and information filtering. It provides the possibility of having different visual components arranged in multiple different ways with little or no code at all.

- **Flexible layout**: This, combined with the perspective generation utilities, provides the final user with a way of defining a particular view for him or her that can be utilized later on in future when he or she logs in. Thanks to the filesystem and security management features combined, the UberFire framework can internally store the preferences for each user's perspectives.

- **Event intercommunication between components**: Thanks to Errai and CDI, all components (both client and server side) can easily interact using events.

Event intercommunication is a very important and simple-to-use component that generates events that can be shared by the client and server. The first thing we need to do is to define our event objects. Let's examine how we defined `NewMessageEvent` in our `uberfire-demo-api` project:

```
@org.jboss.errai.common.client.api.annotations.Portable
public class NewMessageEvent implements Serializable {
    public NewMessageEvent() { … }
    …
}
```

In the previous code fragment, which we reduced to the most important sections, you can see that our event doesn't have to extend any specific class. All it needs is a `@Portable` annotation from Errai to be shared between client and server. Inside the event, any kind of serializable information can be placed to be shared between a client and server.

Later on, these events are captured or fired by specific instances, but the configuration to use them is almost trivial. In the following code fragment, we see how the `MessageListViewImpl` class in the `uberfire-demo-client` project listens for `NewMessageEvent` firings and how it fires another type of event called `NotificationEvent`:

```
public class MessageListViewImpl … {
    …
    @javax.inject.Inject
    public javax.enterprise.event.Event<NotificationEvent>
notification;
    …
```

```
    public void requestCreated(@javax.enterprise.event.Observes
NewMessageEvent e ){
        ...
    }

    public void displayNotification( String text ) {
        notification.fire( new NotificationEvent( text ) );
    }
    ...
}
```

As you can see, all it took to listen to event firings was the creation of a method that had a parameter with the `@Observes` annotation. In the previous code fragment, the method is called `requestCreated`.

Meanwhile, we need two things to fire events:

- A `javax.enterprise.event.Event` object
- A `fire` method needs to be invoked with a new event instance

In the previous code fragment, the `fire` method is invoked from inside the `displayNotification` method. Using the `Event` object is quite simple. Thanks to CDI and Errai, we don't need to do anything else than to inject the instance with the `@Inject` annotation, and then let the framework take care of creating the actual object and setting it to any component.

Extending and reusing the UberFire UI components

One of the greatest advantages of the KIE workbench adoption of UberFire is not the components it provides, but how easy it is to integrate new custom components into an existing workbench.

Since all of the jBPM6 tooling is based on UberFire, adding new components becomes a great advantage for adopters of the tooling. It is also a very significant improvement from the previous versions, where the jBPM tooling was very difficult to change due to its complexity and highly-coupled code. In this version, adding new components is very easy, and we will show how to create new screens for an existing workbench and how to integrate them together.

Model View Presenter

Before we fully dive into the code, we need to understand how it is composed and designed. UberFire component design is based on a very useful design pattern used for building user interfaces called **Model View Presenter** (**MVP**). MVP is based on a highly used pattern called **Model View Controller** (**MVC**), but is devoid of one of its biggest issues, regarding component intercommunication. The idea behind MVP is twofold:

- Each component in a user interface project should have three classes with very specific responsibilities:
  - **Model**: This will handle all the business logic detached from presentation
  - **View**: This will handle visual representations of data regardless of the business logic that created it
  - **Presenter**: This will manage communication between two and more components

- Each different MVP group should communicate with other components (and, to some measure, even with itself) by listening and firing events

This creates a very distinctive structure of classes that can be easily changed, to provide different representations by allowing them to be completely detached from the business logic and from other visual components. The following diagram of MVP shows the basic interactions that happen with this pattern:

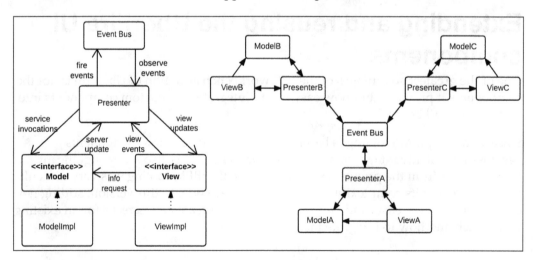

In the preceding figure, we can see how the classes inside one single MVP group interact on the left and how multiple MVP groups interact with each other on the right. We can see how communication is always managed through an event bus that distributes events to their relevant listeners, even with multiple MVP groups. This allows the application to grow exponentially without having to increase the complexity of its already existing components. Each MVP group only has to worry about the events that they care about.

This presents a significant improvement over MVP's predecessor pattern, called MVC. It is similar to MVP, except that it doesn't adopt intercommunication using an event bus. Without said component, each MVC group (as opposed to MVP) should know any other MVC group that requires notification of a particular action, and communication between controllers becomes hard to maintain. In the following figure, we can see an example of this with only five different MVC and MVP groups. Views and models were removed to reduce complexity.

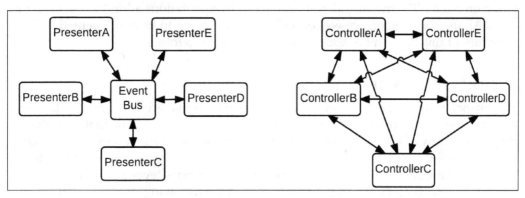

Model View Controller versus Model View Presenter intercommunication channels

As you can see, no matter how many presenters exist, or what events they await, existing presenters that fire said events don't have to change to adjust to a growing component. With controllers, on the other hand, complexity can grow exponentially.

Now that we understand MVP and its advantages, we will make an example component using the UberFire framework and the MVP pattern.

The workbench components

In this section, we will learn how to configure our own visual components inside an UberFire-based application. In order to understand how to build them, we need to understand which types are available, and what are they used for. In the following subsections, we will discuss four of UberFire's most used components for defining user interfaces:

- Workbench screens
- Workbench pop ups
- Workbench editors
- Workbench perspectives

Once we get to know how they work and what they do, we will learn how to build our own user interfaces. Each visual representation in our demonstration will be based on the MVP pattern, and will be marked by annotations added to the Presenter class. All the components we will describe here are going to be implemented in the code files of this book in the `appendix/uberfire-demo` folder.

Workbench screens

Workbench screens are pieces of visual representation that are fitted in a particular window. From a UI point of view, they are nonfloating components that fit in the display window of the web application. They are simple UI containers, so they can define virtually anything inside them. Classes that should be used as workbench screens in the UberFire framework are marked with a class-level annotation and a couple of method-level annotations, as shown in the following code fragment:

```
@Dependent
@WorkbenchScreen(identifier = "myParticularScreenID")
public class MyParticularScreenPresenter {

    ...

    @WorkbenchPartTitle
    public String getTitle() {
        return "My Particular Screen";
    }

    ...

    @WorkbenchPartView
    public IsWidget getView() {

        ...

    }

    ...
```

```
    @WorkbenchMenu
    public WorkbenchMenuBar getBar() {

        ...

    }
}
```

There is a lot to comment about the annotations used in the preceding code fragment. Let's analyze them briefly:

- `@Dependent`: This annotation is not part of UberFire API, but a part of CDI. CDI marks this class as a **dependent scoped CDI bean** that should be freshly instantiated every time a new instance is called for. This annotation is in contrast with `@ApplicationScoped`, which marks a CDI bean that should be created only one time over the life of the application.

- `@WorkbenchScreen`: This annotation is used to declare that the class defines a screen in the application. It has one attribute called `identifier` that defines a unique name for this screen, which is used later for external reference by other components.

- `@WorkbenchPartTitle`: This annotation denotes the method that returns the screen's title. Every screen must have a `@WorkbenchPartTitle` method.

- `@WorkbenchPartView`: This annotation denotes the method that returns the panel's view. The view can be any class that extends GWT's `Widget` class or implements GWT's `IsWidget` interface (a basic interface to refer to a UI component built in GWT). Every screen must have an `@WorkbenchPartView` method.

- `@WorkbenchMenu`: This is an optional annotation to mark a method that will return a menu for the specific screen. It helps to make all menus in all screens appear in a similar fashion. The returned type of the annotated method should be an instance of the `org.uberfire.client.workbench.widgets.menu.WorkbenchMenuBar` class.

Using these annotations, we can define different components in any part of the code, without the need to depend on specific aggregations or class hierarchies and still add new screens in an easy way.

Workbench pop ups

Workbench pop ups are very similar to workbench screens, with the single difference of appearing on a pop-up window instead of as a part of a composite screen. Pop ups will become modal from the UberFire perspective, not letting the user click on any other component of the particular screen until the pop up is closed.

It also requires a @WorkbenchPartTitle and a @WorkbenchPartView annotation to register a title and a view for the pop up and an identifier to invoke it from outside, just like screens. Because those methods can be implemented by any class, creating widgets that could be used both from a screen or a pop up becomes very simple. This is shown in the following code example:

```
@Dependent
@WorkbenchPopup(identifier = "myOwnPopupID")
public class MyOwnPopupPresenter {

    ...

    @WorkbenchPartTitle
    public String getTitle() {
        return "My Own Popup";
    }

    ...

    @WorkbenchPartView
    public IsWidget getView() {

        ...

    }

}
```

As you can see from the comparison of the last two code fragments, workbench screens and pop ups are virtually the same except for the final layout in the UberFire framework.

Workbench editors

Workbench editors are special kinds of UI components that perform some kind of editing functionality for a specific file type or group of file types. It extends the functionality of common screens to associate the opening of an editor with a specific file that needs to be stored on the server side. They provide some extra needed configuration to bind a specific editor with a particular file and file type. Here's an example:

```
@WorkbenchEditor(identifier = "myEditorForTypeX",
        supportedTypes = { XClientType.class })
public class MyEditor {
    @WorkbenchPartTitle
    public String getTitle() {
        return "MyEditor";
    }
    @WorkbenchPartView
    public IsWidget getEditorView() {

        ...

    }
```

```
@OnStartup
public void onStart(final Path path) {
    ...
}
...
}
```

In the preceding code, there are a few things that are different from workbench screens:

- `@WorkbenchEditor`: This annotation is used to declare that the class defines an editor in the application. It has two attributes—one called `identifier` that defines a unique name for this editor and for external reference by other tools and another called `supportedTypes`, which should receive an array of all file types that the editor can work with. File types are represented using the `org.uberfire.client.workbench.type.ClientResourceType` class that can be extended to add support for new file types.

- `@OnStartup`: This is one of UberFire's lifecycle annotations. They are better explained in the next subsection. It marks a method that will be called when the editor is created. For the special case of editors, the annotated method can receive a parameter of type `org.uberfire.backend.vfs.Path`, which denotes the file with which the editor will be working.

Workbench perspectives

UberFire workbench UI components are arranged as **Workbench | Perspective | Panel | Workbench** screen. Perspectives dictate the position and size of workbench panels, and therefore provide a place to put our workbench screens and editors. Defining a perspective is very simple:

```
@ApplicationScoped
@WorkbenchPerspective(
    identifier = "myCustomPerspective",
    isDefault = false)
public class CustomPerspective {

    @Perspective
    public PerspectiveDefinition getPerspective() {
        final PerspectiveDefinition p =
            new PerspectiveDefinitionImpl(
                PanelType.ROOT_LIST);
        p.setTransient(true);
        p.setName(getClass().getName());
```

```
        p.getRoot().addPart(
            new PartDefinitionImpl(
                new DefaultPlaceRequest("myParticularScreenID")
            )
        );
        return p;
    }
}
```

The preceding code defines a perspective that will contain our previously defined screen with the identifier `"myParticularScreenID"`. The necessary components of a perspective are as follows:

- `@WorkbenchPerspective`: This annotation is used to declare that the class defines a perspective in the application. It has two attributes—one called `identifier` that defines a unique name for this perspective and for external reference by other tools and another called `isDefault`, which determines whether it should be opened by default when the workbench loads. Only one default perspective is allowed in each workbench.

- `@Perspective`: This annotated method must return an `org.uberfire.workbench.model.PerspectiveDefinition` object. These objects will allow different layout dispositions to be formed in a tree-like structure, and they will reference different screens by their identifier using a `PlaceRequest` object.

In this way, when the workbench opens a perspective, it will know that it should open a series of particular screens, all referenced by an ID and placed in special places of the open window.

The lifecycle annotations

All the visible UberFire components (perspectives, editors, pop ups, and screens) are defined in a way that makes them very detached from any core UberFire functionality. All you have to do is annotate certain methods to let UberFire connect them for you to all the right places. However, we just started with configuration annotations, and we still have to see a very important group of annotations that are used to define what to do on specific events that the workbench will send to your components.

Whenever a perspective changes, a screen is created, an editor is closed, or when the workbench needs to shut down, we need a way to tell our components how to react or even pass specific information about the event. For events as common as opening, closing, or focusing on a component, UberFire provides us with a series of lifecycle annotations that are visible in the following diagram:

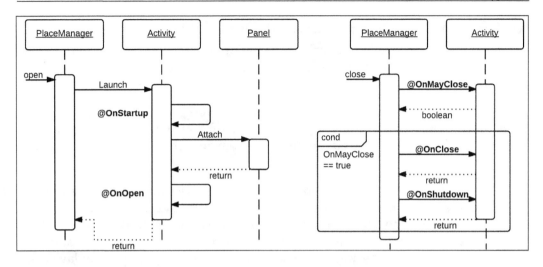

The annotations shown in the preceding diagram are as follows:

- **@OnStartup**: When the component is initialized, methods marked with this annotation are called. For workbench editors, the method should have a VFS path object as a parameter and for all other workbench parts it should have zero parameters. It is commonly used to initialize server components.

- **@OnOpen**: When the workbench component is displayed, this method will be called. The method should have zero arguments and return void, and is commonly used to start visual representations.

- **@OnFocus**: Methods annotated with this will be called when the workbench component receives focus. It should also have zero arguments and return void.

- **@OnLostFocus**: Whenever the user clicks on another component, the current one will lose focus and the method annotated with this will be called.

- **@OnMayClose**: Methods annotated with this should return a Boolean value. They should decide whether the component is in a state where it can be closed or not. Based on that, the workbench will decide whether to continue closing the component.

- **@OnClose**: When a component is closed, the method annotated with this will be called — usually to clean visual resources.

- **@OnShutdown**: This annotation is called to release resources on both the client and server side regarding the current component.

Using these annotations, we can define user interactions that are very detached from the actual workbench's final implementation. This helps a lot in making scalable UI components with a lot of embedded functionality.

Creating a screen and a pop up

Now that we have seen all the UberFire annotation components, we can start seeing in detail the components created in the uberfire-demo project provided with the book.

In our example, we create a user interface to show a very simple functionality; a screen that shows us a list of messages with a pop up that allows us to create a new message. Messages are stored as simple String elements. The project is divided into three subprojects:

- **uberfire-demo-api**: This subproject defines a service interface for reading all messages and adding a new one (called DemoServiceEntryPoint) and an event type for sending a new message back and forth (called NewMessageEvent). You can see in the code that the event class is marked with the @Portable annotation, to make it accessible through both Java and GWT JavaScript code. Also, the service interface is marked with the @Remote annotation, which lets Errai know that the GWT code will try to invoke it.

- **uberfire-demo-backend**: This subproject defines an implementation for the service interface defined in the uberfire-demo-api project. The implementation is based on holding a list in memory and adding values to it. What's really interesting about it is that it's marked with a @Service annotation that lets Errai know this is an implementation for an Errai server-side service.

- **uberfire-demo-client**: This subproject defines the user interfaces. Here's where we will use most of the UberFire components previously explained.

For this example, uberfire-demo-client is the subproject that will be most useful for us. We have created two components in it, a screen (to display a message list) and a popup (to create a new message). Let's take a look at specific utilities that the **Message List** screen uses by looking at a code fragment of MessageListPresenter:

```
@Dependent
@WorkbenchScreen(identifier = "uberFireDemo.MessageListScreen")
public class MessageListPresenter {
    public interface MessageListView extends
                UberView<MessageListPresenter> {
        void displayNotification(String text);
        DataGrid<String> getDataGrid();
    }
    @Inject
    private PlaceManager placeManager;
```

```
    @Inject
    private MessageListView view;
    ...
    @WorkbenchMenu
    public Menus getMenus() {
        return MenuFactory
            .newTopLevelMenu(constants.NewMessage())
            .respondsWith(new Command() {
                @Override
                public void execute() {
                    placeManager.goTo(
                        new DefaultPlaceRequest(
                            "uberFireDemo.NewMessagePopup" ) );
                }
            }).endMenu().build();
    }
  }
}
```

There are a few components in this code fragment that we still haven't seen and are very useful when working with UberFire components:

- **UberView interface**: This is an extension of the `IsWidget` interface, which adds a method to initialize a view based on a presenter object. You can see that we extend it to add methods that will be useful for our specific case.

- **Injection of MessageListView instance**: This is because the view object is also generated and injected through Errai and CDI. As you can see in the code, the view implementation is template-based and we're working with an HTML file (`MessageListViewImpl.html`). The templating is handled by mappings between both the files marked by `data-field` attributes in the HTML file, and `@DataField` annotated attributes in the Java class.

- **WorkbenchMenu generation**: This is to show how we can create menus that have any commands we wish. In the preceding code, we show how to use a very useful utility called `PlaceManager` (which is also injected through Errai and CDI), which is a utility manager to tell the workbench to go to another particular view or to get parameters from the current URL. In our case, we're using it to go to the popup for creating a new message.

The code in the view implementation is then only an initialization and exposure of GWT components (in our case, those components are just a table with strings in it).

The other component, the pop up, has a very similar structure. Let's analyze this code fragment of the `NewMessagePresenter` class:

```
@Dependent
@WorkbenchPopup(identifier = "uberFireDemo.NewMessagePopup")
public class NewMessagePresenter {

    ...
    @Inject
    private Caller<DemoServiceEntryPoint> demoService;
    @Inject
    private Event<NewMessageEvent> newMsgEvent;
    ...
    public void sendMessage(String message) {
        this.demoService.call( new RemoteCallback<Void>() {
            @Override
            public void callback( Void response ) {
                //send event
                newMsgEvent.fire(
                    new NewMessageEvent( view.getMessage() ) );
            }
        } ).sendMessage( message );
    }
}
```

For brevity's sake, we removed the most similar parts to the previous component. Let's discuss what's new in this class:

- `Caller`: This interface is a wrapper from Errai to handle server-side service invocations as an asynchronous communication. As we have mentioned, GWT code will be translated by a compiler into JavaScript code. This means that service calls will eventually be made through JavaScript using Ajax, and their behavior should be asynchronous. Later on, in the `sendMessage` method, we will learn how we use that wrapper with a `RemoteCallback` parameter to handle the response.

- `Event`: This interface is a way to let Errai handle event firing. We're using it to communicate with the message list presenter in a detached fashion.

Creating a perspective

Creating a perspective is done exactly as explained before. In our case, we create a perspective to include only our message list screen. Here's the code found in our `MessageListPerspective` class:

```
@ApplicationScoped
@WorkbenchPerspective(
    identifier = "uberFireDemo.MessageListPerspective",
    isDefault = false)
public class MessageListPerspective {
    @Perspective
    public PerspectiveDefinition getPerspective() {
        final PerspectiveDefinition p =
            new PerspectiveDefinitionImpl(PanelType.ROOT_LIST);
        p.setTransient(true);
        p.setName("My Customized panel of Messages");
        p.getRoot().addPart(new PartDefinitionImpl(
            new DefaultPlaceRequest(
                "uberFireDemo.MessageListScreen")));
        return p;
    }
}
```

As you can see, all we do is create a method annotated with `@Perspective` to return a `PerspectiveDefinition` instance that will have our message list screen in it, and we mark it to not be the default perspective.

Integrating components with the existing workbenches

Workbenches are Maven-based web projects that depend extensively on UberFire and its internal configurations to work. Due to UberFire being in an alpha state, workbench definition is something that might still change a lot. It is because of this reason that we will not see how to create our own workbenches in detail. Instead, we are going to see the necessary steps to add new components built with UberFire in an already existing workbench. This is less prone to change to keep compatibility with already defined components. If you wish to build your own workbench from scratch, visit `http://www.uberfireframework.org` for more help with that aspect.

Review the `jbpm-console-ng-showcase` project inside the `uberfire-demo` folder. This is one workbench already available in the open source jBPM6 repositories to which we have added `uberfire-demo` as an extra component.

The steps taken to add new components to an UberFire based workbench are as follows:

1. The first step needed to let GWT compile our Java components into JavaScript modules in the workbench is to add the component release IDs to the workbench as dependencies. In this case, we can do this by adding `uberfire-demo-client` and `uberfire-demo-backend` dependencies into a particular workbench's `pom.xml` file.

2. Maven will trigger the GWT code translation to JavaScript, but will need to know all the dependencies that need to be translated to JavaScript. To do so, we need to add two `compileSourcesArtifact` tags to the GWT Maven plugin configuration — one for `uberfire-demo-api`, and one for `uberfire-demo-client`.

3. GWT uses special XML files to define modules and dependencies between them. We have defined two of them in our demonstration projects (`UberfireDemoAPI.gwt.xml` and `UberfireDemoClient.gwt.xml`). In order to make the GWT code know that it will use those modules, we need to make the specific workbench GWT XML file that has those modules (and any other we define) as dependencies, using the `inherits` tag:

   ```
   <inherits name="path.to.my.UberfireModule"/>
   ```

4. GWT projects define one class as an entry point for all incoming user calls (marked with the `@EntryPoint` annotation) where we will need to add some form of linking to our components. In the case of our `jbpm-console-ng-showcase` project, we added a navigation bar item called MY ADDED ITEMS in the `ShowcaseEntryPoint` class.

5. Thanks to the project being a Maven-based GWT web project, we can test it directly by running the following command from the `uberfire-demo/jbpm-console-ng-showcase` folder:

   ```
   mvn clean install gwt:run
   ```

> By running the web project like this, you will be using a special plugin component for quick development of GWT applications, and you will need a plugin in your navigator to see the application running. In order to not need this plugin, you will need to do a full compilation of the GWT application to JavaScript. You can do this by passing the system property `Dfull` to the maven command previously mentioned. Now, the WAR file compiled will be runnable without that extra plugin, but in order to run it you'll need to deploy it in an application server.

As this book is being written, there are three Drools and jBPM6-related workbench applications that you can use to add your own components:

- org.drools...drools-wb-webapp for Drools 6 UI components

- org.jbpm...jbpm-console-ng-showcase for jBPM6 UI components

- org.kie...kie-wb-webapp for both Drools and jBPM6 UI components at the same time

All of them could be extended to add new UberFire components in the way we explained in this section.

Summary

The UberFire framework provides a wide variety of functionalities to explain the definition and execution environment for different types of applications, which makes it so suitable for defining the UI to apply the BPM discipline. We hope you learned how to use, configure, and possibly extend the KIE workbench by understanding its base frameworks to get the most out of it.

Index

E

Thank you for buying
jBPM6 Developer Guide

About Packt Publishing

Packt, pronounced 'packed', published its first book "*Mastering phpMyAdmin for Effective MySQL Management*" in April 2004 and subsequently continued to specialize in publishing highly focused books on specific technologies and solutions.

Our books and publications share the experiences of your fellow IT professionals in adapting and customizing today's systems, applications, and frameworks. Our solution based books give you the knowledge and power to customize the software and technologies you're using to get the job done. Packt books are more specific and less general than the IT books you have seen in the past. Our unique business model allows us to bring you more focused information, giving you more of what you need to know, and less of what you don't.

Packt is a modern, yet unique publishing company, which focuses on producing quality, cutting-edge books for communities of developers, administrators, and newbies alike. For more information, please visit our website: www.packtpub.com.

About Packt Open Source

In 2010, Packt launched two new brands, Packt Open Source and Packt Enterprise, in order to continue its focus on specialization. This book is part of the Packt Open Source brand, home to books published on software built around Open Source licenses, and offering information to anybody from advanced developers to budding web designers. The Open Source brand also runs Packt's Open Source Royalty Scheme, by which Packt gives a royalty to each Open Source project about whose software a book is sold.

Writing for Packt

We welcome all inquiries from people who are interested in authoring. Book proposals should be sent to author@packtpub.com. If your book idea is still at an early stage and you would like to discuss it first before writing a formal book proposal, contact us; one of our commissioning editors will get in touch with you.

We're not just looking for published authors; if you have strong technical skills but no writing experience, our experienced editors can help you develop a writing career, or simply get some additional reward for your expertise.

Business Process Management with JBoss jBPM
A Practical Guide for Business Analysts

ISBN: 978-1-84719-236-3   Paperback: 220 pages

Develop business process models for implementation in a business process management system

1. Map your business processes in an efficient, standards-friendly way.

2. Use the jBPM toolset to work with business process maps, create a customizable user interface for users to interact with the process, collect process execution data, and integrate with existing systems.

3. Use the SeeWhy business intelligence toolset as a Business Activity Monitoring solution, to analyze process execution data, provide real-time alerts regarding the operation of the process, and for ongoing process improvement.

Oracle BPM Suite 11g: Advanced BPMN Topics

ISBN: 978-1-84968-756-0   Paperback: 114 pages

Master advanced BPMN for Oracle BPM Suite including inter-process communication, handling arrays, and exception management

1. Cover some of the most commonly misunderstood areas of BPMN.

2. Gain the knowledge to write professional BPMN processes.

3. A practical and concise tutorial packed with advanced topics which until now had received little or no documentation for BPM Suite developers and architects.

Please check **www.PacktPub.com** for information on our titles